对外汉语教材系列
Chinese as Foreign Language Series

初级汉语口语

上 册

ELEMENTARY SPOKEN CHINESE

Part One

戴桂芙　刘立新　李海燕　编著
by Dai Guifu Liu Lixin Li Haiyan
蔡庆年　英文翻译
Translated by Cai Qingnian

北京大学出版社
PEKING UNIVERSITY PRESS

图书在版编目(CIP)数据

初级汉语口语.上册/戴桂芙等编著.—北京:北京大学出版社,1997.10
ISBN 978-7-301-03526-9

Ⅰ.初… Ⅱ.戴… Ⅲ.汉语-口语-对外汉语教学-教材 Ⅳ.H195.4

中国版本图书馆CIP数据核字(1997)第19345号

书　　　名:	初级汉语口语(上册)
著作责任者:	戴桂芙　刘立新　李海燕　编著
插图作者:	杨　威　兆　元
责任编辑:	郭　力　沈浦娜
标准书号:	ISBN 978-7-301-03526-9/H·0375
出版发行:	北京大学出版社
地　　　址:	北京市海淀区成府路205号　100871
网　　　址:	http://www.pup.cn
电子邮箱:	zpup@pup.pku.edu.cn
电　　　话:	邮购部 62752015　发行部 62750672　编辑部 62752028　出版部 62754962
印　刷　者:	北京大学印刷厂
经　销　者:	新华书店
	787毫米×1092毫米　16开本　17.875印张　350千字
	1997年10月第1版　2011年11月第22次印刷
定　　　价:	40.00元

未经许可,不得以任何方式复制或抄袭本书之部分或全部内容。
版权所有,侵权必究　举报电话:010—62752024
　　　　　　　　　　电子邮箱:fd@pup.pku.edu.cn

目　录

序 ……………………………………………………………… (3)
前言 …………………………………………………………… (5)
第 一 课　你好 …………………………………………… (1)
　　　　　　你知道吗？(1) 中国人的姓名 …………… (6)
第 二 课　现在几点了？ ………………………………… (7)
第 三 课　食堂在哪儿？ ………………………………… (16)
第 四 课　一共多少钱？ ………………………………… (22)
　　　　　　你知道吗？(2) 生活中的数字 …………… (28)
第 五 课　一起去好吗？ ………………………………… (30)
第 六 课　她病了 ………………………………………… (36)
第 七 课　我喜欢喝茶 …………………………………… (41)
第 八 课　你干什么呢？ ………………………………… (47)
第 九 课　我去邮局寄信 ………………………………… (54)
　　　　　　你知道吗？(3) 时间和地点的顺序 ……… (59)
第 十 课　今天天气怎么样？ …………………………… (60)
第 十 一 课　您贵姓？ …………………………………… (67)
第 十 二 课　一个星期有多少节课？ …………………… (73)
第 十 三 课　请问,去动物园怎么走？ ………………… (79)
　　　　　　你知道吗？(4) 中国人对人的称呼 ……… (84)
第 十 四 课　喜欢吃什么？ ……………………………… (85)
第 十 五 课　请你做我的辅导,好吗？ ………………… (93)
第 十 六 课　我有点儿不舒服 …………………………… (99)
　　　　　　你知道吗？(5) 寒暄与客套 ……………… (105)
第 十 七 课　我看不懂 …………………………………… (107)
第 十 八 课　我在学习书法呢 …………………………… (113)

1

第十九课	周末你打算怎么过？	(120)
第二十课	今天比昨天冷一点儿	(126)
第二十一课	他们是做什么工作的？	(133)
	你知道吗？(6) 家庭与称谓	(139)
第二十二课	你今年多大了？	(142)
第二十三课	离这儿有多远？	(150)
	你知道吗？(7) 方位与文化	(156)
第二十四课	她又聪明又用功	(158)
第二十五课	便宜点儿吧	(166)
第二十六课	怎么了？	(174)
	你知道吗？(8) 儿化与语义	(181)
第二十七课	要是下雨怎么办呢？	(183)
第二十八课	天气越来越冷了	(192)
第二十九课	我没买着火车票	(200)
第三十课	杯子叫我打碎了	(207)
词语表		(214)
会话、课文英译		(245)

序

随着改革开放的深入发展,对外汉语教学也日益受到人们的重视。来华的留学生人数也在增加。这些留学生中,虽然也有要通过汉语学习中国文化的,但其中有不少是要利用汉语和中国通商或进行政治、外交等诸方面的活动的。在这种情况下,口语能力就显得特别重要。许多留学生都希望在最短期间内学好一口流利的普通话以便进行工作。

我们的汉语教学起步较晚。五六十年代虽然已有不少国家的留学生,可以说都是要打好汉语基础再入系深造的。我们对口语会话能力并未给以特殊的重视。文化大革命以后,开始有些口语课本出现,这些口语课本都是在会话内容上强调要贴近留学生生活、要能介绍中国文化、要能教给留学生得体的汉语、要能引起学生兴趣等等,等等。

诚然,上述各方面对口语教材都是非常重要的。但是要提高口语教学质量,改善口语教材的编写,却是更重要的问题。

1996年起戴桂芙同志和两位青年教师在教授初级口语的同时,开始边实践、边总结、边研究、边编写,写成了今天这部初级口语课本。在编写课文时,她们没有忘记课文要贴近学生生活、要介绍中国文化、要语言得体、活泼有趣等等。因为这是所有口语教师都十分注意的。我认为她们把过去以词语为单位的教学法改革为以句型为单位的教学法才是最重要而有意义的改革。

为什么要把句型本位作为口语教学的出发点?这种变动有什么道理?我认为教材离不开学生的特点。成人学习外语都是想短期速成、目标明确。在一定的语言环境下教给学生恰当的句型,叫他们会话,这是符合学生要求的,也是便于学生掌握的。这样的教学效果肯定会较好的。

因为有句型本位的训练,初级口语也能训练学生成段表达的能力。这也有利于培养学生用汉语进行思维的能力,从而为他们尽早掌握符合汉语习惯的口语创造条件。

戴桂芙、刘立新和李海燕三位同志善于深思、勇于创新,为口语教学开新路。我祝她们取得更大成绩,为对外汉语教学立新功!

邓　懿

一九九七年七月

前　言

　　本教材是我们自1996年初开始编著的口语系列教材初级阶段的课本，教学对象是零起点的学生。分上下两册，每册30课，可供每周8～10学时、每学期18～20周的课堂教学使用一个学年。教材内容选取留学生关心和感兴趣的话题，语言遵守规范化原则，词汇数量上册每课20～30个，下册每课30～40个，两册共计2000个左右。选词范围以《汉语水平词汇和汉字等级大纲》为标准，主要选用其中的甲级词汇。

　　遵循语言学习规律，服从初级口语教学法原则，参照教学实践的有效经验，我们采用了以下两个编写原则：第一，变传统的以词语为本位、从语义到语用为以句子为本位、从语用到语义；第二，在学习初级口语常用句式、简单对话的同时，就开始进行成段表达的训练。目的是从一开始就为培养学生用汉语进行思维打下基础，并为他们尽快掌握符合中国人表达习惯的自然、得体的汉语口语创造条件。

　　为贯彻以上两条原则，在编写体例上，没有专门设计语音教学阶段，从第一课就开始直接学习说话，在语流当中学习和纠正发音的问题；语音、语调自始至终都是教学的重点之一，在练习中，我们注意设计了有关项目；每课的课文部分，由会话和简短的叙述性语段组成，语段是根据会话的内容和常用句式编写的；每课都有一个小标题，这个标题不是全课话题内容的总括，只是从会话中选取的一个具有代表性的句式；为了将学生的注意力集中在学习句子上，每课出现的新词语不编排在课文之后，全部作为附录置于书后；考虑到学生理解和自学的方便，会话和语段同时编排汉字和拼音；会话和语段全部备有英语译文，作为附录编于书后；注释是对课文中的语言点和文化点的说明；每课中的大量练习，形式生动多样，图文并用，具有交际价值；"你知道吗"是配合课文并结合学生的兴趣和需要编写的口语常识或文化知识，可作为教学的参考和补充，也可作为课外学习材料。

　　本教材在编写过程中，听取了北京大学对外汉语教学中心一些老师和北京大学出版社沈浦娜、郭力两位编辑不少很好的意见和建议；邓懿教授欣然为之作序；蔡庆年老师应邀为课文、注释和"你知道吗"进行了英文释义，马瑙甘女士审阅了以上这三部分的英文释义。在此向以上各位一并致以衷心的感谢。

戴桂芙　刘立新　李海燕
一九九七年六月于北京大学

第一课　你好!

(开学第一天,在校园里)

杰　夫:你好!
安　妮:你好!
杰　夫:我叫杰夫。你叫什么名字?
安　妮:我叫安妮。

(在教室里)

田老师:你们好! 我姓田。
安　妮:⎫
　　　　⎬您好! 田老师!
杰　夫:⎭
田老师:(对杰夫说)你叫什么名字?
杰　夫:我叫杰夫。
田老师:(对安妮说)你呢?
安　妮:我叫安妮。

（在教室外）

王　平：你们好！
杰　夫：
安　妮：｝你好！

杰　夫：你叫什么名字？
王　平：我叫王平。你们是……？
安　妮：我是安妮，他是杰夫。

（杰夫对王平说）

　　我叫杰夫，她叫安妮。我们都是留学生，我们的老师姓田。

Dì-yī kè　Nǐ Hǎo!
(Kāixué dì-yī tiān, zài xiàoyuán li)

Jiéfū：Nǐ hǎo!
Ānní：Nǐ hǎo!
Jiéfū：Wǒ jiào Jiéfū. Nǐ jiào shénme míngzi?
Ānní：Wǒ jiào Ānní.

(Zài jiàoshì li)

Tián lǎoshī：Nǐmen hǎo! Wǒ xìng Tián.
Ānní：
Jiéfū：｝Nín hǎo! Tián lǎoshī!

Tián lǎoshī：(Duì Jiéfū shuō) Nǐ jiào shénme míngzi?
Jiéfū：Wǒ jiào Jiéfū.
Tián lǎoshī：(Duì Ānní shuō) Nǐ ne?
Ānní：Wǒ jiào Ānní.

(Zài jiàoshì wài)

Wáng Píng：Nǐmen hǎo!
Jiéfū：
Ānní：｝Nǐ hǎo!

Jiéfū：Nǐ jiào shénme míngzi?
Wáng Píng：Wǒ jiào Wáng Píng. Nǐmen shì……?
Ānní：Wǒ shì Ānní, tā shì Jiéfū.

(Jiéfū duì Wáng Píng shuō)

　　Wǒ jiào Jiéfū, tā jiào Ānní. Wǒmen dōu shì liúxuéshēng, wǒmen de lǎoshī xìng Tián.

注释 Notes

1. "你好"：

见面时的问候语。第一次见面或平时见面时都可以用,回答是"你好"。

A greeting said when meeting someone for the first time or coming across an acquaintance. The response is also "你好".

2. "你叫什么名字"：

问对方的姓名,一般不用于比自己年长或比自己地位高的人。回答是："我叫……"或"我是……"。常常是连名带姓一起回答。

Used to ask someone for his or her full name, but not those older than yourself or in a higher position. The answer is "我叫……" or "我是……", usually giving both the surname and the first name.

3. "你呢"：

"呢"表示疑问的语气。在一定的上下文中,前边可以只有一个名词成分,省略疑问词。如："我是中国人,你呢?"其中的"你呢"意思是"你是哪国人?"复数时可以说："你们呢?""他们呢?"

In certain context, the particle "呢" can be added to a noun or pronoun to form an elliptical question and the interrogative word is omitted. For example: "我是中国人,你呢?" "你呢" means "你是哪国人?" in the context. In the plural form: "你们呢?" "他们呢?"

4. 你们是……(你是……)：

不认识对方时,客气地问对方的姓名、身份等,带有疑问的语气,"是"的发音一般比较长。

Used to ask in a polite manner for the name and identity of someone you don't know. The word "是" should be dragged out.

练习 Exercises

一、发音练习：Pronunciation Drills:

1. 辨音练习：Discriminate the following syllables

①ao an ②in ing ③ei en eng

2．单音节练习：One – syllable drills：

nǐ　nín　wǒ　tā　dōu　xìng　ne　shì　jiào

3．双音节练习：Two – syllable drills：

nǐ hǎo　nín hǎo　wǒmen　nǐmen　lǎoshī　míngzi

二、用正确的语调读下边的句子：Read the following sentences in correct intonation：

1．你好！

2．你们好！

3．您好！田老师！

4．我姓田。

5．你叫什么名字？

6．我是安妮，他是杰夫。

7．我叫王平。你们是……？

三、替换练习：Substitution drills：

1．<u>你</u>好！
　　您
　　你们
　　老师
　　田老师

2．我是<u>王平</u>。
　　　杰夫
　　　你们的汉语老师
　　　学生
　　　留学生

3．我叫<u>杰夫</u>，你呢？
　　我是留学生
　　我叫安妮

4．我姓<u>田</u>。
　　　张
　　　李
　　　刘

　　　　陈

5. 我们都<u>是</u> <u>留学生</u>。
　　　　是　学生
　　　　是　老师
　　　　姓　张
　　　　姓　李

四、选出合适的应答句：Choose the correct answers：

1. 你好!
　　☐你好!
　　☐我好!
　　☐好!

2. 你叫什么名字?
　　☐叫杰夫。
　　☐杰夫。

3. 我叫杰夫,你呢?
　　☐我是学生。
　　☐我叫安妮。

4. 你们是……?
　　☐我们是。
　　☐我是安妮,他是王平。

五、说出相应的上句：Ask the questions accordingly：

1. 甲:_____?
　　乙:我叫王平。

2. 甲:_____?
　　乙:我姓张。

六、根据实际情况完成下面的一段话：

Complete the passages according to your real situation：

你们好！我姓____，叫_____。我的老师姓____，叫_____。

七、用四句话在全班同学面前介绍你自己。

Introduce yourself to your classmates in four sentences.

你知道吗？ (1)　　　　　　中国人的姓名

　　中国人的姓大多是单姓，即用一个汉字来表示，最常用的有："张 Zhāng、王 Wáng、李 Lǐ、赵 Zhào、钱 Qián、刘 Liú、周 Zhōu、郑 Zhèng、高 Gāo、郭 Guō、牛 Niú、马 Mǎ、齐 Qí、杨 Yáng"等等。也有用两个汉字表示的姓，叫做复姓，常见的如："欧阳 Ōuyáng、司马 Sīmǎ、东方 Dōngfāng、上官 Shàngguān"等等。中国人姓名的排列次序是姓在前，名在后，如："张兰""李卫东"。名字既有一个汉字的，也有两个汉字的，如："王平""赵大明""欧阳玉青"等。孩子一般还有小名，多用两个重叠的字，如："明明""兰兰"等，或在名字的后一字前面加上一个"小"字，如"小青""小明"等。名字所用的字，都有一定的意义。

Do You Know? (1)　　　　　**Chinese Names**

　　Chinese surnames are mostly one‐character names. The most common ones are Zhang, Wang, Li, Zhao, Qian, Liu, Zhou, Zheng, Gao, Guo, Niu, Ma, Qi, Yang and so on. There are also two‐character surnames called compound surnames. The common ones are Ouyang, Sima, Dongfang, Shangguan and so on. In Chinese names, the surname always comes first and the first name second, for example, "Zhang Lan", "Li Weidong". People are given one‐character names as well as two‐character names, for example, "Wang Ping", "Zhao Daming", "Ouyang Yuqing"... Children are often given pet names, mostly composed of reduplicated characters, such as "Mingming", "Lanlan"... or with the word "xiao" preceding the last word of the name, such as "Xiaoqing", "Xiaoming". People often use meaningful characters for names.

第二课　现在几点了?

(在路上)

彼　得:早上好!
安　妮:早上好!
彼　得:你叫什么名字?
安　妮:我叫安妮。你呢?
彼　得:我叫彼得。你是哪国人?
安　妮:我是英国人。你是美国人吗?
彼　得:不,我是法国人。

(彼得和安妮正说着话,杰夫走过来)

安　妮:杰夫,你好!
杰　夫:你好! 安妮! 他是谁?
安　妮:他是彼得。
杰　夫:你好,彼得! 我叫杰夫!
彼　得:你好! 你是美国人吧?
杰　夫:对。你在几班?

彼　得：一班。你们呢？
安　妮：我在二班。
杰　夫：我也在二班。
彼　得：现在几点了？
安　妮：两点了，该上课了。再见！彼得！

（彼得说）

　　我是法国人，安妮是英国人，杰夫是美国人。我在一班，他们在二班。我们两点上课。

　　　　Dì－èr kè　Xiànzài jǐ diǎn le？

（Zài lùshang）

Bǐdé：Zǎoshang hǎo！

Ānní：Zǎoshang hǎo！

Bǐdé：Nǐ jiào shénme míngzi？

Ānní：Wǒ jiào Ānní. Nǐ ne？

Bǐdé：Wǒ jiào Bǐdé. Nǐ shì něi guó rén？

Ānní：Wǒ shì Yīngguórén. Nǐ shì Měiguórén ma？

Bǐdé：Bù, wǒ shì Fǎguórén.

（Bǐdé hé Ānní zhèng shuōzhe huà, Jiéfū zǒu guòlai）

Ānní：Jiéfū, Nǐ hǎo！

Jiéfū：Nǐ hǎo！Ānní！Tā shì shéi？

Ānní：Tā shì Bǐdé.

Jiéfū：Nǐ hǎo, Bǐdé！Wǒ jiào Jiéfū！

Bǐdé：Nǐ hǎo！Nǐ shì Měiguórén ba？

Jiéfū：Duì. Nǐ zài jǐ bān？

Bǐdé：Yī bān. Nǐmen ne？

Ānní：Wǒ zài èr bān.

Jiéfū：Wǒ yě zài èr bān.

Bǐdé：Xiànzài jǐ diǎn le？

Ānní：Liǎng diǎn le, gāi shàngkè le. Zàijiàn！Bǐdé!

（Bǐdé shuō）

　　Wǒ shì Fǎguórén, Ānní shì Yīngguórén, Jiéfū shì Měiguórén. Wǒ zài yī bān, tāmen zài èr bān. Wǒmen liǎng diǎn shàngkè.

注释 Notes

1. "早上好":

    早上(一般在上午九点以前)见面时的打招呼用语,有时也说"早晨好"或"你(您)早",对方回答也是"早上好""早晨好"或"你(您)早"。

    A greeting usually exchanged in early morning before 9 am; "早晨好" or "你(您)早" are sometimes said, too; The answer is also "早上好""早晨好" or "你(您)早".

2. "你是美国人吧":

    "吧",助词,用在句末表示疑问,带有揣测的语气。如:

    "吧" is a particle used to end and form a question or a guess. For example:

    "他不来了吧?""你是老师吧?""他有二十岁了吧?"

3. 百以内的数字表达法:The expression of cardinal numbers within 100:

    一 二 三 四 五 六 七 八 九 十
    十一 十二 十三 十四 十五 十六 十七 十八 十九 二十
    二十一 二十二 …… 三十
    三十一 …… 三十九 四十 …… 五十 …… 九十九 一百

    one, two, three, four, five, six, seven, eight, nine, ten, eleven, twelve, thirteen, fourteen, fifteen, sixteen, seventeen, eighteen, nineteen, twenty, twenty-one, twenty-two, ... thirty, thirty-one, ... thirty-nine, forty, ... fifty, ... ninety-nine, a hundred.

4. "二"和"两":

    "二"和"两"都表示2,说数目时用"二",如:"一,二,三,四"。"两"必须用在量词前面,如:"两个人""两点""两天";十以上的百以内数中的"2"一般用"二",如:"十二个人""二十二点""三十二天",不用"两"。

    The words "二" and "两" both mean two. While "二" is used in counting: one two three four. "两" must be followed by a measure word, such as "两个人", "两点", "两天". But in two digit numerals, "二"is often used instead of "两", for example: "十二个人", "二十二点", "三十二天".

5. 时间的表达:Telling the time:

1:00　一点 one o'clock
1:05　一点零五分（一点过五分）five past one (one five)
1:15　一点一刻（一点十五分）a quarter past one (one fifteen)
1:30　一点半（一点三十分）half past one (one thirty)
1:45　一点三刻（一点四十五分）（差一刻两点）one forty five (quarter to two)
1:55　一点五十五分（差五分两点）（两点差五分）one fifty five (five to two)

练习 Exercises

一、发音练习：Exercises on pronunciation：

1. 辨音练习：Discriminate the following syllables：

①ai an　②ang eng　③uo ui　④e er

2. 单音节练习：One – syllable drills：

jǐ　diǎn　rén　yě　ma　ba　bù　shéi　dōu　zài　bān　yī　èr　nà　nèi

3. 双音节练习：Two – syllable drills：

xiànzài　lǎoshī　Fǎguó　zàijiàn

4. 听听哪个对？Listen and tell which transcription is correct：

一班 yībān	他们 tāmen	美国 Měiguó	留学生 liúxuéshéng	法国 Fǎguó
yíbàn	tāmen	Měiguò	liūxuesheng	Fàguó
yībān	tāmén	Méiguǒ	liúxuéshēng	Fǎguó

什么 shénme	几点 jǐdiàn	老师 lǎoshī	我们 wǒmen	你呢 nǐ ne
shènme	jīdiàn	lǎoshì	wǒmen	nī ne
shénme	jǐdiǎn	láoshì	wòmen	nǐ ne

5. 绕口令：A tongue twister

sì shì sì,　　　　　　四是四，
shí shì shí,　　　　　十是十，
shísì shì shísì,　　　十四是十四，
sìshí shì sìshí.　　　四十是四十。
sìshí búshi shísì,　　四十不是十四，
shísì búshi sìshí.　　十四不是四十。

二、用正确的语调读下边的句子：
Read the following sentences in correct intonation:

1. 早上好！
2. 你是哪国人？
3. 我是英国人。你呢？
4. 你是美国人吗？
5. 他是谁？
6. 你在几班？
7. 我在一班。
8. 现在几点了？
9. 该上课了。
10. 再见！

三、替换练习：Substitution drills：

1. <u>早上</u>好！
　　早晨
　　晚上

2. 我是<u>英国</u>人。
　　　中国
　　　法国
　　　美国
　　　日本
　　　德国
　　　韩国

3. 你是<u>美国人</u>吧？
　　　留学生
　　　老师
　　　安妮
　　　王平

4. 我在<u>一</u>班。
　　　六

□二
　　　□七
　　　□五

5．我们<u>两</u>点上课。
　　　□八
　　　□三
　　　□四

四、选择合适的应答句：Choose the correct answer：

1．现在几点了？
　　　□二点。
　　　□两点。

2．你也是英国人吗？
　　　□我也。
　　　□对，我是。
　　　□也是。

3．你在几班？
　　　□三班。
　　　□三。

4．他是谁？
　　　□他是学生。
　　　□他是美国人。
　　　□他是王平。

五、看图问答：Complete the dialogues according to the pictures：

1．

甲：现在几点了？

乙：_____，该_____了。

2.

甲：_____？
乙：六点。

3.

甲：你在几班？
乙：_____。

4.

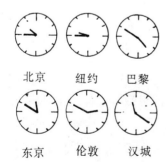

北京　纽约　巴黎

东京　伦敦　汉城

甲：现在是北京时间_____，_____现在几点？
乙：_____。

六、仿照例句对话：Make conversations following the example：

例：甲：杰夫在几班？
　　乙：二班。
　　甲：他是哪国人？
　　乙：美国人。

　　　安妮　　　　　　　　　彼得　　　　　　　　　田中

七、根据实际情况完成下面的一段话：

Complete the following passage according to your own situation：

　　早上好！我叫_____，我是_____人。我在_____班，我们早上____点上课。

八、用第一课和第二课的表达方法再次介绍自己。

Introduce yourself again using the expressions in Lesson One and Two.

九、练习数字的游戏：A game of counting：

　　同学们围坐在一起，有一个人随便说一个十以下的数字，右边的人顺次数下去（范围在百以内），遇到带7或7的倍数的数，用拍一下儿手来代替。错了罚唱一支歌。然后再由唱歌的人重新开始数，速度要快。此游戏锻炼同学们迅速数数的能力。

　　All the students sit in a circle. One of them chooses and says a numeral under 10. The next student sitting at his right side says the following numeral. Each saying a numeral, the students go on counting (within 100) in turn. Anyone who comes to a numeral with 7 or a multiple of 7 must clap instead of saying it. Whoever makes a mistake has to sing a song as a forfeit and then restart the game from a numeral under 10 while increasing the speed. This game helps the students improve their counting skill and speed.

第三课　食堂在哪儿？

（在校园里）

安　妮：请问，这是教学楼吗？

过路人：不，这是办公楼。那是教学楼。

安　妮：谢谢。

过路人：不谢。

（在教学楼里）

安　妮：请问，二班的教室在这儿吗？

一学生：对，就在这儿。

安　妮：谢谢你。

一学生：不用谢。

（在校园里）

山　下：请问，留学生食堂在哪儿？

过路人：在那边。

山　下：哪边？

过路人:留学生宿舍的旁边。
山　下:谢谢。

(在教学楼里)
杰　夫:请问,厕所在哪儿?
一学生:在这个教室的旁边。……哦,不对,在那个教室的旁边。
杰　夫:谢谢。
一学生:不客气。

(安妮说)
　　这是我们的学校。我们的学校很大。这是办公楼,那是教学楼。留学生食堂在宿舍的旁边。

Dì-sān kè　Shítáng zài nǎr?

(Zài xiàoyuán li)
Ānní: Qǐngwèn, zhè shì jiàoxuélóu ma?
Guòlùrén: Bù, zhè shì bàngōnglóu, nà shì jiàoxuélóu.
Ānní: Xièxie.
Guòlùrén: Bú xiè.

(Zài jiàoxuélóu li)
Ānní: Qǐngwèn, èr bān de jiàoshì zài zhèr ma?
Yì xuésheng: Duì, jiù zài zhèr.
Ānní: Xièxie nǐ.
Yì xuésheng: Búyòng xiè.

(Zài xiàoyuán li)
Shānxià: Qǐngwèn, liúxuéshēng shítáng zài nǎr?
Guòlùrén: Zài nèibian.
Shānxià: něibian?
Guòlùrén: Liúxuéshēng sùshè de pángbiān.
Shānxià: Xièxie.

(Zài jiàoxuélóu li)
Jiéfū: Qǐngwèn, cèsuǒ zài nǎr?
Yì xuésheng: Zài zhèige jiàoshì de pángbiān. ……Ò, bú duì, zài nèige jiàoshì de pángbiān.

Jiéfū: Xièxie.

Yī xuésheng: Bú kèqi.

(Ānní shuō)
　　Zhè shì wǒmen de xuéxiào. Wǒmen de xuéxiào hěn dà. Zhè shì bàngōnglóu, nà shì jiāoxuélóu. Liúxuéshēng shítáng zài sùshè de pángbiān.

注释 Notes

1. "请问":
   询问时客气的用语,如:
   Used to inquire about something in a polite way, for example:
   "请问,教室在哪儿?""请问,现在几点?"

2. "不谢、不用谢、不客气":
   都是对"谢谢"的回答。用法相同。
   All used in the same way in response to "谢谢".

3. "就在这儿":
   这里"就"表示情况是这样,不是别的情况,有强调的作用,用在动词的前面,如:
   The word "就" means exactly or precisely here. It precedes the verb "在" for emphasis. For instance:
   "哪位是小王?——我就是。""教室就在这儿。""这个人就是他哥哥。"

4. "哦":
   叹词,读第四声时,表示醒悟、领会、明白了,如:
   Read in the fourth tone, the exclamatory "哦" indicates realization or understanding, for example:
   "哦,我懂了。""哦,我错了。"

练习 Exercises

一、发音练习: Exercises on pronunciation:

1. 辨音练习: Discriminate the syllables:

①xie xue ②gong yong ③ban bian ④dang tang ⑤hen wen ⑥xiao jiao

2. 儿化练习：Drills on the syllables with a retroflex ending：

zhèr   nàr   nǎr   yǎnjìngr   bīnggùnr

yìdiǎnr   yíhuìr   yíkuàir

二、听与读：Listen and read：

Chuáng qián míngyuè guāng,

Yí shì dì shàng shuāng.

Jǔ tóu wàng míngyuè,

Dī tóu sī gùxiāng.

三、熟读下边的两组双音节词,注意重音的位置：
　　Read the two groups of dissyllabics, paying attention to where the accent falls：

1. 前重后轻 Accent on the first syllable：

名字　你们　我们　他们

早上　学生　谢谢　不客气

2. 前轻后重 Accent on the second syllable：

老师　现在　再见　食堂

宿舍　厕所　学校　安妮

四、用正确的语调读下边的句子：
　　Read the following sentences in correct intonation：

1. 请问,这是教学楼吗?
2. 这是办公楼,那是教学楼。
3. 留学生食堂在哪儿?
4. 哪边?
5. 厕所在那个教室的旁边。
6. 谢谢。
7. 不(用)谢。
8. 不客气。

五、仿照例句替换划线的部分：
　　Substitute the underlined parts following the examples.

1. 甲:请问,留学生食堂在哪儿?　　乙:在那边。
　　　　　一班的教室　　　　　　　　这儿

你们的学校　　　　　　　那儿
　　　留学生宿舍　　　　　　食堂的旁边
　　　厕所　　　　　　　　　那个教室的旁边
2.甲:请问,这是<u>教学楼</u>吗?　乙:不,这是<u>办公楼</u>,那是<u>教学楼</u>。
　　　二班的教室　　　　　　一班的教室
　　　留学生宿舍　　　　　　中国学生的宿舍
　　　男厕所　　　　　　　　女厕所

六、看图问答：

　　Look at the pictures and practice questions－and－answers using where or there or beside：
请选用下边的词语：
在　哪儿　那儿　旁边

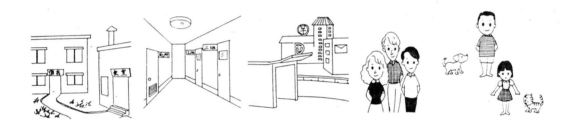

七、找出ＡＢ中有关联的上下句并读出来：

　　Pair the two groups of sentences accordingly and read them aloud：

谢谢!　　　　　　　　　　是。
请问,厕所在哪儿?　　　　不客气。
你是哪国人?　　　　　　在这个教室的旁边。
早上好!　　　　　　　　我叫杰夫。
你叫什么名字?　　　　　早上好!
你是留学生吗?　　　　　我是中国人。
　　　Ａ　　　　　　　　　　Ｂ

八、用教室里的人或物提问方位。请参考下列句式：

　　Ask questions about the positions of people and things in your classroom using the following sentence patterns：

Ａ在哪儿?

(A)在这儿/在那儿/在那边。
A 在 B 的旁边。
这是 A,这(那)是 B。

第四课　一共多少钱?

(在留学生食堂中餐部)
服务员:你要哪个菜?
丽　莎:我要这个。多少钱?
服务员:六块五。
山　下:我要这个,还要那个。
服务员:还要哪个?
山　下:那边,那个! 一共多少钱?
服务员:十五块七。

(安妮和杰夫在逛商店)
杰　夫:我要买这种自行车,你看什么颜色的好?
安　妮:黑的怎么样?
杰　夫:黑的……我喜欢蓝的,我还想看看蓝的。
安　妮:劳驾,这种有蓝的吗?
售货员:哪种?
杰　夫:这种。

售货员：有。蓝的、黑的都有。
杰　夫：我要一辆蓝的。多少钱？
售货员：五百四。

（杰夫说）
　　我要买一辆自行车，我看了黑的，还看了蓝的，我喜欢蓝的。我花五百四十块钱买了一辆蓝的。

Dì-sì kè　Yígòng duōshao qián?

(Zài liúxuéshēng shítáng zhōngcānbù)
Fúwùyuán: Nǐ yào něige cài?
Lìshā: Wǒ yào zhèige. Duōshao qián?
Fúwùyuán: Liù kuài wǔ.
Shānxià: Wǒ yào zhèige, hái yào nèige.
Fúwùyuán: Hái yào něige?
Shānxià: Nèibian, nèige! Yígòng duōshao qián?
Fúwùyuán: Shíwǔ kuài qī.

(Ānní hé Jiéfū zài guàng shāngdiàn)
Jiéfū: Wǒ yào mǎi zhèi zhǒng zìxíngchē, nǐ kàn shénme yánsè de hǎo?
Ānní: Hēi de zěnmeyàng?
Jiéfū: Hēi de……Wǒ xǐhuan lán de, Wǒ hái xiǎng kànkan lán de.
Ānní: Láo jià, zhèi zhǒng yǒu lán de ma?
Shòuhuòyuán: Něi zhǒng?
Jiéfū: Zhèi zhǒng.
Shòuhuòyuán: Yǒu. Lán de、hēi de dōu yǒu.
Jiéfū: Wǒ yào yí liàng lán de. Duōshao qián?
Shòuhuòyuán: Wǔbǎi sì.

(Jiéfū shuō)
　　Wǒ yào mǎi yí liàng zìxíngchē, wǒ kànle hēi de, yě kànle lán de. Wǒ xǐhuan lán de. Wǒ huā wǔbǎi sìshí kuài qián mǎile yí liàng lán de.

注释 Notes

1. "黑的、蓝的"：

"黑的、蓝的"分别表示"黑的自行车、蓝的自行车"。"的"后省略了谈话双方共知的或已出现过的名词性成分。"的"用在形容词、名词、代词、动词等后面,可以代替上文所说的人或物。如:

"Black ones, blue ones" represent the black bikes and the blue bikes respectively. The noun element after the word "的" is omitted either because it is understood by both parties or was mentioned earlier. The word "的" following an adjective, a noun, a pronoun, or a verb represents someone or something mentioned earlier. For example:

"这是我的,那是你的""我买点儿吃的。"

2. "你看":

询问别人的意见,请别人对某事物作出判断时用。回答时可以用"我看……"。如:

Used to solicit an opinion about something from someone. "我看..." can be used as an answer, for example:

甲:"你看这件衣服怎么样?"　　乙:"我看这件衣服挺好的。"

3. "黑的怎么样":

"黑的怎么样?"意思是"你觉得黑的自行车好不好?""怎么样"在本课中用来询问对方的意见。如:

"黑的怎么样?" means "Do you think the black bike is good?" "怎么样" is used in this lesson to solicit an opinion from the other party. More examples:

"你看去故宫怎么样?""买这件衣服怎么样?"

4. 人民币的单位和读法:Units of Ren Min Bi and how to read them:

10.55元	十元五角五分 ten yuan fifty-five fen,	在口语里读成: in oral Chinese:	十块五毛五(分) shí kuài wǔ máo wǔ (fēn)
0.12元	一角二分 twelve fen		一毛二(分) yì máo èr (fēn)
2.05元	两元零五分 two yuan and five fen		两块零五分 liǎng kuài líng wǔ fēn
2.10元	两元一角 two yuan ten fen		两块一(毛) liǎng kuài yī (máo)
3.50元	三元五角 three yuan fifty fen		三块五(毛) sān kuài wǔ (máo)
150.00元	一百五十元		一百五十块

a hundred fifty yuan　　　　　　yìbǎi wǔshí kuài

5."要"：

①动词,买东西时常常说"要",不说"买",如："你要什么?""我要这个,还要那个。""我要一个面包。"在这里"要"的意思和"买"一样,用法也相同。

The verb"要"is more commonly used than"买"by shopping people. For example："你要什么?" "我要这个,还要那个 ." "我要一个面包 ." In this sense, "要"is equivalent to"买"and they are used in the same way.

②能愿动词,用在动词前边,表示想做某事,做某事的愿望和意志。如：

An optative verb preceding a verb, indicating the wish and will to do something. For instance：

"我要买一辆自行车。""他要学游泳。"

练习 Exercises

一、发音练习：Exercises on pronunciation：

1.辨音练习：Discriminate the syllables：

①hai huai ②fu hu ③kua hua ④qiang xiang ⑤ chuan chuang

2."一"的变调练习：Tone‒sandhi drills on "一"：

yì tiān　　yì nián　　yì diǎnr　　yí liàng　　yíge

3.注意不同声调的词语所表示的不同含义：

Notice the different meanings of words with the same initials and finals but read in different tones：

①nǎ 哪　nà 那　　②mǎi 买　mài 卖　　③zhōng 中　zhǒng 种

④bái 白　bǎi 百　　⑤liǎng 两　liàng 辆　　⑥shì 是　　shí 十

二、用正确的语调读下边的句子：

Read the following sentences in correct intonation：

1.我要这个,还要那个。

2.多少钱?

3.一共多少钱?

4.十五块七。

5.我要买(一)辆蓝的(自行车)。

三、快速读出下边的钱数：Read the following sums of money rapidly：

0.21 元　8.00 元　9.10 元　　540.00 元

0.02 元　5.80 元　600.00 元　1702.30 元

四、看图进行买东西的对话：

　　Produce dialogues about shopping in terms of the following price list：

五、替换练习：Substitution drills：

1. 我要买一辆　自行车。
　　　　　　本　字典
　　　　　　双　鞋
　　　　　　支　笔
　　　　　　本　书
　　　　　　斤　苹果

2. 黑的怎么样？
　　白的
　　蓝的
　　这个
　　旁边的那个

3. 你要哪个　菜？
　　　　　本　书
　　　　　双　鞋
　　　　　支　笔
　　　　　辆　车
　　　　　个　房间
　　　　　种　水果

六、先读对话,再模仿表演: Read the dialogue and then perform it:

甲:小姐,我看看那双鞋。
乙:是这双蓝的吗?
甲:不是,旁边的那双。
乙:这双黑的吗?
甲:也不是,那双。
乙:这双吗?
甲:对。多少钱?
乙:八百八。
甲:什么?八百八?不买了,不买了!

七、扩展练习: Extension exercises:

例:Following example:

车
自行车
蓝色的自行车
一辆蓝色的自行车
买了一辆蓝色的自行车
花钱买了一辆蓝色的自行车
花四百块钱买了一辆蓝色的自行车
我花四百块钱买了一辆蓝色的自行车

鞋
笔
本子

八、你们国家的国旗都有什么颜色?各部分颜色代表什么意思?

How many colors are there in the national flag of your country? What does each colored part represent?

九、说说你在中国商店里买过什么东西,并说出5至10种商品的价钱。

Make an account of the things that you have bought in the shops here in China. Tell the prices of 5 to 10 commodities.

****

你知道吗？(2)   生活中的数字

1. 用手势怎么表示数字？

从1到10这十个数字在中国用手势来表示的话，分别是：

2. 从1到10这十个数字在银行、邮局的存、取款单上、账单上和汇款单上都要用汉字分别写成：壹 贰 叁 肆 伍 陆 柒 捌 玖 拾

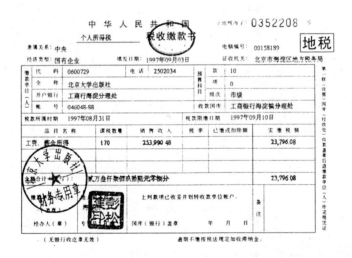

3. "1"在电话号码、房间号码、公共汽车路线等的号码中常读作"yāo"，为的是清晰地区别"1"(yī)和"7"(qī)，如：62751771、103房间、311路公共汽车中的"1"都应读作"yāo"。

Do You Know?   (2)   Numerals In Everyday Life

1. How to gesticulate the numerals 1 to 10 with your hands? The gesticulations of the numerals 1 to 10 are:

2. To fill out a savings account, a check or a money order in a bank or a post office, you

must write the numerals 1 to 10 in their capital forms:

3. In telephone numbers, room numbers and bus numbers, the numeral "1" is often pronounced as [yāo] so as to clearly distinguish "1" [yī] from "7" [qī], for instance: 62751771, Room 103, Bus Nr. 311.

第五课 一起去好吗?

(上课以前)

安　妮:下午你有课吗?

杰　夫:有。

安　妮:下课以后你有空儿吗?

杰　夫:我六点下课,你有什么事?

安　妮:我想去王平那儿,你去不去?

杰　夫:我也想去,晚上我有空儿。

安　妮:晚上一起去好吗?

杰　夫:好。晚上见!

安　妮:晚上见!

(上午第四节下课以后)

安　妮:田老师,现在您有空儿吗?

田老师:对不起,我现在没空儿,你有事吗?

安　妮:(打开书)这几个问题我还不懂。

田老师:我看看,哦,山下说这几个问题他也不懂。明天上课我给你们一起讲讲吧。

安　妮：太好了！明天见！
田老师：明天见！

（安妮对王平说）
　　今天的课有几个问题我还不懂，田老师说明天上课给我们讲讲。明天晚上我和杰夫都有空儿，我们一起去你那儿，好吗？

Dì-wǔ kè　Yìqǐ qù hǎo ma?

（Shàng kè yǐqián）
Ānní：Xiàwǔ nǐ yǒu kè ma?
Jiéfū：Yǒu.
Ānní：Xià kè yǐhòu nǐ yǒu kòngr ma?
Jiéfū：Wǒ liù diǎn xià kè, nǐ yǒu shénme shì?
Ānní：Wǒ xiǎng qù Wáng Píng nàr, nǐ qù bu qù?
Jiéfū：Wǒ yě xiǎng qù, wǎnshang wǒ yǒu kòngr.
Ānní：Wǎnshang yìqǐ qù hǎo ma?
Jiéfū：Hǎo. Wǎnshang jiàn!
Ānní：Wǎnshang jiàn!

（Shàngwǔ dì-sì jié xià kè yǐhòu）
Ānní：Tián lǎoshī, xiànzài nín yǒu kòngr ma?
Tián lǎoshī：Duìbuqǐ, wǒ xiànzài méi kòngr, nǐ yǒu shì ma?
Ānní：(Dǎkāi shū) Zhè jǐ ge wèntí wǒ hái bù dǒng.
Tián lǎoshī：Wǒ kànkan, ò, Shānxià shuō zhè jǐ ge wèntí tā yě bù dǒng. Míngtiān shàng kè wǒ gěi
　　　　　　nǐmen yìqǐ jiǎngjiang ba.
Ānní：Tài hǎo le! Míngtiān jiàn!
Tián lǎoshī：Míngtiān jiàn!

（Ānní duì Wáng Píng shuō）
　　Jīntiān de kè yǒu jǐ ge wèntí wǒ hái bù dǒng, Tián lǎoshī shuō míngtiān shàng kè gěi wǒmen jiǎngjiang. Míngtiān wǎnshang wǒ hé Jiéfū dōu yǒu kòngr, wǒmen yìqǐ qù nǐ nàr, hǎo ma?

注释 Notes

1."晚上见""明天见"：
　　告别的时候，可以用下次见面的时间来表示，如："一会儿见""下星期见""八点见""明年见"等等。

　　Leave-taking may include the time at which you will again see the other party, such as:"一会儿见""下星期见""八点见""明年见"and so on.

2."有空儿":
　　"有空儿"和"有时间"的意思、用法都一样。"明天你有空儿吗?"回答是"有空儿"或"没(有)空儿"。
　　"有空儿" and "有时间" mean the same thing and are used in the same way. For instance:"明天你有空儿吗?" The answer is "有空儿" or "没(有)空儿".

3."这几个问题我还不懂":
　　其中的"几个"表示大概的数量,并且数量不多,如:
　　"几个" indicates a probable number, a few, not many, for example:
　　"我买了几本书。""还有几个人没来。"

练习 Exercises

一、发音练习:Exercises on pronunciation:
1.双音节练习:Two-syllable drills:
xià kè　　shàng kè　　yǒu kòngr　　méi kòngr　　yǐqián　　yǐhòu
2.三声变调练习:Sandhi drills in the 3rd tone:
nǐ hǎo　　nǐ zǎo　　jǐ diǎn　　fǔdǎo　　wǔbǎi

3.听与读:Listen and read:
Tùzi pǎo le. 兔子跑了。
Dùzi bǎo le. 肚子饱了。

二、用正确的语调读下边的句子:
　　Read the following sentences in correct intonation:
1.下午你有课吗?
2.下课以后你有空儿吗?
3.晚上我有空儿。
4.一起去好吗?

5.你有事吗?
5.明天上课我给你们一起讲讲吧。

三、读下边的句子,注意问句和答句在语调上的不同:
   Read the following sentences, paying attention to the differences in intonation between questions and answers:

1.问句句尾上扬(↑)　　　　　　　2.答句句尾下降(↓)
   现在几点?　　　　　　　　　　　现在两点。
   你有空儿吗?　　　　　　　　　　我有空儿。
   你也有课?　　　　　　　　　　　我没有课。
   一起去好不好?　　　　　　　　　好,一起去吧。

四、替换练习:Substitution drills:
1.下课以后你有空儿吗?
   下午两点
   今天晚上
   明天上午

2.我想去杰夫那儿,一起去好吗?
   我想买辆自行车
   我也有课
   我要去食堂

3.这几个问题 我还不懂。
       人　都在二班
       菜　一共十六块钱
       房间 都是教室

五、按正确的顺序把下面的词各组成一句话:
   Rearrange each group of words into a sentence:
1.你的房间　以后　下课　我　去
2.我　辅导　你　给　明天　晚上　八点
3.我　杰夫　和　一起　你　去　那儿
4.田老师　上课　给　我们　在　教室　上午　十点

六、将相关的甲乙句用线连起来组成一段对话：

Rearrange the two groups of sentences into a dialogue by showing their order and connections with arrows:

例：甲：早上好！　　　　　　　　　　　乙：早上好！
　　甲：你去上课吗？　　　　　　　　　乙：对。
　　甲：再见！　　　　　　　　　　　　乙：没空儿。
　　甲：我也有课，一起去吧！　　　　　乙：好。
　　甲：什么时候有空儿？　　　　　　　乙：下午。

1. 甲：今天有空儿吗？　　　　　　　　乙：没空儿。
　　　　　　　　　　　　　　　　　　　乙：不知道。

　　甲：现在几点了？　　　　　　　　　乙：明天。
　　甲：什么时候有空儿？　　　　　　　乙：三点了。

　　甲：明天我去你那儿好吗？　　　　　乙：好。
　　甲：几点上课？　　　　　　　　　　乙：两点。

2. 甲：你有空儿吗？　　　　　　　　　乙：什么事？
　　　　　　　　　　　　　　　　　　　乙：今天。

　　甲：我想去王平那儿，你去吗？　　　乙：对不起，我现在没空儿。
　　甲：我去上课。　　　　　　　　　　乙：一起去吧！

　　甲：昨天呢？　　　　　　　　　　　乙：我不懂。
　　甲：明天呢？　　　　　　　　　　　乙：也没空儿。

　　甲：太好了！
　　甲：你真忙。

七、以杰夫的口气叙述第一段会话。

Reproduce Dialogue 1 in the first person from Jeff's point of view：

八、情景会话：Situational dialogues：

1．你请同学一起去买自行车。

2．你请朋友到自己家玩儿。

第六课　她病了

（上课以前）
杰　　夫：老师，安妮不能来上课了。
田老师：她怎么了？
杰　　夫：她病了，感冒了。
田老师：好，我知道了，谢谢你。

（安妮叫杰夫给她请假）
　　杰夫，我感冒了，今天不能去上课了，你跟老师说说。好吗？

（上课半个小时以后，丽莎敲门）
田老师：请进！
丽　　莎：对不起，我来晚了。
（丽莎入座，她的同桌小声问）
同　　桌：你怎么才来呀？
丽　　莎：我的闹钟睡觉了，所以……
同　　桌：什么？闹钟睡觉？哦，我知道了，你的闹钟停了。

丽　莎:对,我的闹钟停了,我八点才起床,所以来晚了。
田老师:你们有问题吗?
丽　莎:没有,没有,对不起。

(下课以后,彼得跟老师请假)
　　田老师,明天我要去大使馆,不能来上课,跟您请个假。

Dì-liù kè　Tā bìng le

(Shàng kè yǐqián)
Jiéfū: Lǎoshī, Ānní bù néng lái shàng kè le.
Tián lǎoshī: Tā zěnme le?
Jiéfū: Tā bìng le, gǎnmào le.
Tián lǎoshī: Hǎo, wǒ zhīdào le, xièxie nǐ.

(Ānní jiào Jiéfū gěi tā qǐngjià)
　　Jiéfū, wǒ gǎnmào le, jīntiān bù néng qù shàng kè le, nǐ gēn lǎoshī shuōshuo. Hǎo ma?

(Shàng kè bàn ge xiǎoshí yǐhòu, Lìshā qiāo mén)
Tián lǎoshī: Qǐng jìn!
Lìshā: Duìbuqǐ, wǒ lái wǎn le.
(Lìshā rù zuò, tā de tóngzhuō xiǎoshēng wèn)
Tóngzhuō: Nǐ zěnme cái lái ya?
Lìshā: Wǒ de nàozhōng shuìjiào le, suǒyǐ……
Tóngzhuō: Shénme? Nàozhōng shuìjiào? Ò, wǒ zhīdào le, nǐ de nàozhōng tíng le.
Lìshā: Duì, wǒ de nàozhōng tíng le, wǒ bā diǎn cái qǐ chuáng, suǒyǐ lái wǎn le.
Tián lǎoshī: Nǐmen yǒu wèntí ma?
Lìshā: Méiyǒu, méiyǒu, duìbuqǐ.

(Xià kè yǐhòu, Bǐdé gēn lǎoshī qǐngjià)
　　Tián lǎoshī, míngtiān wǒ yào qù dàshǐguǎn, bù néng lái shàng kè, gēn nín qǐng ge jià.

注释 Notes

1."怎么了":
　　询问某种情况发生的原因。例如:"他怎么了?——他病了。"也可以说"他怎么没去?——他累了。"

Used to inquire about the cause of some happening, For example: "他怎么了？——他病了."also can be said "他怎么没去？——他累了."

2."好吗":

用在祈使句的末尾，语气委婉，有商量的口气，如："请你帮我请个假，好吗？""明天给我辅导，好吗？"回答是"好""好的"或"好吧"，不用"对""是"。

Used to end an imperative sentence in a mild and consulting tone, for instance: "请你帮我请个假，好吗？""明天给我辅导，好吗？"The answer should be "好", "好的"or"好吧"instead of "对" or "是".

3."呀":

"呀"，助词，是"啊"在句中受到前一字的韵尾 a o e i ü 的影响而发生的音变，如：

"呀" is a variation of the particle "啊". The pronunciation has changed from [a] to [ya] as a result of liaison from the finals (a o e i u) of the preceding word, for example:

"是你呀？""快来呀！"

4."我来晚了":

"来晚了"用于已经发生的事，如："昨天来晚了。"也可以表示告诫，常用"别来晚了"；"晚(一)点儿来"，用于未发生的事，如："明天我有事，可能晚(一)点儿来。"

"来晚了" can be used in different situations. It may refer to some happening in the past, for instance: "昨天来晚了"; It may convey an admonition: such as "别来晚了"; It may also indicate something still to come, for example: "明天我有事，可能晚(一)点儿来".

练习 Exercises

一、听与读：Listen and read:

Yí wàng èr sān lǐ,
Yān cūn sì wǔ jiā,
Mén qián liù qī shù,
Bā jiǔ shí zhī huā.

二、用正确的语调读下边的句子：
　　Read the following sentences in correct intonation：

1. 安妮不能来上课了。
2. 她怎么了？
3. 安妮病了，她感冒了。
4. 你怎么才来呀？
5. 我八点才起床，所以来晚了。
6. 跟您请个假。

三、替换练习：Substitution drills：

1. 她病了。
　　　感冒
　　　来晚
　　　去大使馆
　　　不能来上课
　　　去教室

2. 你怎么才来？
　　　　　去
　　　　　知道
　　　　　起床
　　　　　请假
　　　　　去食堂

3. 我八点才起床，所以来晚了。
　　我的自行车坏了　　不能骑车去玩儿了
　　她病了　　　　　　不能去上课了
　　彼得要去大使馆　　不能来上课了

四、模拟表演第一段会话。Perform Dialogue 1.

五、模拟表演下边的对话：Perform the following dialogues：

（一）

　　（在教室门口，甲要进教室，乙正要出教室）

　　甲：去哪儿？该上课了。

　　乙：今天咱们不上课了，老师病了。

　　甲：什么病？

　　乙：不知道。

（二）

　　（甲在等乙，乙来了）

　　甲：你怎么才来？

　　乙：你不是说三点见面吗？

　　甲：是呀，你看看现在几点了？

　　乙：三点呀！

　　甲：什么？三点？三点半了！

　　乙：你的表快了吧？

　　甲：什么？是你的表慢了吧？

　　乙：不会，我的表从来不慢。

六、复述第二段会话。Reproduce Dialogue 2.

七、情景会话：Situational dialogues：

向老师口头请假 Ask the teacher for leave under the following circumstances：

1. 病了。
2. 要去大使馆。
3. 妈妈要来北京，你去机场接她。

第七课 我喜欢喝茶

(吃晚饭时)

杰　夫：你喜欢吃什么？
安　妮：豆包子。
杰　夫：什么？我听不懂。
安　妮：豆—包—子。就是包子。
杰　夫：哈哈！小姐，错了！
安　妮：怎么错了？
杰　夫：那叫豆包儿！不叫豆包子。豆包儿不是包子。
安　妮：什么是包子？
杰　夫：肉包子、菜包子才是包子呢。

(杰夫和安妮去彼得的宿舍)

杰　夫：王平，你也在这儿！
王　平：是你们哪！
彼　得：欢迎！欢迎！请坐！
安　妮：好，杰夫，你坐那儿，我坐这儿。

彼　得：杰夫，喝点儿什么？茶还是咖啡？
杰　夫：咖啡，我喜欢咖啡。
安　妮：你这个人，怎么忘了"女士优先"？
彼　得：对不起，小姐，您也喜欢喝咖啡，对吧？
安　妮：先生，您又错了！来中国以后，我喜欢喝茶了！

（杰夫告诉安妮）

　　包子是包子，豆包儿是豆包儿。豆包儿不能叫豆包子，肉包子、菜包子才能叫包子。

（安妮说）

　　以前在英国我喜欢喝咖啡，来中国以后，习惯了喝茶，现在我非常喜欢中国茶。

Dì-qī kè　Wǒ xǐhuan hē chá

(Chī wǎnfàn shí)

Jiéfū: Nǐ xǐhuan chī shénme?

Ānní: Dòu bāozi.

Jiéfū: Shénme? Wǒ tīng bu dǒng.

Ānní: Dòu-bāo-zi. Jiùshì bāozi.

Jiéfū: Hā ha! Xiǎojie, cuò le!

Ānní: Zěnme cuò le?

Jiéfū: Nà jiào dòubāor! Bú jiào dòu bāozi. Dòubāor bú shi bāozi.

Ānní: Shénme shì bāozi?

Jiéfū: Ròu bāozi、cài bāozi cái shì bāozi ne.

(Jiéfū hé Ānní qù Bǐdé de sùshè)

Jiéfū: Wáng Píng, nǐ yě zài zhèr!

Wáng Píng: Shì nǐmen na!

Bǐdé: Huānyíng! Huānyíng! Qǐng zuò!

Ānní: Hǎo, Jiéfū, nǐ zuò nàr, wǒ zuò zhèr.

Bǐdé: Jiéfū, hē diǎnr shénme? Chá háishi kāfēi?

Jiéfū: Kāfēi, wǒ xǐhuan kāfēi.

Ānní: Nǐ zhèi ge rén, zěnme wàng le "Nǚshì yōuxiān"?

Bǐdé: Duìbuqǐ, xiǎojie, nín yě xǐhuan hē kāfēi, duì ba?

Ānní: Xiānsheng, nín yòu cuò le! Lái Zhōngguó yǐhòu, wǒ xǐhuan hē chá le!

（Jiéfū gàosu Ānní）

Bāozi shì bāozi, dòubāor shì dòubāor. Dòubāor bù néng jiào dòu bāozi，ròu bāozi、cài bāozi cái néng jiào bāozi.

（Ānní shuō）

Yǐqián zài Yīngguó wǒ xǐhuan hē kāfēi, lái Zhōngguó yǐhòu, xíguàn le hē chá，xiànzài wǒ fēicháng xǐhuan Zhōngguó chá.

注释 Notes

1. "小姐"：

一般是对年轻女子的称呼。有时前边可以加上姓,如："李小姐、刘小姐"。本课是跟比较熟悉的朋友开玩笑。

Used to address young women, could be preceded by a surname, for example：. "李小姐""刘小姐". In this dialogue, it is used jokingly between familiar friends.

2. "先生"：

对男子的称呼。前面可以加上姓,如：

Used to address men, could be preceded by a surname, for example：

"王先生早！""张先生好！"

3. "哪"：

"哪",助词,是"啊"的音变,在句中"啊"的前一字韵尾是"-n"时,"啊"变成"哪",如：

A variation of the particle"啊"; Preceded by a final with the nasal ending "-n", "啊" [a] becomes "哪" [na] as a result of liaison. For example：

"你看哪！""汉语真难哪！"

4. "一点儿"：

表示不定的数量,如："多买一点儿吧","一"常被省略,如："吃点儿东西""喝点儿茶"。

Indicating an indefinite amount, for instance："多买一点儿吧", "一" is often omitted, for instance："吃点儿东西""喝点儿茶".

练习 Exercises

一、"不"的变调练习：Tone sandhi drills on "不"：

bù chī   bù tīng   bù shuō   bù gāoxìng

bù nán   bù míngbai   bù néng   bù lái

bù dǒng   bù zǎo   bù wǎn   bù hǎochī

bú shì   bú huì   búyòng xiè   bú kèqi   bú guì   bú duì

二、听与读：Listen and read：

① nán de（男的）　　　lán de（蓝的）
② nǚ de（女的）　　　lǜ de（绿的）
③ Hénán（河南）　　　Hélán（荷兰）
④ zhīdào（知道）　　　chídào（迟到）
⑤ wǒ wèn nǐ（我问你）　　wǒ wěn nǐ（我吻你）

三、用正确的语调读下边的句子：Read aloud the following sentences in correct intonation：

1. 你喜欢吃什么？
2. 我听不懂。
3. 怎么错了？
4. 欢迎！欢迎！
5. 喝点儿什么？茶还是咖啡？
6. 我喜欢喝咖啡。
7. 以前我喜欢喝咖啡，现在我非常喜欢中国茶。

四、看图回答：Answer the questions with the help of the pictures：

1. 你喜欢喝什么？

2.吃点儿什么?

五、替换练习：Substitution drills：

1.你喜欢吃什么?
　　　　喝
　　　　干
　　　　买
　　　　看
　　　　学

2.我喜欢喝茶。
　　　　吃包子
　　　　看书
　　　　骑自行车
　　　　喝咖啡

3.你喜欢茶 还是 咖啡?
　　　　中国茶　日本茶
　　　　肉包子　豆包儿
　　　　蓝的　　黑的

六、以彼得的口气复述第二段会话。

Reproduce Dialogue 2 in the first person from Peter's point of view.

45

七、看图说话：Say something about the pictures：

我喜欢_____。
我不喜欢_____。

八、选择合适的词语填空，然后背诵全文：

Fill in the blanks with proper expressions, then recite the passage：

习惯　喜欢　非常　以前　以后

来中国_____，我不_____喝茶，我只喜欢喝咖啡。来中国_____，我也_____喝茶了。我觉得茶_____好喝，我每天都喝很多茶。

九、口头表达：Narration：

说说你或你的朋友、家里人都喜欢喝什么饮料。

Talk about yourself, your friends or your family members：what kind of drinks do they like?

第八课　你干什么呢？

(安妮的宿舍外，杰夫敲门)

杰　夫：安妮，在吗？
安　妮：(开门)是你呀，请进！坐吧！
杰　夫：谢谢！你怎么了？好像不太高兴？
安　妮：我有点儿想家。
杰　夫：想家了？那听(一)会儿音乐怎么样？
安　妮：好。咱们听着音乐聊天儿吧。

(在杰夫的宿舍门口)

丽　莎：杰夫！杰夫！
杰　夫：谁呀？进来！
丽　莎：你干什么呢？
杰　夫：做练习呢！
丽　莎：你听着音乐，能做好练习吗？
杰　夫：我听着音乐，练习做得更好！
丽　莎：真的吗？我问你一个问题，你能回答对吗？

杰　夫：你问吧！

（杰夫对彼得说）
　　昨天晚上我去安妮那儿，我看她有点儿不高兴。问她为什么，她说想家了。我说，听会儿音乐吧。我们听着音乐聊了一会儿天儿，都很高兴，她就不太想家了。

Dì-bā kè　Nǐ gàn shénme ne？

(Ānní de sùshè wài, Jiéfū qiāo mén)
Jiéfū：Ānní, zài ma？
Ānní：(Kāi mén) Shì nǐ ya, qǐng jìn！Zuò ba！
Jiéfū：Xièxie！Nǐ zěnme le？Hǎoxiàng bú tài gāoxìng？
Ānní：Wǒ yǒu diǎnr xiǎng jiā.
Jiéfū：Xiǎng jiā le？Nà tīng (yí)huìr yīnyuè zěnmeyàng？
Ānní：Hǎo. Zánmen tīngzhe yīnyuè liáo tiānr ba.

(Zài Jiéfū de sùshè ménkǒu)
Lìshā：Jiéfū！Jiéfū！
Jiéfū：Shéi ya？Jìnlai！
Lìshā：Nǐ gàn shénme ne？
Jiéfū：Zuò liànxí ne！
Lìshā：Nǐ tīngzhe yīnyuè, néng zuòhǎo liànxí ma？
Jiéfū：Wǒ tīngzhe yīnyuè, liànxí zuò de gèng hǎo！
Lìshā：Zhēnde ma？Wǒ wèn nǐ yí ge wèntí, nǐ néng huídá duì ma？
Jiéfū：Nǐ wèn ba！

(Jiéfū duì Bǐdé shuō)
　　Zuótiān wǎnshang wǒ qù Ānní nàr, wǒ kàn tā yǒudiǎnr bù gāoxìng. Wèn tā wèi shénme, tā shuō xiǎng jiā le. Wǒ shuō, tīng huìr yīnyuè ba. Wǒmen tīngzhe yīnyuè liáole yíhuìr tiānr, dōu hěn gāoxìng, tā jiù bú tài xiǎng jiā le.

注释 Notes

1."在吗"：
　　找人时常用的问话，如：打电话找小王："小王在吗"；一边敲门一边问："杰夫在吗？"
　　A question often asked when looking for someone, for example：Making a phone

call：“小王在吗？" knocking at the door and asking：“杰夫在吗？".

2."有点儿"：

　　副词,用在动词或形容词的前面,表示轻微、稍微,常常用在不如意的事情上,如：

　　Adverbial preceding a verb or an adjective, meaning slightly, a bit; often used to qualify undesirable things, for example：

　　"衣服有点儿脏了。""我有点儿累。""衣服有点儿长。"

3."那听会儿音乐怎么样"：

　　"那"表示顺着上文的意思或根据上文的条件、情况,说出应该出现的结果或做出的决定。上文可以是对方的话,也可以是自己提出来的假设或前提。也可以用"那么",意思一样。如：

　　"那" means then or in that case which modifies the conclusion or the decision made as a result of the previous condition or situation. It could be said by the other party or assumed by oneself. "那么"is also used in the same way. For example：

　　"他不来了。——那咱们先走吧。"
　　"邮局关门了。——那今天不能取包裹了。"

4."咱们"和"我们"：

　　"咱们"和"我们"都是代词,动作的主体包括谈话的对方时用"咱们",即总称己方(我或我们)和对方(你或你们)；不包括对方时用"我们"。但有时用"我们"也可以包括对方。

　　"咱们" and "我们" are both pronouns. "咱们" is used when the action involves not only the speaker (I or we) but also the other party (you); And "我们" normally does not include the other party. Sometimes "我们" may also include the other party.

5."干什么呢""做练习呢"：

　　这里的"呢"是助词,用在陈述句的末尾,表示动作正在进行或情况正在继续,如：

　　"呢" here is a particle used to end a declarative sentence, indicating the continuity of the action or the state of affair, for example：

　　"他正在看书呢。""外边正下着雨呢。"

6."真的吗"：

对某件事或某种现象表示怀疑或惊讶,如:

Used to express doubt or surprise at some happening or phenomenon, for example:

甲:我的自行车丢了。　　　甲:今天有听写。
乙:真的吗?　　　　　　　乙:真的?

"真的"也可以用在动词或形容词前面,强调确认,如:

"真的" may also come before a verb or an adjective, to emphasize or confirm something, for example:

"他真的没来?""真的很好。"

练习 Exercises

一、听与读:Listen and read:

①tā pǎo le	(他跑了)	(He ran away.)
tā bǎo le	(他饱了)	(He is full.)
②mǎi yì bāo yān	(买一包烟)	(Buy a pack of cigarettes.)
mǎi yì bāo yán	(买一包盐)	(Buy a pack of salt.)
③wǒ xiàng wǒ māma	(我像我妈妈)	(I take after my mother.)
wǒ xiǎng wǒ māma	(我想我妈妈)	(I miss my mother.)
④wǒ mǎi bēizi	(我买杯子)	(I want some cups.)
wǒ mǎi bèizi	(我买被子)	(I want a quilt.)
⑤zhè shì wǒ de tóngwū	(这是我的同屋)	(This is my roommate.)
zhè shì wǒ de dòngwu	(这是我的动物)	(This is my pet animal.)

二、用正确的语调读下边的句子:Read the following sentences in correct intonation:

1. 你好像不太高兴?
2. 我有点儿想家。
3. 咱们听着音乐聊天儿吧。
4. 你干什么呢?
5. 做练习呢!
6. 真的吗?
7. 我们听着音乐聊了一会儿天儿,她就不太想家了。

三、模仿例句看图说话:Look at the pictures and produce dialogues following the examples:

(一)例:甲:你干什么呢?

乙：做练习呢！

(二)例：甲：他怎么了？
　　　　乙：他病了。

四、替换练习：Substitution drills：

1. 请<u>进</u>!
　　　坐
　　　喝茶
　　　喝咖啡
　　　回答

2. 他好像<u>不太高兴</u>？
　　　　想家了
　　　　不知道
　　　　在做练习
　　　　没听懂

3. 她<u>不想家</u>了。
　　　不高兴

51

去上课
来中国
病
不舒服

4. 我有点儿想家。
这种鞋　贵
他　　　感冒
我的表　快
我　　　听不懂
她　　　不高兴

5. 听着音乐　聊天儿
喝　茶　　看电视
骑　车　　唱歌
抽　烟　　看书

五、下面的话你能说得更简单吗？Can you simplify the following statements?
例：听一会儿音乐吧！→听会儿音乐吧！
1. 我正在做作业呢！
2. 你是谁呀？请进来！
3. 我的名字叫安妮。
4. 我在一班，你们在几班？
5. 你喝点儿什么？喝茶还是喝咖啡？

六、模拟表演第一段会话。Perform Dialogue 1.

七、用丽莎的口气复述第二段会话。
Reproduce Dialogue 2 in the first person from Lisa's point of view.

八、根据自己的情况回答下面的问题：
Answer the following questions according to your own situation:
1. 来中国以后，你想家吗？为什么？

2. 想家的时候,你干什么?
3. 你能听着音乐做练习吗?你觉得这样做好不好?
4. 你喜欢和朋友聊天儿吗?为什么?

第九课　我去邮局寄信

（在宿舍门口）

杰　　夫：安妮，你要去哪儿？

安　　妮：我去邮局寄信。

杰　　夫：我也要寄几封信。

安　　妮：一块儿去吧！

杰　　夫：（看表）已经五点了，邮局关门了吧？

安　　妮：五点半才关门呢。

（到了学校邮局）

安　　妮：我买两张五块四的邮票。

营业员：一共十块八。

杰　　夫：小姐，这封信寄到美国，这封寄上海，这封本市。

营业员：这封五块四，这两封都是五毛。

（在邮局门口）

安　　妮：丽莎，你也来邮局寄信？

丽　莎：不，我来取一个包裹。
安　妮：是你家里寄来的吗？
丽　莎：是啊！
安　妮：那你得去学校外边的大邮局取。
丽　莎：安妮，能跟我一起去吗？
安　妮：真对不起，我现在没空儿……
丽　莎：没关系，我自己去吧！

（安妮说）
　　我和杰夫都要去寄信，杰夫不知道邮局几点关门，我说，现在才五点，邮局开着门呢，我们一起去吧。到了邮局，我们先买邮票。杰夫寄三封信，一共六块四，我寄两封，十块八。

（杰夫说）
　　丽莎家里给她寄了一个包裹，她不知道学校里边的邮局不能取国外寄来的包裹，安妮告诉她得到学校外边的大邮局去取。

Dì-jiǔ kè　Wǒ qù yóujú jì xìn

（Zài sùshè ménkǒu）
Jiéfū：Ānní, nǐ yào qù nǎr？
Ānní：Wǒ qù yóujú jì xìn.
Jiéfū：Wǒ yě yào jì jǐ fēng xìn.
Ānní：Yíkuàir qù ba！
Jiéfū：(Kàn biǎo) Yǐjīng wǔ diǎn le, yóujú guān ménr le ba？
Ānní：Wǔ diǎn bàn cái guān ménr ne.

（Dàole xuéxiào yóujú）
Ānní：Wǒ mǎi liǎng zhāng wǔ kuài sì de yóupiào.
Yíngyèyuán：Yígòng shí kuài bā.
Jiéfū：Xiǎojie, zhèi fēng xìn jì dào Měiguó, zhèi fēng jì Shànghǎi, zhèi fēng běn shì.
Yíngyèyuán：Zhèi fēng wǔ kuài sì, zhèi liǎng fēng dōu shì wǔ máo.

（Zài yóujú ménkǒur）
Ānní：Lìshā, nǐ yě lái yóujú jì xìn？
Lìshā：Bù, wǒ lái qǔ yí ge bāoguǒ.
Ānní：Shì nǐ jiā li jì lái de ma？

Lìshā: Shì a!
Ānní: Nà nǐ děi qù xuéxiào wàibian de dà yóujú qǔ.
Lìshā: Ānní, néng gēn wǒ yìqǐ qù ma?
Ānní: Zhēn duìbuqǐ, wǒ xiànzài méi kòngr……
Lìshā: Méi guānxi, wǒ zìjǐ qù ba!

(Ānní shuō)

　　Wǒ hé Jiéfū dōu yào qù jì xìn, Jiéfū bù zhīdào yóujú jǐ diǎn guān ménr, wǒ shuō, xiànzài cái wǔ diǎn, yóujú kāizhe ménr ne, wǒmen yìqǐ qù ba. Dàole yóujú, wǒmen xiān mǎi yóupiào. Jiéfū jì sān fēng xìn, yígòng liù kuài sì, wǒ jì liǎng fēng, shí kuài bā.

(Jiéfū shuō)

　　Lìshā jiā li gěi tā jìle yí ge bāoguǒ, tā bù zhīdào xuéxiào lǐbian de yóujú bù néng qǔ guówài jì lái de bāoguǒ, Ānní gàosu tā, děi dào xuéxiào wàibian de yóujú qù qǔ.

注释 Notes

1. "是啊":

　　表示肯定的应答。如果只回答"是",语气显得生硬。

　　Indicating an affirmative answer. The one-word answer "是" would sound a bit blunt.

2. "没关系":

　　对方表示歉意说"对不起"时,可以用"没关系""不要紧"来回答。

　　Used in reply to an apology, the answer is "没关系"or"不要紧".

3. 方位词:

　　"里边、外边、上边、下边、前边、后边"等方位词中,"边"一般可以换成"面"。与名词相连接时用在名词的后边,常常省略"边"或者"面",如:

　　In some Chinese localizers: inside, outside, on, under, in front of, behind, etc., the word "边" can be replaced by "面". When preceded by a noun, "边" or "面" can be omitted, for example:

　　"家里、房间里、桌子上、国外、床下、门前。"

练习 Exercises

一、用正确的语调读下边的句子：Read the following sentences in correct intonation：

1. 你要去哪儿？
2. 我去邮局寄信。
3. 邮局关门了吧？
4. 我来取一个包裹。
5. 是你家里寄来的吗？
6. 你得去学校外边的大邮局取。
7. 邮局开着门呢。
8. 到了邮局，我们先买邮票。

二、读下边的句子，注意句子的重音：Read the following sentences taking care of where to stress：

1. 我是法国人，他是英国人。
2. 他在二班，我也在二班。
3. 我的宿舍就在这儿。
4. 厕所在那个教室旁边。
5. 他们都是留学生。
6. 先生，您又错了。
7. 五点半才关门呢。
8. 以前我喜欢喝咖啡，现在我非常喜欢喝中国茶。

三、用线连出相应的口语表达法，并各说出一句话：
   Draw a line between each oral expression and its equivalent and make sentences with both：

1. 什么时候   a. 一块儿
2. 一起   b. 几点
3. 一元钱   c. 一块
4. 有时间   d. 有空儿

四、替换练习：Substitution drills：

1. 我去邮局 寄信。
     教室   上课
     食堂   买饭

　　　　宿舍　休息

2. 邮局　关门了吧?
　　他们　下课
　　老师　回家
　　你　　想家
　　他　　不高兴

3. 你得去学校外边的邮局取。
　　　去办公楼问老师
　　　去学校里边的商店买
　　　去宿舍旁边的食堂吃
　　　回答这个问题
　　　先买邮票

4. 我来取一个　包裹。
　　买　张　邮票
　　买　点儿　菜
　　寄　封　信
　　问　个　问题

五、模拟对话表演：Perform the following dialogues:

(第一天)

甲:信来了!

乙:有我的吗?

甲:没有。

乙:怎么又没有我的信呢?

甲:那是因为你没给别人写过信吧?

(第二天)

甲:你的信!

乙:太好了! 哎,这是我寄的呀?

甲:是呀,你看看怎么又寄回来了?

乙:哦,忘了贴邮票了!

六、模拟表演第一段会话。Perform Dialogue 1.

七、用丽莎的口气复述第三段会话。
Reproduce Dialogue 3 in the first person from Lisa's point of view.

八、你去过邮局吗？说说你在那儿办事的经过。
Have you been to the post office? Talk about your experience there.

***

你知道吗？ (3)   时间和地点的顺序

　　今天是几月几号？回答是：1997年10月19号。写信的时候，信封上的地址怎么写？"中国北京市北京大学勺园3号楼103房间"。
　　你看出来了吗？时间和地点的顺序都是从大到小排列的。这跟你们国家的习惯一样不一样？

Do You Know? (3)   **How To Write a Date and an Address?**

What's the date today? Today is 1997, October 19th. How to address a letter? "P. R. C. Beijing Peking University Shaoyuan Building No. 3 Room 103".

Do you see now? The sequence of the elements of a date or an address goes from large to small. Is it same as in your country?

```
┌─────────────────────────────────┐
│  1 0 0 8 7 1                    │
│                                 │
│    北京市北京大学勺园3号楼103房间  │
│                                 │
│         何麦克    收             │
│                                 │
│       上海市复旦大学中文系        │
│                    2 0 0 4 3 3  │
└─────────────────────────────────┘
```

第十课　今天天气怎么样?

(早上,彼得从外边回来)
杰　夫:今天天气怎么样?
彼　得:不错。
杰　夫:热吗?
彼　得:不太热。
杰　夫:有风吗?
彼　得:没有。

(安妮跟王平谈天气)
安　妮:这里冬天冷不冷?
王　平:很冷。
安　妮:风大不大?
王　平:非常大。
安　妮:夏天怎么样?
王　平:热极了。
安　妮:哦,冬天和夏天天气都不好。

王　平：可是还有春天和秋天呢。

（李文静妈妈的朋友王阿姨从南方老家来，顺便看看李文静）
李文静：王阿姨，您怎么来了？
王阿姨：听说你病了，我来看看你。你怎么病了？
李文静：我不习惯这儿的天气。
王阿姨：现在身体怎么样？
安　妮：已经好了。
王阿姨：学习忙不忙？
李文静：不太忙。
王阿姨：生活习惯了吗？
李文静：还有点儿不习惯。可是没关系。
王阿姨：食堂的饭好吃吗？
李文静：还可以。

（李文静说）
　　王阿姨，您来看我，我非常高兴。请告诉我的爸爸妈妈：这里冬天很冷，风非常大，夏天热极了，我有点儿不习惯。现在我身体不错，学习不太忙。

Dì-shí kè Jīntiān tiānqì zěnmeyàng？

(Zǎoshang, Bǐdé cóng wàibian huílai)
Jiéfū: Jīntiān tiānqì zěnmeyàng？
Bǐdé: Bú cuò.
Jiéfū: Rè ma?
Bǐdé: Bú tài rè.
Jiéfū: Yǒu fēng ma?
Bǐdé: Méiyǒu.

(Ānní gēn Wáng Píng tán tiānqì)
Ānní: Zhèlǐ dōngtiān lěng bu lěng?
Wáng Píng: Hěn lěng.
Ānní: Fēng dà bu dà?
Wáng Píng: Fēicháng dà.
Ānní: Xiàtiān zěnmeyàng?
Wáng Píng: Rè jíle.

Ānní: Ò, dōngtiān hé xiàtiān tiānqì dōu bù hǎo.
Wáng Píng: Kěshì hái yǒu chūntiān hé qiūtiān ne.

(Lǐ Wénjìng māma de péngyou Wáng āyí cóng nánfāng lǎojiā lái, shùnbiàn kànkan Lǐ Wénjìng)
Lǐ Wénjìng: Wáng āyí, nín zěnme lái le?
Wáng āyí: Tīngshuō nǐ bìng le, wǒ lái kànkan nǐ. Nǐ zěnme bìng le?
Lǐ Wénjìng: Wǒ bù xíguàn zhèr de tiānqì.
Wáng āyí: Xiànzài shēntǐ zěnmeyàng?
Lǐ Wénjìng: Yǐjing hǎo le.
Wáng āyí: Xuéxí máng bu máng?
Lǐ Wénjìng: Bú tài máng.
Wáng āyí: Shēnghuó xíguàn le ma?
Lǐ Wénjìng: Hái yǒudiǎnr bù xíguàn, kěshì méi guānxi.
Wáng āyí: Shítáng de fàn hǎochī ma?
Lǐ Wénjìng: Hái kěyǐ.

(Lǐ Wénjìng shuō)
　　Wáng āyí, nín lái kàn wǒ, wǒ fēicháng gāoxìng. Qǐng gàosu wǒ de bàba māma: Zhèlǐ dōngtiān hěn lěng, fēng fēicháng dà, xiàtiān rè jíle, wǒ yǒudiǎnr bù xíguàn. Xiànzài wǒ shēntǐ bú cuò, xuéxí bú tài máng.

注释 Notes

1. "天气怎么样""身体怎么样":

　　"天气怎么样"意思是"天气好不好";"身体怎么样"意思是"身体好不好"。这里"怎么样"是用来询问事物的状况或性质的,再如:"玩得怎么样?""学习怎么样?"等等。

　　"天气怎么样" means "Is the weather good or not?" "身体怎么样" means "Are you keeping fit or not?" The expression "怎么样" is used to inquire the state or quality of something. More examples: "玩得怎么样?" "学习怎么样?" etc.

2. "不错":

　　"不错"是比较好的意思。如:

　　"不错" means pretty good. For instance:

　　"身体不错。""天气不错。""学习不错。"

3. "还可以":

表示情况一般,不太好也不太坏。

Indicating a moderate state, not very good nor very bad.

4."阿姨":

对与母亲年龄相当、没有亲属关系的妇女的称呼,前面可以加上姓,也可以不加,如:

Used to address an unrelated female of one's mother's generation; sometimes preceded by a surname, for example:

"李阿姨来了。""王阿姨呢?"

练习 Exercises

一、用正确的语调读下边的句子: Read the following sentences in correct intonation:

1. 今天天气怎么样?
2. 热吗?
3. 风大不大?
4. 现在身体怎么样?
5. 生活习惯了吗?
6. 有点儿不习惯。
7. 食堂的饭好吃吗?
8. 还可以。

二、发音练习: Exercises on pronunciation:

(一)圈出各组中与其他词语声调不同的两个词:
Circle two words or expressions in each group, which tone is different from the rest:
1. 现在 再见 所以 上课 教室 宿舍 包裹 下课 睡觉 寄信
2. 英国 喝茶 没有 欢迎 非常 开门 阿姨 生活 练习 关门
3. 学校 一共 习惯 问题 一块儿 邮票 国外 不错 身体 不用

(二)将声调相同的词语归类:Sort out the dissyllables in the same tone:
昨天　冬天　知道　这里　听说　自己
回答　邮局　学习　音乐　天气
明天　聊天儿　夏天　豆包儿　一起

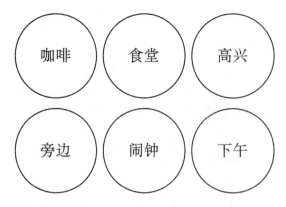

(三)轻声练习：Neutral–tone drills：

他们 师傅 包子 先生 真的 妈妈
什么 名字 还是 咱们
你们 我们 你呢 早上 晚上 怎么 喜欢 里边
谢谢 外边 告诉 爸爸
没关系 为什么 不客气 对不起

(四)半上声练习：Semi–rising tone drills：

1. (三声＋一声)老师 想家 好吃
   (三声＋二声)哪国 美国 法国 起床 以前
   (三声＋四声)请问 以后 有空儿 感冒 请进 请假 好像 本市
   (三声＋轻声)你们 我们 你呢 早上 晚上 怎么 喜欢 里边 已经

三、请参考下边的句式看图说话：

　　Practice the following sentence patterns referring to the pictures：

A：……怎么样？
B：很/非常/……极了

四、替换练习：Substitution drills：

1. 今天天气怎么样？

这儿的天气
　　食堂的菜
　　你们的教室
　　你买的自行车

2. 今天<u>很</u>热。
　　非常
　　有点儿
　　不太

五、参照例句,用类似的句式提问:
　　Ask similar questions as the example, using the following noun phrases:
例:这里冬天冷不冷?
　　1. 这儿的风
　　2. 这儿的夏天
　　3. 你的学习
　　4. 你的生活
　　5. 食堂的饭
　　6. 你的宿舍
　　7. 你的教室

六、根据实际情况回答问题: Answer the following questions according to the real situation:
1. 今天天气怎么样?
2. 你觉得这里的天气怎么样?
3. 今天有风吗?
4. 你来中国以后身体怎么样?
5. 你现在学习忙不忙?
6. 留学生食堂的饭怎么样?
7. 你习惯这里的生活吗?

七、将第一段会话和第二段会话合起来复述。
　　Reproduce Dialogue 1 and Dialogue 2 put together.

八、以王阿姨的口气向李文静的父母介绍李文静的情况。

Tell Li Wenjing's parents about Li's situation in the first person from Aunt Wang's point of view.

九、请根据第三段会话谈一谈：你和李文静的感觉一样吗？请谈谈你来北京以后的生活。

Talk about yourself referring to Dialogue 3: Do you feel the same way as Li Wenjing? Talk about your life in Beijing after you got here.

第十一课　您贵姓?

(在办公室门口)
安　妮:请问,这是留学生办公室吗?
刘老师:是。请进! 有什么事吗?
安　妮:老师,我想问问我的学生证办好了没有?
刘老师:你叫什么名字?
安　妮:安妮。
刘老师:你就是安妮? 你的学生证还没办好,你明天来取吧。
安　妮:谢谢。老师,您贵姓?
刘老师:我姓刘。
安　妮:刘老师明天见!

(在校园里,杰夫、安妮和王平、李文静相遇)
王　平:杰夫、安妮,来认识一下儿,这是李文静。
杰　夫:李文静,你好! 我叫杰夫。
安　妮:我叫安妮,认识你很高兴。
李文静:你们好! 你们俩都是新来的留学生吧?

杰　夫：⎫
安　妮：⎬是啊。

杰　夫：(小声对王平)是女朋友吧？
王　平：(小声对杰夫)哪里,女的朋友。
李文静：你们说什么呢？
王　平：⎫
杰　夫：⎬没说什么。

(在回宿舍的路上)
李文静：安妮,你是第一次来中国吗？
安　妮：是第二次。第一次是来旅行的。
李文静：来中国以前你学了多长时间汉语了？
安　妮：两个星期。
李文静：学汉语难不难？
安　妮：发音不难,语法也不太难。就是汉字,太难了。

(安妮说)
　　今天又认识了一个新朋友,是王平介绍给我们的。她叫李文静,是王平的同学。认识她我很高兴。

Dì-shíyī kè　Nín guìxìng？

(Zài bàngōngshì ménkǒu)
Ānní：Qǐng wèn, zhè shì liúxuéshēng bàngōngshì ma？
Liú lǎoshī：Shì. Qǐng jìn！Yǒu shénme shì ma？
Ānní：Lǎoshī, wǒ xiǎng wènwen wǒ de xuéshēngzhèng bànhǎo le méiyǒu？
Liú lǎoshī：Nǐ jiào shénme míngzi？
Ānní：Ānní.
Liú lǎoshā：Nǐ jiùshì Ānní？Nǐ de xuéshēngzhèng hái méi bànhǎo, nǐ míngtiān lái qǔ ba.
Ānní：Xièxie. Lǎoshī, nín guì xìng？
Liú lǎoshī：Wǒ xìng Liú.
Ānní：Liú lǎoshī míngtiān jiàn！

(Zài xiàoyuán li, Jiéfū、Ānní hé Wáng Píng、Lǐ Wénjìng xiāngyù)
Wáng Píng：Jiéfū, Ānní, lái rènshi yí xiàr, zhè shì Lǐ Wénjìng.
Jiéfū：Lǐ Wénjìng, nǐ hǎo！Wǒ jiào Jiéfū.

Ānní：Wǒ jiào Ānní, rènshi nǐ hěn gāoxìng.

Lǐ Wénjìng：Nǐmen hǎo！Nǐmen liǎ dōu shì xīn lái de liúxuéshēng ba？

Jiéfū：
Ānní： } Shì a.

Jiéfū：(Xiǎoshēng duì Wáng Píng) Shì nǚ péngyou ba？

Wáng Píng：(Xiǎoshēng duì Jiéfū) Nǎlǐ, Nǚ de péngyou.

Lǐ Wénjìng：Nǐmen shuō shénme ne？

Wáng Píng：
Jiéfū： } Méi shuō shénme.

(Zài huí sùshè de lùshang)

Lǐ Wénjìng：Ānní, nǐ shì dì-yī cì lái Zhōngguó ma？

Ānní：Shì dì-èr cì. Dì-yī cì shì lái lǚxíng de.

Lǐ Wénjìng：Lái Zhōngguó yǐqián xuéle duō cháng shíjiān Hànyǔ le？

Ānní：Liǎng ge xīngqī.

Lǐ Wénjìng：Xué Hànyǔ nán bu nán？

Ānní：Fāyīn bù nán, yǔfǎ yě bú tài nán. Jiùshì Hànzì, tài nán le.

(Ānní shuō)

Jīntiān yòu rènshi le yí ge xīn péngyou, shì Wáng Píng jièshào gěi wǒmen de. Tā jiào Lǐ Wénjìng, shì Wáng Píng de tóngxué. Rènshi tā wǒ hěn gāoxìng.

注释 Notes

1. "您贵姓"：

客气地问对方的姓。"贵"是敬词。回答时可以只说自己的姓："我姓……"，也可以说出全名："我叫……"。不能说"我贵姓……"。

A polite form of asking someone's name. "贵" is a term of respect. The answer could be the surname only："我姓……", or the full name："我叫……". But never say "我贵姓……".

2. "是女朋友吧"：

"女朋友""男朋友"指恋人，如果是一般的朋友，介绍时说："这是我的一个朋友"；为了避免误解，在谈到异性朋友时，有人也强调说"女的朋友""男的朋友"。

Girlfriend or boyfriend means lover. One may introduce an ordinary friend by saying, "这是我的一个朋友"; Some may introduce a friend of the opposite sex as "女的朋友" or "男的朋友" for emphasis so as to avoid misunderstanding.

3."哪里,是女的朋友":

在这儿"哪里"表示否定:"不,不是。"

"哪里" is a negative answer here:"No, she is not."

4."就是":

"就是"表示强调实际情况是这样。如:

The expression"就是" is used to emphasize something, for example:

"她就是安妮。""左边那位就是。"

5."俩":

口语词"俩"的意思是"两个",如:"我们俩""有三个包子,我吃了俩。"注意:"俩"的后边不再接"个"或其他量词。

"俩", informal, means "two", for example:"我们俩","有三个包子,我吃了俩。" Notice that "俩" no longer needs "个" or any other measure word after it.

练习 Exercises

一、用正确的语调读下边的句子,注意重音:

Read the following sentences in correct intonation, paying attention to the stresses:

1. 您贵姓?
2. 认识你很高兴。
3. 你们俩都是新来的留学生吧?
4. 你是第一次来中国吗?
5. 学汉语难不难?
6. 今天又认识了一个新朋友,是王平介绍给我们的。
7. 她是王平的同学。

二、替换练习: Substitution drills:

1. 我想问问我的学生证办好了没有?

　　　　他叫什么名字

　　　　留学生办公室在哪儿

　　　　你晚上有空儿没有

　　　　食堂几点关门

　　　　几月几号放假

2. 你们俩都是新来的留学生吧?
　　　　来过中国
　　　　去大使馆
　　　　习惯喝茶
　　　　是法国人
　　　　喜欢吃中国菜

三、体会加点儿词语的意思,模仿完成对话:
　　Make sure of the meanings of the dotted words and expressions and complete the dialogues:
1.①甲:她是你的女朋友吧?
　　乙:哪里,女的朋友。
　②甲:你是第一次来中国吧?
　　乙:_____。
2.①甲:学汉语难不难?
　　乙:发音不难,语法也不太难,就是汉字,太难了。
　②甲:在中国学习生活习惯吗?
　　乙:_____,就是_____。
3.①甲:你们说什么呢?
　　乙:没说什么。
　②甲:你看什么呢?
　　乙:_____。

四、用"新"搭配词语,并各说一句话:
　　Make a sentence with each of the following collocations beginning with the word "新":
新来的
新买的
新学的
新朋友
新老师
新学生
新食堂

五、表演第二段会话。Perform Dialogue 2.

71

六、熟读下面的话：Read the following passage repeatedly：

　　今天下午我去了留学生办公室，看见一位姓刘的老师。她说我的学生证已经办好了。我真高兴。

七、互问互答：Practice questions and answers with your classmate：
1．您贵姓？
2．你知道留学生办公室在哪儿吗？你去过吗？
3．你是第一次来中国吗？
4．来中国以前你学了多长时间汉语了？
5．学汉语难不难？什么最难？

八、用下边的句子作开头进行成段表达：
　　Produce a short narrative with each of the following as the first sentence：
①我来中国一个月了，……
②我有一位新朋友，……

第十二课　一个星期有多少节课？

（在安妮宿舍）

丽　莎：安妮，快起床！

安　妮：几点了？

丽　莎：七点三刻了！

安　妮：糟糕！我第一节有课，唉，又得饿着肚子去了。

（在去教室的路上）

彼　得：安妮，去上课吗？

安　妮：嗯。

彼　得：这学期你有几门课？

安　妮：三门。语法、口语和听力。你有几门？

彼　得：两门。我没有听力课。

安　妮：你一个星期有多少节课？

彼　得：二十节。

安　妮：两门也二十节？

彼　得：对，每门十节。今天你有几节课？

第十二课 一个星期有多少节课？

（在安妮宿舍）

丽莎：安妮，快起床！

安　妮：几点了？

丽莎：七点三刻了！

安　妮：糟糕！我第一节有课，哎，又得饿着肚子去了。

（在去教室的路上）

彼得：安妮，去上课吗？

安　妮：嗯。

彼得：这学期你有几门课？

安　妮：三门。语法、口语和听力。你有几门课？

彼得：两门。我没有听力课。

安　妮：你一个星期有多少节课？

彼得：二十节。

安　妮：两门也二十节？

彼得：对，每门十节。今天你有几节课？

安　妮：上午两节，下午两节，一共四节。

（彼得说）

　　我在一班，安妮在二班。我有两门课，她有三门课。每个星期我们都有二十节课。我们班人太多，有十六个学生，她们班人少，只有十二个。

（田老师介绍说）

　　一个学年有两个学期：第一学期在下半年，从九月到第二年一月，共有二十周；第二学期在上半年，从二月到七月，共有十八周。冬天放寒假，夏天放暑假。

Dì-shí'èr kè　Yí ge xīngqī yǒu duōshao jié kè？

(Zài Ānní sùshè)
Lìshā：Ānní, kuài qǐchuáng！
Ānní：Jǐ diǎn le？
Lìshā：Qī diǎn sān kè le！
Ānní：Zāogāo！Wǒ dì-yī jié yǒu kè, ài, yòu děi èzhe dùzi qù le.

(Zài qù jiàoshì de lùshang)
Bǐdé：Ānní, qù shàng kè ma？
Ānní：Ǹg.
Bǐdé：Zhè xuéqī nǐ yǒu jǐ mén kè？
Ānní：Sān mén. Yǔfǎ、kǒuyǔ hé tīnglì. Nǐ yǒu jǐ mén kè？
Bǐdé：Liǎng mén. Wǒ méiyǒu tīnglì kè.
Ānní：Nǐ yí ge xīngqī yǒu duōshao jié kè？
Bǐdé：Èrshí jié.
Ānní：Liǎng mén yě èrshí jié？
Bǐdé：Duì, měi mén shí jié. Jīntiān nǐ yǒu jǐ jié kè？
Ānní：Shàngwǔ liǎng jié, xiàwǔ liǎng jié, yígòng sì jié.

(Bǐdé shuō)
　　Wǒ zài yī bān, Ānní zài èr bān. Wǒ yǒu liǎng mén kè, tā yǒu sān mén kè. Měi ge xīngqī wǒmen dōu yǒu èrshí jié kè. Wǒmen bān rén tài duō, yǒu shíliù ge xuésheng, tāmen bān rén shǎo, zhǐ yǒu shí'èr ge.

(Tián lǎoshī jièshào shuō)
　　Yí ge xuénián yǒu liǎng ge xuéqī：Dì-yī xuéqī zài xià bànnián, cóng jiǔyuè dào dì-èr nián

yīyuè, gòng yǒu èrshí zhōu; Dì-èr xuéqī zài shàng bànnián, cóng èryuè dào qīyuè, gòng yǒu shíbā zhōu. Dōngtiān fàng hánjià, xiàtiān fàng shǔjià.

注释 Notes

1. "糟糕":

发现事情的结果很坏、很不如意时用,如:

Used to indicate something terrible or undesirable, for example:

"糟糕,我把钥匙忘在房间里了。"

2. "从二月到七月":

"从……到……"可以表示时段:如"从八点到九点""从十岁到十五岁";也可以表示距离,如:"从北京到上海""从这儿到那儿"等。

It indicates a period of time, for instance: "从8点到9点""从10岁到15岁"; or a distance, for instance: "从北京到上海""从这儿到那儿"and so on.

3. "嗯":

叹词,发音是"ng",声调不一样时,表达的感情也不同:"ǹg"表示答应、同意,如:"嗯,你说得对。";"ńg"表示疑问,如:"嗯,你说什么?";"ēg"表示沉思,如:"嗯,我想想。"

Interjection, the pronunciation is "ng". Spoken in different tones, the exclamation "嗯" expresses different emotions: In the fourth tone, it indicates a response or consent, for instance: "嗯,你说得对。", In the second tone, it conveys a question or doubt, for instance: "嗯,你说什么?" In the first tone, it conveys contemplation, for instance: "嗯,我想想。"

4. "上半年""下半年":

"上"指前一半时间或刚过去的一段时间,如:

"上"indicates the first half of a length of time or a length of time in the immediate past, for instance:

"上半年、上学期、上半个月、上(个)月、上星期二"。

"下"指后一半时间或即将到来的一段时间,如:

"下"indicates the second half of a length of time or a length of time yet to come, for instance:

"下半年、下学期、下半个月、下(个)月、下星期二"。

5."几"和"多少"：

(1)"几"：询问数量，估计数量不太多时用，如："教室里有几个人？""一斤香蕉几块钱？""现在几点？"；"几"一般表示小于十的数，如："买了几本书？""这孩子十几岁了？"

注意：在"几"的后边一般要用上量词。

"几"inquires about the number, usually a small number, for example："教室里有几个人？""一斤香蕉几块钱？""现在几点？"；"几"indicates a few, a numeral below 10, for instance："买了几本书？""这孩子十几岁了？"

N.B. the word"几"is normally followed by a measure word.

(2)"多少"：疑问代词"多少"中的"少"读轻声。可以询问数量，也可以表示不定的数量。"多少"后边的量词可以省去不用。如：

In the interrogative pronoun"多少", the second word"少"is in the neutral tone. It may inquire about the amount, or an indefinite amount. The measure word following"多少"is often omitted. For example：

"你们班有多少(个)学生？""这些东西一共多少(块)钱？""学多少会多少。"

练习 Exercises

一、用正确的语调读下边的句子：Read the following sentences in correct intonation：

1. 快起床！
2. 糟糕！
3. 这学期你有几门课？
4. 一个星期你有多少节课？
5. 每个星期我们都有二十节课。

二、读下边这段话：Read the following passage：

（一、二节课间，安妮对一个同学说）今天我又起晚了。已经七点三刻了，丽莎叫我，我才起床。八点上课，没时间吃早饭了，所以我又饿着肚子来了。哎，你有饼干吗？没有？唉，午饭我得多吃点儿。

三、替换练习：Substitution drills：

1. 我又得饿着肚子去(上课)了。

　　　起床

　　　买茶叶

　　　　　练习汉字
　　　　　去银行换钱

2. 糟糕！<u>我第一节有课</u>,<u>又得饿着肚子去了</u>。
　　　　　我的钥匙没了
　　　　　又忘了做练习了
　　　　　又该考试了
　　　　　邮局已经关门了

3. 从<u>今年九月</u>到<u>明年一月</u>　<u>是第一学期</u>。
　　早上　　　晚上　　　他都在房间里
　　八点　　　十点　　　我有空儿
　　九点半　　十一点半　我得上课
　　宿舍　　　教室　　　得走五分钟

四、体会"上"与"下"在不同句子中的不同含义：
　Make sure of the different meanings of "上" and "下" in different sentences：

1. 我每天上四节课。
2. 上次我没去,这次我去。
3. 下课以后你去哪儿?
4. 下星期我们还在这儿辅导,好吗?

五、完成对话：Complete the dialogues：

1. 甲：下午你有课吗?
　　乙：_____(没)
2. 甲：星期五你有几节课?
　　乙：_____(只有)

六、体会加点词的用法,用相同的句式做新的对话：
　Make sure of the use of the dotted words and produce new dialogues in the same sentence patterns：

1. 甲：今天你有几节课?
　　乙：四节。
2. 甲：一个星期有多少节课?
　　乙：二十节。

七、合理发问：下边是一些问题的应答语，设想一下儿问句是什么？

　　Probable questions: The following are the answers to certain questions, what should the questions probably be?

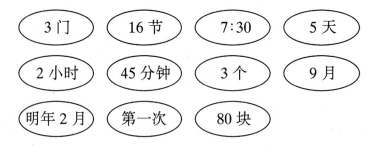

八、互问互答： Practice questions and answers with a classmate：

1. 你每天几点起床？
2. 这学期你有几门课？都是什么课？
3. 你一个星期上几节课？
4. 今天你有哪几门课？
5. 你们班有多少人？
6. 这个学期有多少周？从什么时候到什么时候？
7. 寒假什么时候开始？
8. 中国的学期时间和你的国家一样吗？

九、选用下边的词语成段表达：

　　Make a short oral composition choosing from the following words and expressions：

节　门　每　学年　学期　周　放　寒假　暑假

（我这个学期有……门课……）

第十三课　请问,去动物园怎么走?

(在一家大商场里)
彼　　得:小姐,请问哪儿卖鞋?
营业员:三楼,右边。
彼　　得:谢谢。
营业员:不用谢。

(在马路上)
安　　妮:大爷,请问,去动物园怎么走?
一老人:往前走,马路左边就是。
安　　妮:远吗?
一老人:不远,走五分钟就到了。
安　　妮:谢谢您。
一老人:不客气。

(在学校医院里)
杰　　夫:同学,请问牙科在哪儿?

一同学：我也不太清楚，好像在二楼，你再问问别人吧。

（杰夫上了二楼）

杰　夫：大夫，请问牙科是在二楼吗？

大　夫：是，往前走，再往右拐，左边第二个门就是。门上写着呢。

杰　夫：太谢谢了。

（杰夫告诉安妮）

　　昨天我去医院看牙，我不知道牙科在哪儿。我问了两个人才找到。牙科在二楼，上楼以后往前走再往右拐，左边第二个门就是。

Dì-shísān kè　Qǐng wèn, qù Dòngwùyuán zěnme zǒu?

（Zài yì jiā dà shāngchǎng li）

Bǐdé: Xiǎojie, qǐng wèn nǎr mài xié?

Yíngyèyuán: Sān lóu, yòubian.

Bǐdé: Xièxie.

Yíngyèyuán: Búyòng xiè.

（Zài mǎlù shang）

Ānní: Dàye, qǐng wèn, qù Dòngwùyuán zěnme zǒu?

Yì lǎorén: Wǎng qián zǒu, mǎlù zuǒbian jiùshì.

Ānní: Yuǎn ma?

Yì lǎorén: Bù yuǎn, zǒu wǔ fēnzhōng jiù dào le.

Ānní: Xièxie nín.

Yì lǎorén: Bú kèqi.

（Zài xuéxiào yīyuàn li）

Jiéfū: Tóngxué, qǐng wèn yákē zài nǎr?

Yì tóngxué: Wǒ yě bú tài qīngchu, hǎoxiàng zài èrlóu, nǐ zài wènwen biérén ba.

（Jiéfū shàngle èrlóu）

Jiéfū: Dàifu, qǐng wèn yákē shì zài èr lóu ma?

Dàifū: Shì, wǎng qián zǒu, zài wǎng yòu guǎi, zuǒbian dì-èr ge mén jiùshì. Ménshang xiězhe ne.

Jiéfū: Tài xièxie le.

（Jiéfū gàosu Ānní）

　　Zuótiān wǒ qù yīyuàn kàn yá, wǒ bù zhīdào yákē zài nǎr. Wǒ wènle liǎng ge rén cái zhǎodào. Yákē zài èrlóu, shàng lóu yǐhòu wǎng qián zǒu zài wǎng yòu guǎi, zuǒbian dì – èr ge mén jiùshì.

注释 Notes

1. "问问"：

动词的重叠。表示动作的动词可以重叠，表示动作的时间很短或者表示动作很轻松，很随便，有时也表示尝试。单音节动词重叠的形式是："AA"，如："看看""想想""尝尝"，双音节动词重叠形式是"ABAB"，如："休息休息""介绍介绍"；还有一类双音节动词的重叠形式是"AAB"，如："散散步""睡睡觉"。重叠的动词一般不能作定语或状语。

Reduplication of verbs：Verbs of action can be reduplicated to indicate the briefness of the action, or the relaxed or casual nature of the action, sometimes it indicates the effort of trying. One – syllable verbs reduplicate in the form of "AA", for example："看看"，"想想"，"尝尝"; Two – syllable verbs reduplicate in the form of "ABAB", for example："休息休息"，"介绍介绍"; Another type of two – syllable verbs reduplicate in the form of "AAB", for example："散散步"，"睡睡觉". Reduplicated verbs cannot be used as attributives or adverbials.

2. "同学"：

在学校里对学生的称呼。前面不加姓。如：

A common term of address for students on the campus. It is not preceded by any surname. For example：

"同学，请问，教学楼在哪儿？"

3. "三号楼"、"三楼"和"三层"的区别：

"三号楼"指大楼的号码儿；"三层"是指楼一共有三层，如："这是一座三层楼"，也可以指楼的第三层，如："办公室在三层"；"三楼"只是指"第三层"。再如：

"三号楼" indicates the number of the building；"三层" means there're altogether three storeys in the building, for example："这是一座三层楼", it also means the third storey, for example："办公室在三层"; "三楼" means the third storey only, More instance：

"学校里有三座宿舍楼，（一号楼、二号楼、三号楼）我住在三号楼，三号楼有五层，我住在三层（三楼）314 号房间。"

练习 Exercises

一、读下边的句子，注意自然连读与句中停顿：
Read the following sentences, paying attention to liaison and pauses in them:

1. 请问，去动物园怎么走？
2. 往前走，马路左边就是。
3. 远吗？
4. 请问牙科是在二楼吗？
5. 我不知道牙科在哪儿。
6. 太谢谢了！

二、替换练习： Substitution drills:

1. <u>牙科</u> <u>好像</u> <u>在二楼</u>。
   学校里　　没邮局
   这儿　　　不卖吃的
   他俩　　　不认识

2. 你再<u>问问</u>别人吧。
   　　想想
   　　休息休息
   　　看看书
   　　给我介绍介绍

3. 请问<u>牙科</u>是<u>在二楼</u>吗？
   　　王老师　住在这儿
   　　动物园　在前边
   　　银行　　在马路右边

三、回答问题： Answer the questions:

1. 你的宿舍在几楼？
2. 从你的宿舍到教室远吗？
3. 你知道校医院在哪儿吗？
4. 你家住几楼？

四、选用下边的句式和圈内的词语问路:
Ask the way using the following sentence patterns and the words and expressions in the circle：

请问,去……怎么走?
………在哪儿?
哪儿有………?

五、画一画,说一说,你们学校教学楼或宿舍楼的位置和布局是怎样的。
Draw a plan of your school and talk about the positions and layout of your classroom buildings or dormitory buildings.

参考用语:上楼　左　右　拐　往　厕所　教室

六、看图说话:Make an oral composition with the help of the drawing:
这是一家医院的平面图,请说说牙科、内科、外科分别在哪儿。
This is the plane of a hospital, explain where the Dentistry Department, the Internal Medicine Department and the Surgical Department are each located.

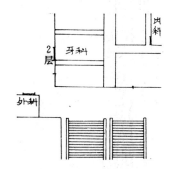

七、成段表达:介绍一个你熟悉的地方,并说说去那儿怎么走?
Make an oral composition about a place you know well and explain how to get there in a few parts：
分三部分:1.那个地方在哪儿?

2. 那个地方怎么样?

3. 去那儿怎么走?

八、附加练习:我理想的家

An additional exercise: My Ideal Home

要求:画出图,说说你希望住在什么样的楼层和房间里。

Requirements: Draw a picture and explain on which floor and in what kind of a room you'd like to live.

你知道吗? (4)　　中国人对人的称呼

1. 对陌生人:对年轻的女子,一般叫"小姐";对比自己年纪大的女子,可分别用"大姐""阿姨""大妈"或"大娘"来称呼;对男子一般叫"先生"。对年老的男子叫"大爷",对小孩儿叫"小朋友"。另外,还有"师傅""同志"等,除了对小孩儿以外所有的人都可以用。

2. 对认识的人:在姓的后面加上他(她)的职位,如:"李老师""王大夫""张主任""赵经理"等。年纪比较大的人,可以在姓前加"老"来称呼,如:"老王""老张";年纪大的人称呼年轻人,可在姓前加"小",如:"小刘""小钱"等;比较熟悉的朋友之间,可以只叫名字,不叫姓,如:对"赵大明"可以只叫"大明"。如果是单姓单名,那么就连姓一起叫,如:"王平"。

Do You Know? (4)　　**Chinese Ways of Addressing People**

1. Addressing strangers: Young women are generally addressed as "小姐"; Women older than yourself could be addressed as "大姐","阿姨","大妈" or "大娘" according to their age; Men are generally addressed as "先生". Older men are addressed as "大爷" and children as "小朋友"."师傅" and"同志" could be used to address everybody except children.

2. Addressing people one knows: Add surname to their posts or titles, for example:"李老师""王大夫""张主任""赵经理" etc. The word "老" could be added to older people's surname, for example:"老王""老张"; The word "小" could be added to the surname of younger people, for example:"小刘""小钱"and so on; Familiar friends can address each other by their name only, without the surname, for example:"大明"instead of"赵大明". But if the name contains only a one-word surname and a one-word name, then the full name in preferred, for example:"王平".

第十四课 喜欢吃什么？

（在一家饭馆里）

杰　夫：两位小姐，喜欢吃什么？
安　妮：我喜欢又酸又甜的。
杰　夫：你呢，丽莎？
丽　莎：我喜欢辣一点儿的。

（杰夫叫服务员）

杰　夫：小姐，又酸又甜的有什么菜？
服务员：有番茄肉片、糖醋鱼，还有古老肉。
丽　莎：要个番茄肉片吧。
杰　夫：辣的来个鱼香肉丝。
安　妮：再来个青菜好不好？
杰　夫：香菇菜心怎么样？
安　妮：好，我爱吃。
服务员：一共三个菜，还喝点儿什么？
杰　夫：喝茶吧。
服务员：请等一会儿。

（杰夫对彼得说）

　　昨天我和安妮、丽莎一起去饭馆吃饭，要了一个又酸又甜的番茄肉片，一个鱼香肉丝，是辣的，还要了一个青菜，味道也不错。那个饭馆的菜又好吃又便宜。

（在宿舍门口）
杰　　夫：安妮，这么早，去哪儿啊？
安　　妮：我去逛逛早市。
杰　　夫：早市？那儿都卖什么东西？
安　　妮：蔬菜、水果、衣服什么的，都卖。
杰　　夫：有水果？便宜吗？
安　　妮：便宜！比别的地方都便宜！
杰　　夫：真的？我也去！我要买点儿香蕉，我最爱吃香蕉了！
安　　妮：那一起去吧！
杰　　夫：行，走吧！

（安妮说）

　　我喜欢逛早市，因为那儿的东西又多又便宜。杰夫喜欢吃香蕉，他想买点儿香蕉，就跟我一起去了，这是他第一次逛早市。

Dì-shísì kè　Xǐhuan chī shénme？

(Zài yì jiā fànguǎnr li)
Jiéfū：Liǎng wèi xiǎojie, xǐhuan chī shénme？
Ānní：Wǒ xǐhuan yòusuān-yòutián de.
Jiéfū：Nǐ ne, Lìshā？
Lìshā：Wǒ xǐhuan là yìdiǎnr de.
(Jiéfū jiào fúwùyuán)
Jiéfū：Xiǎojie, yòusuān-yòutián de yǒu shénme cài？
Fúwùyuán：Yǒu Fānqié-ròupiàn、Tángcùyú, hái yǒu Gǔlǎoròu.
Lìshā：Yào ge Fānqié-ròupiàn ba.
Jiéfū：Là de lái ge Yúxiāng-ròusī.
Ānní：Zài lái ge qīngcài hǎo bu hǎo？
Jiéfū：Xiānggū-càixīn zěnmeyàng？
Ānní：Hǎo, wǒ ài chī.
Fúwùyuán：Yígòng sān ge cài, hái hē diǎnr shénme？
Jiéfū：Hē chá ba.

Fúwùyuán: Qǐng děng yíhuìr.

(Jiéfū duì Bǐdé shuō)
　　Zuótiān wǒ hé Ānní、Lìshā yìqǐ qù fànguǎn chī fàn, yàole yí ge yòusuān-yòutián de Fānqié-ròupiàn, yí ge Yúxiāng-ròusī, shì là de, hái yào le yí ge qīngcài, wèidao yě búcuò. Nà ge fànguǎn de cài yòu hǎochī yòu piányi.

(Zài sùshè ménkǒu)
Jiéfū: Ānní, zhème zǎo, qù nǎr a?
Ānní: Wǒ qù guàngguang zǎoshì.
Jiéfū: Zǎoshì? Nàr dōu mài shénme dōngxi?
Ānní: Shūcài、shuǐguǒ、yīfu shénme de, dōu mài.
Jiéfū: Yǒu shuǐguǒ? Piányi ma?
Ānní: Piányi! Bǐ biéde dìfang dōu piányi!
Jiéfū: Zhēnde? Wǒ yě qù! Wǒ yào mǎi diǎnr xiāngjiāo, wǒ zuì ài chī xiāngjiāo le!
Ānní: Nà yìqǐ qù ba!
Jiéfū: Xíng, zǒu ba!

(Ānní shuō)
　　Wǒ xǐhuan guàng zǎoshì, yīnwèi nàr de dōngxi yòu duō yòu piányi. Jiéfū xǐhuan chī xiāngjiāo, tā xiǎng mǎi diǎnr xiāngjiāo, jiù gēn wǒ yìqǐ qù le, zhè shì tā dì-yī cì guàng zǎoshì.

注释 Notes

1. "有点儿"和"一点儿"的区别:
　　(1)"有点儿"用在形容词或动词的前面,表示略微,稍微,多用于不如意的事情。如:
　　"有点儿" comes before an adjective or a verb, meaning "a bit", "a little", "slightly". It's often used to qualify something undesirable. For instance:
　　"他有点儿不高兴。""衣服有点儿长。"
　　(2)"一点儿"用在动词的后面,表示数量少或者使语气缓和,如:"我只买一点儿。""吃(一)点儿什么?";用在形容词的后面,表示稍微,有所比较,如:"今天比昨天热一点儿。""我要长一点儿的(衣服)。"
　　注意:" 点儿"不用在动词和形容词的前面,如:不能说"一点儿喜欢""一点儿高兴"。
　　"一点儿" comes after a verb meaning a few or a little. It is sometimes used to soften the mood, for example: "我只买一点儿。""吃(一)点儿什么?"; When fol-

lowing an adjective, it is used to form the comparative degree, for example:"今天比昨天热一点儿.""我要长一点儿的(衣服)."

N.B."一点儿"does not come before verbs or adjectives, for example:" * 一点儿喜欢"or" * 一点儿高兴".

2.表示列举或举例子的句式(一):

Sentence patterns for listing or giving examples (一):

(1)"什么的":用在一个成分或几个成分的后面,表示列举没有完,(一般用在句尾),如:

Following an item or several items listed (usually ending the sentence), it indicates the listing isn't finished yet, for instance:

"打打球,唱唱歌什么的,他都喜欢。""饺子,包子什么的,我都爱吃。"

(2)"有……(有……)还有……":表示列举,"还有"用在最后一项前,如:

Used for listing, "还有" comes before the last item being listed, for instance:

"我们班的学生有日本人,有韩国人,还有美国人。"

3."再来(一)个青菜好不好":

这儿的"来"是"要"的意思,在饭馆点菜或在商店买食品、饮料时常用。如:

"来" here means want, It is often used while ordering dishes in a restaurant or buying food and drinks in a shop. For example:

"来两瓶啤酒。"

4."比":

用"比"表示比较的句式是:"A 比 B+形容词性成分",如:

The sentence pattern for making comparison with the preposition"比" is:"A 比 B + adjective element". For example:

"小王比小张高。""今天比昨天冷一点儿。"

注意:它的否定形式是:"小张没有小王高。"不能说"小张比小王不高。"

N.B. The negative form is "小张没有小王高." " * 小张比小王不高" is a faulty sentence.

练习 Exercises

一、读下边的句子,注意语调和停顿:
Read the following sentences, paying attention to your intonation and where to pause:

1. 两位小姐,喜欢吃什么?
2. 我喜欢又酸又甜的。
3. 我喜欢辣一点儿的。
4. 再来个青菜好不好?
5. 那个饭馆的菜又好吃又便宜。
6. 我最爱吃香蕉了!
7. 我喜欢逛早市,因为那儿的东西又多又便宜。

二、替换练习: Substitution drills:

1. 我喜欢<u>辣</u>一点儿的(<u>菜</u>)。

  甜 香蕉
  大 房间
  早 课
  热 茶
  小 包子

2. 有<u>番茄肉片</u>、<u>糖醋鱼</u>,还有<u>古老肉</u>。

  大的   小的
  男的   女的
  黑的   蓝的
  美国人 日本人 韩国人

3. <u>蔬菜</u>、<u>水果</u>、<u>衣服</u>什么的,都<u>卖</u>。

 苹果 香蕉 葡萄 爱吃
 美国 法国 西班牙 想去
 辣的 甜的 酸的 有
 邮局 饭馆 商店 不远

4. (<u>这儿</u>)比<u>别的地方</u> <u>便宜</u>。
 今天 昨天 热

  他的发音 我   好
  上午的课 下午的课 多
  写汉字   说汉语   难

5. 我最爱<u>吃香蕉</u>了。
    看电视
    买东西
    写汉字
    吃辣的

6. <u>我喜欢逛早市</u>，因为<u>那儿的东西又多又便宜</u>。
  我今天没去上课 我病了
  我没去他家   这几天没空儿
  我买了很多水果 我最爱吃水果
  他来晚了   他的闹钟停了

7. 来一<u>个</u> <u>鱼香肉丝</u>。
   碗 米饭
   斤 香蕉
   瓶 啤酒
   斤 饺子

三、完成对话：Complete the dialogues：

1. 甲：你认识小王吗？
  乙：认识，他_____（又……又……，比……都……）
2. 甲：那个饭馆怎么样？
  乙：_____（又……又……，比……都……）
3. 甲：你的房间怎么样？
  乙：_____（又……又……，比……都……）
4. 甲：你喜欢什么水果？
  乙：_____（……，……什么的，都……）
5. 甲：你喜欢旅行吗？还有什么地方你想去？
  乙：_____。（……，……还有……，都……）

四、回答问题：Answer the questions：

1. 你吃过哪些中国菜？

2．你爱吃什么味道的菜？

3．你爱去哪个饭馆？那儿的菜怎么样？

4．你最爱吃什么水果？

五、情景会话：和同学去一家饭馆，商量点菜（要求至少点四菜一汤）。请选用下边的词语和句式：

　　Situational dialogue：Discuss with your classmates in a restaurant what dishes to order（at least four dishes and a soup），using some of the following words, expressions and sentence patterns.

词语：酸　　　　　　　　　　　句式：我喜欢……
　　　甜　　　　　　　　　　　　　　要一个……
　　　辣　　　　　　　　　　　　　　来一个……
　　　爱吃　　　　　　　　　　　　　……怎么样？
　　　味道　　　　　　　　　　　　　再来一个……好不好？
　　　青菜　　　　　　　　　　　　　一共……
　　　最

六、成段表达：Narration：

1、介绍一下"早市"。

2、介绍一个买东西的好地方。

3、介绍一家你喜欢的饭馆。

七、你能看懂下边的菜单了吗？（价格略）

　　Can you make sense of the following menu?（all the prices left out）

凉菜	海鲜	荤菜	素菜	主食	汤	饮料
松花蛋	锅巴三鲜	腰果鸡丁	香菇菜心	米饭	三鲜汤	啤酒
小葱拌豆腐	清炒虾仁	京酱肉丝	炒土豆丝	馒头	酸辣汤	茅台
拌海带丝	糖醋鱼	东坡肘子	荷兰豆	面条	粟米羹	菊花茶
蒜泥白肉	红焖大虾	扒肘条	鱼香茄子	炒饭		可口可乐
红油三丝	葱烧海参	古老肉		炒面		雪碧
花生米		红烧肉		饺子		椰汁
凉拌西红柿		鱼香肉丝		炸馒头		果茶

liángcài	hǎixiān	hūncài	sùcài	zhǔshí	tāng	yǐnliào
Sōnghuādàn	Guōbāsānxiān	Yāoguǒ-jīdīng	Xiānggū-càixīn	mǐfàn	Sānxiāntāng	píjiǔ
Xiǎocōng bàn Dòufu	Qīngchǎoxiārénr	Jīngjiàngròusī	Chǎotǔdòusī	mántou	Suānlàtāng	Máotái
Bàn Hǎidàisī	Tángcùyú	Dōngpōzhōuzi	Hélándòu	miàntiáo	Sùmǐgēng	júhuāchá
Suànní-Báiròu	Hóngmèndàxiā	Bāzhōutiáo	Yúxiāng-qiézi	chǎofàn		Kěkǒukělè
Hóngyóusānsī	Cōngshāohǎishēn	Gǔlǎoròu		chǎomiàn		Xuěbì
Huāshēngmǐ		Hóngshāoròu		jiǎozi		yēzhī
Liángbàn-Xīhóngshì		Yúxiāngròusī		zhá-mántou		guǒchá

第十五课 请你做我的辅导,好吗?

(在王平的宿舍)

安　妮:你最近忙吗?
王　平:还可以,有什么事吗?
安　妮:我想请你做我的辅导,好吗?
王　平:好哇! 你想辅导什么?
安　妮:我想练习口语,每星期两次,每次一个小时,可以吗?
王　平:没问题! 什么时候辅导好?
安　妮:星期一、四的下午五点到六点,怎么样?
王　平:星期一下午我有课,星期二行吗?
安　妮:行。一个小时多少钱?

(安妮对杰夫说)

　　我要练习口语,所以我请王平做我的辅导。我希望每个星期辅导两次,每次一个小时。王平高兴地答应了。从下个星期起,每星期二、四的下午五点到六点,王平都来我的房间辅导。

(在早市上)

安　妮：这葡萄酸不酸？

小商贩：不酸，甜的。

安　妮：可以尝尝吗？

小商贩：可以，尝吧，不甜不要钱。

(安妮尝了一个葡萄)

安　妮：真甜！来两斤吧。

(在路上)

杰　夫：王平，明天晚上有空儿吗？

王　平：什么事？

杰　夫：明天是我生日，来一起玩儿玩儿吧。

王　平：我一定来。

杰　夫：谢谢！

(王平说)

　　杰夫告诉我，明天是他的生日。他请我去他那儿玩儿，我答应一定去。我要送他一件礼物，还要给他唱《祝你生日快乐》。

Dì–shíwǔ kè　Qǐng nǐ zuò wǒ de fǔdǎo, hǎo ma?

(Zài Wáng Píng de sùshè)

Ānní: Nǐ zuìjìn máng ma?

Wáng Píng: Hái kěyǐ, yǒu shénme shì ma?

Ānní: Wǒ xiǎng qǐng nǐ zuò wǒ de fǔdǎo, hǎo ma?

Wáng Píng: Hǎo wa! Nǐ xiǎng fǔdǎo shénme?

Ānní: Wǒ xiǎng liànxí kǒuyǔ, měi xīngqī liǎng cì, měi cì yí ge xiǎoshí, kěyǐ ma?

Wáng Píng: Méi wèntí! Shénme shíhou fǔdǎo hǎo?

Ānní: Xīngqī yī、sì de xiàwǔ wǔ diǎn dào liù diǎn, zěnmeyàng?

Wáng Píng: Xīngqī yī xiàwǔ wǒ yǒu kè, xīngqī èr xíng ma?

Ānní: Xíng. Yí ge xiǎoshí duōshao qián?

(Ānní duì Jiéfū shuō)

　　Wǒ yào liànxí kǒuyǔ, suǒyǐ wǒ qǐng Wáng Píng zuò wǒ de fǔdǎo. Wǒ xīwàng měi ge xīngqī fǔdǎo liǎng cì, měi cì yí ge xiǎoshí. Wáng Píng gāoxìng de dāying le. Cóng xià ge xīngqī qǐ, měi xīngqī èr、sì de xiàwǔ wǔ diǎn dào liù diǎn, Wáng Píng dōu lái wǒ de fángjiān fǔdǎo.

（Zài zǎoshì shang）

Ānní：Zhè pútao suān bu suān？

Xiǎo shāngfàn：Bù suān, tián de.

Ānní：Kěyǐ chángchang ma？

Xiǎo shāngfàn：Kěyǐ, cháng ba, bù tián bú yào qián.

（Ānní cháng le yí ge pútao）

Ānní：Zhēn tián！Lái liǎng jīn ba.

（Zài lùshang）

Jiéfū：Wáng Píng, míngtiān wǎnshang yǒu kòngr ma？

Wáng Píng：Shénme shì？

Jiéfū：Míngtiān shì wǒ shēngri, lái yìqǐ wánrwanr ba.

Wáng Píng：Wǒ yídìng lái.

Jiéfū：Xièxie！

（Wáng Píng shuō）

　　Jiéfū gàosu wǒ, míngtiān shì tā de shēngri. Tā qǐng wǒ qù tā nàr wánr, wǒ dāying tā yídìng qù. Wǒ yào sòng tā yí jiàn lǐwù, hái yào gěi tā chàng《Zhù nǐ shēngri kuàilè》.

注释 Notes

1. "没问题"：

表示痛快地答应或没有任何困难，如：

A positive answer indicating readiness to comply or "there wouldn't be any difficulty", for example：

"这件事请你帮个忙，行吗？——没问题。""他一个人去没问题。"

2. "好吗？""行吗？""可以吗？"：

　　都是询问对方是否许可，也可以说"好不好？""行不行？""可（以）不可以？"肯定的回答分别是"好""行""可以"；否定的回答一般都是"不行"。

　　"行吗？"一般只用在句尾，如："帮我寄一封信，行吗？"；"可以吗"也用在句尾，但也可以分开用作"可以……吗"，如："这儿可以抽烟吗？"

All these expressions are used to ask for permission, "好不好？""行不行？""可（以）不可以？" can also be asked. The affirmative reply is "好""行""可以"; The negative reply is often "不行".

"行吗？" is often used to end a request, for example："帮我寄一封信，行吗？";

"可以吗" is used to end a request too, but also in the following way:"可以……吗", for example:"这儿可以抽烟吗?"

3."什么时候……好?"

意思是"什么时候更合适"。"……好"表示说话人通过比较,选择更合适的办法或更满意的情况。如:

The question "……好?" is asked to make a better choice, for example:

甲:"去哪儿好?"　　　　甲:"买哪件衣服好?"
乙:"去颐和园吧。"　　　乙:"还是买那件红色的好。"

4.重量单位:

一公斤＝2(市)斤＝1000 克　　1(市)斤＝10 两

在市场上,常用"斤""两";在商场里常用"克"。

Units of weight:1 kilogram = 2（市）斤 = 1000 gram

While"斤"and"两"are often used in the marketplace,"克"is often used in stores and supermarkets.

练习 Exercises

一、读下边的句子,注意自然连读与语气停顿:

Read the following sentences, noting the natural liaison and where to pause:

1.你最近忙吗?

2.我想请你做我的辅导,好吗?

3.好哇!

4.每次一个小时,可以吗?

5.什么时候辅导好?

6.可以尝尝吗?

7.星期一、四的下午五点到六点,怎么样?

8.祝你生日快乐!

9.没问题!

二、读一读,想一想,体会句子的语调、重音不同时句子含义的区别:

Read and think, paying attention to the intonation of the sentence and the differences in meaning when different words are being stressed.

1.已经上课了。

已经上课了？
已经上课了！

2. 他又来了。(不是你来,也不是我来)
   他又来了。(不是第一次来)
   他又来了。(不是去了,不是走了)

3. 我是学生。(不是别人)
   我是学生。(肯定)
   我是学生。(不是老师)

三、替换练习：Substitution drills：

1. 我想请你做我的辅导,好吗?
   有空儿去我家坐坐
   书我明天还给你
   再来一个辣点儿的菜
   咱们一块儿去

2. 每次　　一个小时,　可以吗?
   星期　　一次　　　　行吗
   人　　　一个　　　　行不行
   件　　　二百块　　　好不好
   课　　　学习三天　　怎么样

3. 什么时候辅导　好?
         去你家
         去旅行
         买票
         去早市

4. 每(个)星期　辅导两次。
   月　　　　　去一次
   年　　　　　旅行两个月
   天　　　　　上四节课
   小时　　　　三十块钱

5. 从下个星期起,每星期二、四的下午五点到六点,王平都来我的房间辅导。

97

现在　　　　我就是一班的学生了
明天　　　　每天七点半上课
这学期　　　我要找一个辅导
十八岁　　　我就开始学汉语了

四、用第三人称复述第一段会话：Reproduce Dialogue 1 in the third person：
"安妮想请一个辅导，……"

五、情景表演第二段会话："在早市上" Perform Dialogue 2："In the morning market"

六、回答问题：Answer the questions：
1. 你最近忙吗？
2. 你有辅导吗？什么时间辅导？
3. 你的生日是什么时候？
4. 朋友过生日你送给他什么礼物？
5. 你最喜爱的生日礼物是什么？

七、情景会话：Situational dialogues：
1. 请朋友参加你的生日晚会。
2. 请一个中国学生做你的辅导。
3. 请朋友帮你一个忙。

参考句式：……行吗？　　　　可以……吗？
　　　　　……可以吗？　　　什么时候……好？
　　　　　……怎么样？　　　……有空儿吗？
　　　　　……好吗？

《祝你生日快乐》

第十六课　我有点儿不舒服

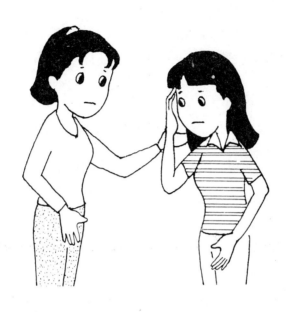

（在课堂上）
学　生：对不起，老师，我有点儿不舒服，想回房间休息休息，可以吗？
老　师：怎么了？
学　生：头有点儿疼。
老　师：好吧，回去好好儿睡一觉，也许就好了。
学　生：谢谢老师。

（下课以后）
山　下：安妮，你们考试了吗？
安　妮：上星期五考了。
山　下：怎么样？考得好吗？
安　妮：不太好。上星期我有点儿不舒服，没好好儿准备。
山　下：没关系，不是还有下（一）次吗？

（在中国学生的宿舍里）
张　新：李文静，听说你不舒服，好点儿了吗？

李文静：多谢你的关心，现在好多了。
张　新：我想出去散散步，你去不去？
李文静：对不起，我不能去，有个朋友要来看我。
张　新：是谁这么关心你呀！男朋友吧？
李文静：……（不语）
张　新：哈哈，你不说话我就知道，我准说对了。
李文静：你知道什么呀？你快走吧！
张　新：我哪儿敢慢走哇！哎，别忘了，好好儿招待招待他。

（安妮对山下说）
　　上星期五我们考试了。可是，考试以前我有点儿不舒服，没好好儿准备，所以考得不太好，下次一定努力。

Dì-shíliù kè　Wǒ yǒudiǎnr bù shūfu
(Zài kètáng shang)
Xuésheng：Duìbuqǐ, lǎoshī, wǒ yǒudiǎnr bù shūfu, xiǎng huí fángjiān xiūxi xiūxi, kěyǐ ma？
Lǎoshī：Zěnme le？
Xuésheng：Tóu yǒudiǎnr téng.
Lǎoshī：Hǎo ba, huíqu hǎohāor shuì yí jiào, yěxǔ jiù hǎo le.
Xuésheng：Xièxie lǎoshī.

(Xià kè yǐhòu)
Shānxià：Ānní, nǐmen kǎoshì le ma？
Ānní：Shàng xīngqīwǔ kǎo le.
Shānxià：Zěnmeyàng？Kǎo de hǎo ma？
Ānní：Bú tài hǎo. Shàng xīngqī wǒ yǒudiǎnr bù shūfu, méi hǎohāor zhǔnbèi.
Shānxià：Méi guānxi, bú shi hái yǒu xià (yí) cì ma？

(Zài Zhōngguó xuésheng de sùshè li)
Zhāng Xīn：Lǐ Wénjìng, tīngshuō nǐ bù shūfu, hǎo diǎnr le ma？
Lǐ Wénjìng：Duō xiè nǐ de guānxīn, xiànzài hǎo duō le.
Zhāng Xīn：Wǒ xiǎng chūqu sànsan bù, nǐ qù bu qù？
Lǐ Wénjìng：Duìbuqǐ, wǒ bù néng qù, yǒu ge péngyou yào lái kàn wǒ.
Zhāng Xīn：Shì shéi zhème guānxīn nǐ ya！Nánpéngyou ba？
Lǐ Wénjīng：……（Bù yǔ）
Zhāng Xīn：Hā ha, nǐ bù shuō huà wǒ jiù zhīdao, wǒ zhǔn shuōduì le.
Lǐ Wénjìng：Nǐ zhīdao shénme ya？Nǐ kuài zǒu ba！

Zhāng Xīn: Wǒ nǎr gǎn màn zǒu wa! Āi, bié wàng le, hǎohāor zhāodài zhāodài tā.

(Ānní duì Shānxià shuō)
　　Shàng xīngqīwǔ wǒmen kǎoshì le. kěshì, kǎoshì yǐqián wǒ yǒudiǎnr bù shūfu, méi hǎohāor zhǔnbèi, suǒyǐ kǎo de bú tài hǎo, xià cì yídìng nǔlì.

注释 Notes

1. "好好儿"：
　　后面接动词，表示尽力地、认真地或尽情地做某事，如：
"好好儿" followed by a verb means to do something conscientiously or heartily, for example：
　　"好好儿想想""好好儿准备考试""好好儿玩儿几天""好好儿休息休息"。

2. "不太"或"不大"：
　　后面接形容词或部分动词，表示轻微的否定，如：
The two expressions followed by an adjective or a verb indicate a slightly negative attitude, for example：
　　"他不太(不大)舒服。""这个问题我不太(不大)明白。""今天不太(不大)冷。"

3. "哪儿敢慢走哇"：
　　是反问句，意思是"不敢慢走"，有强调的作用，再如："我哪儿知道哇"意思是"我不知道"。
　　A rhetorical question for emphasis, which means "I dare not go slowly." Another example："我哪儿知道" means "I don't know."

4. "不是还有下(一)次吗"：
　　也是反问句，意思是"还有下(一)次"；再如："那不是小王吗"，意思是："那是小王"。
　　A rhetorical question, meaning "there is a next time"; another example："那不是小王吗" means "that is Xiao Wang".

5. "哇"：
　　助词，是"啊"受前一字的韵尾"u"或"ao"的影响而发生的音变，如：
　　"哇"：particle, a variation of "啊", as a result of liaison from the final [u] or [ao] of the preceding word, for example：

"好哇!""走哇!"

6. 简单趋向补语:

"来"和"去"用在动词后补充说明动作的方向,是简单趋向补语,一般读轻声。如果动作是朝说话人进行,用"来",反之用"去"。如:"请上来"(说话人在楼上);"等一会儿,我马上下去"(说话人在楼上)。

如果动词后有地点宾语,不能说:"请上来楼""他回去家了"。要说:"请上楼来""他回家去了"。

The simple directional complement:"来" or "去" following a verb here is a simple directional complement indicating the direction of the action. They're often pronounced in the neutral tone. "来"indicates the action is coming towards the speaker, otherwise"去" is used . For example:"请上来"(when the speaker is upstairs) or "等一会儿,我马上下去"(when the speaker is upstairs).

If the verb takes an object of localte, notice the correct word order. You can say,"请上楼来""他回家去了". But "请上来楼","他回去家了"are faulty sentences.

7."哎":

叹词,表示惊讶或不满意,如:"哎! 真没想到。""哎! 你怎么才来?"表示提醒,如:"哎,别忘了,明天有考试!"

"哎"is an exclamation indicating surprise:"哎! 真没想到。" or dissatisfaction:"哎! 你怎么才来?" or to remind:"哎,别忘了,明天有考试!"

练习 Exercises

一、读下边的句子,注意重音:Read the following sentences and take care of the stress:
1. 我有点儿不舒服。
2. 头有点儿疼。
3. 考得好吗?
4. 现在好多了。
5. 是谁这么关心你呀!

二、替换练习:Substitution drills:
1. 你回去好好儿睡一觉,也许就好了。

| 你听听音乐 | 不想家 |
| 你去听一次 | 不想听第二次 |

你们好好儿聊聊　　　　　是好朋友
　　　你好好儿准备准备　　　　考好

2. 听说<u>你不舒服</u>。
　　　他出国了
　　　小王结婚了
　　　你病了
　　　她父母要来北京

3. <u>我准</u>说对<u>了</u>。
　　你　　不知道我是谁
　　他　　说错了
　　她　　考得好
　　我　　感冒了
　　学校　放假了

4. <u>这次考得</u>不太好。
　　这几天天气
　　最近他身体
　　那辆自行车
　　我的发音

5. 我想<u>出去散散步</u>，你去不去?
　　　进去问问
　　　去早市逛逛
　　　回去休息休息
　　　出去走走
　　　上去看看

6. 多谢<u>你的关心</u>。
　　　你来看我
　　　你的帮助
　　　你送给我这么漂亮的礼物
　　　你跟我一起来

三、替换划线部分的词语，然后扩展句子：
　　Substitute the underlined part and then extend the sentence accordingly：

1. 我想<u>回房间休息休息</u>。→真累呀，我想回房间休息休息。
　　　　去湖边走走
　　　　去商店逛逛
　　　　到外边看看
　　　　出去散散步

2. 下次一定<u>努力</u>。→这次考得不好，下次一定努力。
　　　　不忘
　　　　好好儿写
　　　　考好
　　　　早点儿来

3. <u>好好儿招待招待他</u>。→他这么关心你，好好儿招待招待他。
　　　　谢谢他们
　　　　看看书
　　　　学学做菜
　　　　练练发音
　　　　准备准备考试

四、下边是外国留学生常说错的句子，你能改正过来吗？
　　Can you correct the following faulty sentences often spoken by foreign students?

1. 小王比小李不高。
2. 今天一点儿冷。
3. 我现在学习在北大。
4. 明年我回去日本。

五、用下边的叙述方式复述第三段会话。
　　Reproduce Dialogue 3 in the following way of narration：
　　　　张新听说……，所以她想……，可是……

六、体会 A 部分中带点儿词语的意思,并将 B 部分中的各句用相似的句式说出来:
Make sure of the meaning of the dotted word or expression in each of the sentences in Part A and reproduce each of the sentences in Part B in the right sentence pattern:

A　1．我哪儿敢慢走哇!
　　2．他哪儿是我的男朋友哇?
　　3．不是还有下一次吗?
　　4．你不是不舒服吗?快回去休息吧。

B　1．我没有结婚。
　　2．我不是中国人。
　　3．他不认识王平。
　　4．他很关心张新。
　　5．我已经告诉李文静了。
　　6．银行还没关门呢。

七、根据下边的话题线索设计小对话:
Produce a short dialogue according to each subject clue:
1．考试前生病了 → 没好好儿准备 → 没考好
2．感冒了 → 休息 → 好多了
3．朋友来了 → 要去机场接朋友 → 不能辅导了

八、说一说:Talk about the following topics:
1．最近你考试了吗?
2．每次考试前你都好好儿复习吧?
3．你喜欢散步吗?
4．头疼的时候你喜欢在房间里休息还是喜欢去外边走走?

九、成段表达:谈谈你最近的学习和身体情况。
Narration:Talk about your recent studies and health.

你知道吗? (5)　　　　寒暄与客套

中国人见面的时候,相互间有很多寒暄语,如:"你好!好久不见,最近好吗?""工作怎么样?忙吗?""身体好吗?家里人都好吧?"或者:"你去哪儿?""吃(饭)了

吗?""孩子学习怎么样?""听说你前些天去外地了,什么时候回来的?""你好像瘦了?""几天不见,你更漂亮了!""冷吗?你穿得太少了,小心别感冒!""这件衣服挺漂亮的,是新买的吧?"等等。这时对方可以据实回答,也可以简单回答说:"还可以""挺好的""不太忙""我出去了一趟""吃了"等。如果有谁这样问你,这就表示他对你的关心,是他在跟你寒暄,你可不要觉得奇怪。

在见面时,中国人不常说"你好""早上好"等,而常根据时间、情况问要做的或正在做的事情,如:"上课去呀""出去呀""回来啦""洗衣服呢""吃饭呢"等。

告别的时候,常说的客套话有:"我还有点儿别的事,改天咱们好好儿聊聊。""有空儿来家里玩儿。"但这并不一定是真的邀请,而是客套。只有一方提出具体时间,才是真的请对方去家里做客。

Do You Know? (5) Amenities and Civilities

When Chinese people meet, various amenities and civilities are exchanged, for instance: "How are you? We haven't seen each other for a long time. How are you doing lately?" "How about your work? Have you been busy?" "Are you keeping fit? Are your family well?" or "Where are you going?" "Have you dined?" "How are the children doing in their studies?" "I heard that you went away a few days ago, when did you get back?" "You seem to be losing weight?" "Haven't seen you for a few days and you become more pretty!" "Aren't you cold? You're wearing so little, be careful not to catch a cold!" "This is a pretty dress, a new one?" and so on. The other party may give a truthful and factual answer or just a brief answer like: "Passable", "Quite well", "Not very busy", "I went away", "I had dinner." These questions indicate that the person asking them is concerned about you or interested in you. So you shouldn't feel strange or upset since they're just amenities.

When coming across someone, the Chinese don't often say, "How are you" or "Good morning". They are used to asking questions about what you are doing or what you're about to do, according to the time or situation, for instance: "Going to class", "Going out", "You're back", "Washing your clothes" "Having dinner" and etc.

In leaving-taking, the common civilities include: "I have something else to attend to, so let's have a good chat some other time." "Come and visit us when you have time." But this may just be a polite formula, not necessarily an invitation. Only when the date and time is given is it meant for an invitation.

第十七课　我看不懂

(吃晚饭时)

杰　夫：你每天晚上都干什么?
丽　莎：写汉字啦,做作业啦,复习旧课啦,预习新课啦,……
杰　夫：你真是个用功的好学生。
丽　莎：那你晚上一般干什么?
杰　夫：看电视,聊天儿。
丽　莎：我也喜欢聊天儿。
杰　夫：你不喜欢看电视吗?
丽　莎：不喜欢。
杰　夫：为什么?
丽　莎：看不懂。

(星期四下午在宿舍楼外边)

安　妮：周末你想干什么?
山　下：爬山。一起去,怎么样?
安　妮：你喜欢爬山?

山　下：对，你不喜欢吗？
安　妮：爬山太累了。我喜欢逛街。
山　下：我觉得逛街比爬山更累！

（在安妮宿舍，王平正给她辅导）
安　妮：你辅导得真好！我都听懂了。
王　平：你回答得也不错。我嗓子都说疼了，休息会儿吧！
安　妮：真对不起，我光顾让你辅导了，忘了拿饮料了。你喜欢喝什么？
王　平：有什么喝什么吧，能解渴就行。
安　妮：我这儿有一瓶可乐，还有一瓶矿泉水。
王　平：你不是喜欢喝可乐吗？那我就来矿泉水好了。

（丽莎对安妮说）
　　晚上杰夫喜欢看电视、聊天儿。我也喜欢聊天儿，可是不太喜欢看电视，因为我看不懂。

（安妮对丽莎说）
　　周末山下喜欢爬山，我觉得爬山太累，我喜欢逛街，可是山下说逛街更累。

Dì-shíqī kè　Wǒ kàn bu dǒng

(Chī wǎnfàn shí)
Jiéfū：Nǐ měitiān wǎnshang dōu gàn shénme？
Lìshā：Xiě Hànzì la, zuò zuòyè la, fùxí jiùkè la, yùxí xīnkè la, ……
Jiéfū：Nǐ zhēn shì ge yòng gōng de hǎo xuésheng.
Lìshā：Nà nǐ wǎnshang yìbān gàn shénme？
Jiéfū：Kàn diànshì, liáo tiānr.
Lìshā：Wǒ yě xǐhuan liáo tiānr.
Jiéfū：Nǐ bù xǐhuan kàn diànshì ma？
Lìshā：Bù xǐhuan.
Jiéfū：Wèi shénme？
Lìshā：Kàn bu dǒng.

(Xīngqīsì xiàwǔ zài sùshèlóu wàibian)
Ānní：Zhōumò nǐ xiǎng gàn shénme？
Shānxià：Pá shān. Yìqǐ qù, zěnmeyàng？

Ānní: Nǐ xǐhuan pá shān?
Shānxià: Duì, Nǐ bù xǐhuan ma?
Ānní: Pá shān tài lèi le. Wǒ xǐhuan guàng jiē.
Shānxià: Wǒ juéde guàng jiē bǐ pá shān gèng lèi!

(Zài Ānní sùshè, Wáng Píng zhèng gěi tā fǔdǎo)
Ānní: Nǐ fǔdǎo de zhēn hǎo! Wǒ dōu tīngdǒng le.
Wáng Píng: Nǐ huídá de yě búcuò. Wǒ sǎngzi dōu shuōténg le, xiūxi huìr ba!
Ānní: Zhēn duìbuqǐ, wǒ guāng gù ràng nǐ fǔdǎo le, wàngle ná yǐnliào le. Nǐ xǐhuan hē shénme?
Wáng Píng: Yǒu shénme hē shénme ba, néng jiě kě jiù xíng.
Ānní: Wǒ zhèr yǒu yì píng kělè, hái yǒu yì píng kuàngquánshuǐ.
Wáng Píng: Nǐ bú shì xǐhuan hē kělè ma? Nà wǒ jiù lái kuàngquánshuǐ hǎo le.

(Lìshā duì Ānní shuō)
　　Wǎnshang Jiéfū xǐhuan kàn diànshì、liáo tiānr. Wǒ yě xǐhuan liáo tiānr, kěshì bú tài xǐhuan kàn diànshì, yīnwèi wǒ kàn bu dǒng.

(Ānní duì Lìshā shuō)
　　Zhōumò Shānxià xǐhuan pá shān, wǒ juéde pá shān tài lèi, wǒ xǐhuan guàng jiē, kěshì Shānxià shuō guàng jiē gèng lèi.

注释 Notes

1."嗓子都说疼了":

"都……了"意思是:"已经……了"。如:

"都……了" means "already". Another example:

"饭都凉了,你快吃吧。""都八点了,该上课了。"

2."真是个好学生""真好""真对不起":

"真"是"的确""确实"的意思,强调程度深。如:

The word "真" means "really" emphasizing the degree, for example:

"天气真冷。""我真不能再吃了。"

3."有什么喝什么":

两个"什么"前后照应,前一个决定后一个,意思是"有咖啡就喝咖啡,有茶就喝茶"等等。如:

"什么" and "什么" correspond with each other, the first deciding the second.

The sentence means "I'll have coffee if you have coffee. I'll have tea if you have tea". More examples:

"想吃什么吃什么""学什么会什么"。

4. "那我就来矿泉水好了"：

"好了"表示同意、赞许或者结束等语气。如：

"好了" indicates agreement, approval or conclusion, for example：

"就这么办好了。""好了，别说了。"

5. "能解渴就行"：

"能……就行"表示起码的条件。如：

"能……就行"：indicates the elementary condition. For example：

"你能来就行。""能吃饱就行。"

练习 Exercises

一、用正确的语调读下边的句子：Read the following sentences in correct intonation：

1. 你晚上一般干什么?
2. 我也喜欢聊天儿。
3. 爬山太累了,我喜欢逛街。
4. 我觉得逛街比爬山更累!
5. 你辅导得真好!
6. 你回答得也不错。
7. 你不是喜欢喝可乐吗? 那我就来矿泉水好了。

二、根据课文意思,判断句中重读部分：

Decide where to stress in each of the following sentences according to the text.

1. 一起去,怎么样?
2. 你真是个用功的好学生。
3. 周末你想干什么?
4. 有什么喝什么吧。

三、替换划线部分的词语：Substitute the underlined parts：

1. 你真是个<u>用功的好学生</u>。
   　　是个好孩子

喜欢爬山
　　　爱喝茶
　　　是我的好朋友

2. 我觉得<u>逛街</u>　比　<u>爬山</u>　更　<u>累</u>！
　　　这件　　　那件　　　漂亮
　　　这次考试　上次　　　难
　　　听音乐　　不听音乐　想家
　　　热天　　　冷天　　　不舒服

3. <u>我嗓子</u>　　都　<u>说疼</u>了。
　　菜　　　　　　凉
　　早饭　　　　　忘吃
　　新买的本子　　用完
　　家里寄来的钱　花光

4. 我光顾<u>让你辅导</u>了,<u>忘了拿饮料了</u>。
　　　聊天儿　　忘了做饭了
　　　看电视　　没听见你叫我
　　　看信　　　没听见他说的话
　　　说话　　　忘了上课的时间

5. <u>有</u>什么<u>喝</u>什么吧。
　　喜欢　买
　　爱吃　吃
　　想写　写
　　喜欢　听

6. <u>(饮料)能解渴</u>就行。
　　你写的我能看懂
　　这件事问小王
　　到他家坐汽车去
　　取包裹有学生证

7. 你不是<u>喜欢喝可乐</u>吗？那我就来<u>矿泉水</u>好了。

111

这个周末你	没空儿	我下个周末再来
你	最喜欢吃甜的	咱们就来一个甜的菜
今天	没取钱	我们明天取了钱再买电视
明天	要交作业	咱们现在就做

四、体会下边各句中"都……了"的意思有什么不同:

Does "都 … … 了" in the following sentences have any different meanings?

1. 这些我都认识了。
2. 都十二点了,快睡吧。
3. 这些菜我都吃过了,味道好极了。
4. 我的肚子都饿了,咱们先去吃饭吧。
5. 你讲得真好,我们都明白了。

五、读例句,然后用"一般"再说五个句子:

Read the five illustrative sentences, then make five more sentences with "一般":

例1. 我一般自己做饭。
　　2. 我周末一般去看我的父母。
　　3. 我一般六点起床。
　　4. 他一般一星期去逛一次早市。
　　5. 他一般不喜欢和同学一块儿玩儿。
　　　………

六、成段表达:你喜欢下列活动中的哪一项?最不喜欢哪一项?简单说说为什么。

Narration: Of the following activities, which one do you like best? Which one do you dislike most? Give your reasons briefly.

参考用词:words and expressions for reference

觉得　因为　一般　喜欢　爱　不太　更　比

第十八课　我在学习书法呢

（在教学楼）

王　平：昨天晚上你去哪儿了？我去找过你，可是你不在。
张　伟：几点？
王　平：八点。
张　伟：八点我正在教室上课呢。
王　平：晚上上什么课？
张　伟：我在学习书法呢。
王　平：九点半上完课了吧，你怎么也不在？
张　伟：九点半？我正洗澡呢。洗完澡，已经十点了……有什么事吗？
王　平：没什么事。想找你聊聊天儿。

（张伟说）

　　昨天晚上八点，我在教室上书法课。下课以后，我又去洗了个澡。洗完澡，已经十点了，所以王平找了我两次，都没找到我。

(王平跟张伟去安妮的宿舍找安妮)

王　平:请问,安妮在吗?

丽　莎:她刚才出去了,一会儿就回来,请进来等一会儿吧。

王　平:好吧,打扰了。

丽　莎:别客气,请坐! 你看报纸吗?(递给他一张英文报纸)

王　平:谢谢。哎,我念几句,你听听。我的发音怎么样?

丽　莎:很不错嘛!

王　平:上课的时候,英语老师也这么说。

张　伟:你呀,说你胖你就喘上了。

丽　莎:你说什么? 他哪儿胖啊?

(张伟、王平大笑,安妮进来)

安　妮:什么事? 这么可笑? 抱歉! 抱歉! 让你们久等了!

王　平:没什么! 没什么!

(丽莎对安妮说)

　　刚才他们等你的时候,王平拿着英文报纸边看边念,我说他发音很不错,他告诉我老师也这么说,张伟就说"说你胖你就喘上了"。我以为这句话的意思是说王平长得胖呢。我们三个人正笑这个呢,你就回来了。

Dì-shíbā kè　Wǒ zài xuéxí shūfǎ ne

(Zài jiàoxuélóu)

Wáng Píng：Zuótiān wǎnshang nǐ qù nǎr le? Wǒ qù zhǎoguo nǐ, kěshì nǐ bú zài.

Zhāng Wěi：Jǐ diǎn？

Wáng Píng：Bā diǎn.

Zhāng Wěi：Bā diǎn wǒ zhèngzài jiàoshì shàng kè ne.

Wáng Píng：Wǎnshang shàng shénme kè？

Zhāng Wěi：Wǒ zài xuéxí shūfǎ ne.

Wáng Píng：Jiǔ diǎn bàn shàngwán kè le ba, nǐ zěnme yě bú zài？

Zhāng Wěi：Jiǔ diǎn bàn？ Wǒ zhèng xǐ zǎo ne. Xǐwán zǎo, yǐjing shí diǎn le……Yǒu shénme shì ma？

Wáng Píng：Méi shénme shì. Xiǎng zhǎo nǐ liáoliao tiānr.

(Zhāng Wěi shuō)

　　Zuótiān wǎnshang bā diǎn, wǒ zhèngzài jiàoshì shàng shūfǎ kè. Xià kè yǐhòu, wǒ yòu qù xǐle ge zǎo. Xǐwán zǎo, yǐjing shí diǎn le, suǒyǐ Wáng Píng zhǎole wǒ liǎng cì, dōu méi zhǎodào wǒ.

(Wáng Píng gēn Zhāng Wěi qù Ānní de sùshè zhǎo Ānní)

Wáng Píng：Qǐng wèn, Ānní zài ma？

Lìshā：Tā gāngcái chūqu le, yíhuìr jiù huílai, qǐng jìnlai děng yíhuìr ba.

Wáng Píng：Hǎo ba, dǎrǎo le.

Lìshā：Bié kèqi, qǐng zuò！Nǐ kàn bàozhǐ ma？（Dìgěi tā yì zhāng Yīngwén bào）

Wáng Píng：Xièxie. Āi, wǒ niàn jǐ jù, nǐ tīngting. wǒ de fāyīn zěnmeyàng？

Lìshā：Hěn búcuò ma！

Wáng Píng：Shàng kè de shíhou, Yīngyǔ lǎoshī yě zhème shuō.

Zhāng Wěi：Nǐ ya, Shuō nǐ pàng nǐ jiù chuǎnshang le.

Lìshā：Nǐ shuō shénme？Tā nǎr pàng a？

(Zhāng Wěi、Wáng Píng dà xiào, Ānní jìnlai)

Ānní：Shénme shì？Zhème kěxiào？Bàoqiàn！Bàoqiàn！Ràng nǐmen jiǔděng le！

Wáng Píng：Méi shenme！Méi shenme！

(Lìshā duì Ānní shuō)

Gāngcái tāmen děng nǐ de shíhou, Wáng Píng názhe Yīngwén bàozhǐ biān kàn biān niàn, wǒ shuō tā fāyīn hěn búcuò, tā gàosu wǒ lǎoshī yě zhème shuō, Zhāng Wěi jiù shuō "shuō nǐ pàng nǐ jiù chuǎnshang le". Wǒ yǐwéi zhè jù huà de yìsi shì shuō Wáng Píng zhǎng de pàng ne. Wǒmen sān ge rén zhèng xiào zhèige ne, nǐ jiù huílai le.

注释 Notes

1."正在……呢"：

表示动作正在进行，而且动作要持续一段时间，"正在"常和语气词"呢"一起用。如：

Indicating the progressive aspect of a continuous action, "正在" is often used together with the modal particle "呢", for example：

"他正在睡觉呢。""我正在看电视呢。"

2."抱歉"：

意思是"对不起"，不过，用"抱歉"显得更文雅一点儿。

"抱歉" means "sorry", but, "抱歉" sounds more cultured.

3."说你胖你就喘上了"：

这是一句口头俗语，比喻有的人在听到别人说自己的好话时就更加逞能、显示自己的言行。

A common saying, a figure of speech implying one tries to parade one's ability or show off after being praised.

4."嘛":

表示事情本来就是这样,如:"现在你已经说得很不错了嘛。"有时也表示道理、原因显而易见,常用在句末或小句末,加强肯定的语气。如,"他是第一次来嘛。(当然不知道这儿的情况了)"又如:

"嘛": The particle indicates that something is obvious, for example: "已经说得很不错了嘛。" Sometimes it also indicates that the cause or reason of something is obvious, It's often used at the end of a sentence or a clause to strengthen some positive remark, for example: "他是第一次来嘛。(Of course he wouldn't know the situation here)" Another example:

甲:"今天人真多!"
乙:"星期天嘛,人能不多吗?"

5."让你们久等了":

客气话,"久"意思是"很长时间",见对方等自己时用。如:"对不起,让您久等了!"回答是"没关系""别客气"。

A polite remark, "久" means "a long time". The remark is often made when people find someone waiting for them. For instance: "对不起,让您久等了。" The response is "没关系" "别客气".

6."没什么":

对方表示感谢或道歉时的应答语。如:

A response to words of gratitude or an apology from others. For instance:

甲:"太谢谢你了。"　　甲:"真对不起。"
乙:"没什么。"　　　　乙:"没什么。"

7."(一)边……(一)边……":

表示两个动作同时进行。如:

Indicating that two actions are going on at the same time. For example:

"他(一)边走(一)边唱。"
"他(一)边学习,(一)边工作,终于读完了大学。"

练习 Exercises

一、用正确的语调读下边的句子,注意连读部分:
Read the following sentences in correct intonation, paying attention to liaison:

1. 你怎么这么说?
2. 八点我正在教室上课呢。
3. 我在学习书法呢。
4. 九点半? 我正洗澡呢。
5. 打扰了。
6. 你呀,说你胖你就喘上了。
7. 他哪儿胖啊?
8. 什么事? 这么可笑?
9. 抱歉! 抱歉! 让你们久等了!
10. 没什么! 没什么!

二、下边几个句子有几种读法,注意重音不同,意思不同:
There are different ways in reading the following sentences. Notice that the meaning changes as the stress changes.

1. 他哪儿胖啊!
   他哪儿胖啊!

2. 今天天气怎么样?
   今天天气怎么样?

3. 你叫什么名字?
   你叫什么名字?

4. 我姓王。
   我姓王。

三、替换练习:Substitution drills:

1. 我在<u>学习书法</u>呢。
      辅导
      看电视

听音乐
做饭
和朋友聊天儿

2. 你 呀 ，<u>说你胖你就喘上了</u>。
又来晚了
九点半了还不起床
又忘了钥匙放在哪儿了
昨天学的今天就忘了

3. <u>我</u>以为<u>这句话的意思是说王平长得胖</u>呢。
他　　你是小张的哥哥
她　　自己没考好
我们　你已经回国了
他们　咱们不想去

4. <u>王平拿着英文报纸边看边念</u>。
同学们在晚会上　　说　笑
孩子们听着音乐　　唱　跳
小王拿起笔　　　　念　写
我们坐下来　　　　吃　聊

四、根据课文回答问题：Answer the questions according to the text:
(一)1. 昨天晚上王平为什么找不到张伟？
　　2. 张伟最近在学什么？
　　3. 王平找张伟有什么事？

(二)1. 安妮为什么不知道张伟他们笑什么？
　　2. 丽莎夸王平英语好，王平怎么说的？
　　3. 为什么张伟对王平说："说你胖你就喘上了"？

五、模拟表演第一段会话。Perform Dialogue 1.

六、听到下边的话后你怎样应答？What would you say in response to the following remarks?

1. 对不起,打扰你了。
2. 抱歉抱歉,让你久等了。
3. 你的英语不错嘛!

七、以安妮的口气复述第二段会话：

Reproduce Dialogue 2 in the first person from Anne's viewpoint：

"我回宿舍的时候,王平他们正在笑……

八、小游戏:趣味组句(An interesting game：Grouping words into sentences：)

每人发 ABC 三种纸条,A 条上写自己的姓名,B 条上写地名,C 条上写动词词组,然后分类放入老师手中的 ABC 三个大盒中。学生轮流抽取每盒中的一个条子,组成一句话:(姓名) 正在 (地方)(干什么) 呢。大声读出来,看哪个句子合理、有意思,然后把不合理的句子改正过来。

Give each student three slips of paper. Tell them to write his or her name on the first, the name of a place on the second , and a verb on the third. Sort the slips of paper into three boxes labeled A, B, and C. Taking turns, the students draw one note from each box and put the three words together into a sentence in the following pattern：(Name) is (doing what) in (a place) and read it aloud. Point out the logical and interesting sentences and correct the illogical ones.

第十九课　周末你打算怎么过

（在食堂，安妮、杰夫边吃边聊）

安　妮：杰夫，快到周末了，这个周末你打算怎么过？
杰·夫：我想做一次小小的旅行！
安　妮：去哪儿？
杰　夫：一个有山有水的好地方。
安　妮：你一个人去吗？
杰　夫：我已经约了王平，我们俩一起去。
安　妮：我周末还没有什么安排，能跟你们一起去吗？
杰　夫：当然可以啦！我还以为你又要去逛街呢！

（在宿舍里）

丽　莎：安妮，旅行回来了？好玩儿吗？
安　妮：好玩儿极了，就是有点儿累。
丽　莎：你还没吃晚饭吧，走，咱们吃饭去吧。
安　妮：我想先洗个澡，再去吃晚饭。
丽　莎：好吧，我等你。不过，你得快一点儿，食堂快关门了。

（安妮对丽莎说）

周末我和杰夫、王平一起去旅行了。我们去了一个非常美丽的地方，那儿有山有水，很好玩儿，就是有点儿累。现在我先洗个澡，咱们再一起去吃晚饭，请你等我一会儿。

（在学校外边的小饭馆）

王　平：（正在喝汤，见安妮和丽莎进来）二位小姐，怎么也来这儿吃了？
丽　莎：我等她洗澡，食堂关门了，只好出来吃了。
安　妮：你也刚来吧？一块儿吃好了。
王　平：谁说我刚来，你想让我再吃一顿哪！
丽　莎：你不是在喝汤吗？喝一碗汤就饱了？
王　平：（哈哈大笑）你以为吃中餐也是先喝汤啊！
安　妮：你别笑，我们真的不大清楚吃中餐都有哪些习惯，你快给我们介绍介绍吧。
王　平：那我就告诉你：吃中餐的时候，一般是先上凉菜，边喝酒边吃凉菜，过一会儿再上热菜，最后才喝汤，有时候再上点儿水果。

Dì-shíjiǔ kè　Zhōumò nǐ dǎsuan zěnme guò

（Zài shítáng, Ānní、Jiéfū biān chī biān liáo）
Ānní：Jiéfū, kuài dào zhōumò le, zhèige zhōumò nǐ dǎsuan zěnme guò？
Jiéfū：Wǒ xiǎng zuò yí cì xiǎoxiǎo de lǚxíng！
Ānní：Qù nǎr？
Jiéfū：Yí ge yǒu shān yǒu shuǐ de hǎo dìfang.
Ānní：Nǐ yí ge rén qù ma？
Jiéfū：Wǒ yǐjing yuēle Wáng Píng, wǒmen liǎ yìqǐ qù.
Ānní：Wǒ zhōumò hái méiyǒu shénme ānpái, néng gēn nǐmen yìqǐ qù ma？
Jiéfū：Dāngrán kěyǐ la！Wǒ hái yǐwéi nǐ yòu yào qù guàng jiē ne！

（Zài sùshè li）
Lìshā：Ānní, lǚxíng huílai le？Hǎowánr ma？
Ānní：Hǎowánr jíle, jiùshi yǒudiǎnr lèi.
Lìshā：Nǐ hái méi chī wǎnfàn ba, zǒu, zánmen chī fàn qù ba.
Ānní：Wǒ xiǎng xiān xǐ ge zǎo, zài qù chī wǎnfàn.
Lìshā：Hǎo ba, wǒ děng nǐ. Búguò, nǐ děi kuài yìdiǎnr, shítáng kuài guān mén le.

（Ānní duì Lìshā shuō）

Zhōumò wǒ hé Jiéfū、Wáng Píng yìqǐ qù lǚxíng le. Wǒmen qùle yí ge fēicháng měilì de dìfang, nàr yǒu shān yǒu shuǐ, hěn hǎowánr, jiùshi yǒudiǎnr lèi. Xiànzài wǒ xiān xǐ ge zǎo, zánmen zài yìqǐ qù chī wǎnfàn, qǐng nǐ děng wǒ yíhuìr.

(Zài xuéxiào wàibian de xiǎo fànguǎnr)

Wáng Píng:（Zhèngzài hē tāng, jiàn Ānní hé Lìshā jìnlai）Èr wèi xiǎojie, zěnme yě lái zhèr chī le?

Lìshā: Wǒ děng tā xǐzǎo, shítáng guān mén le, zhǐhǎo chūlai chī le.

Ānní: Nǐ yě gāng lái ba? Yíkuàir chī hǎo le.

Wáng Píng: Shéi shuō wǒ gāng lái, Nǐ xiǎng ràng wǒ zài chī yí dùn na!

Lìshā: Nǐ bú shi zài hē tāng ma? Hē yì wǎn tāng jiù bǎo le?

Wáng Píng:（Hāhā dàxiào）Nǐ yǐwéi chī zhōngcān yě shì xiān hē tāng a!

Ānní: Nǐ bié xiào, wǒmen zhēn de bú dà qīngchu chī zhōngcān dōu yǒu něixiē xíguàn, nǐ kuài gěi wǒmen jièshao jièshao ba.

Wáng Píng: Nà wǒ jiù gàosu nǐ: chī zhōngcān de shíhou, yìbān shì xiān shàng liángcài, biān hē jiǔ biān chī liángcài, guò yíhuìr zài shàng rècài, zuìhòu cái hē tāng, yǒushíhou zài shàng diǎnr shuǐguǒ.

注释 Notes

1. "快……了":

   表示"将要……""很快就要……",如:

   "快……了" means "will" or "will soon", for example:

   "你等一会儿,他快回来了。""快放假了。""我来北京快两年了。"

2. "先上凉菜,再上热菜":

   "先……再……"表示时间和动作的先后顺序。如:

   "先……再……", Indicating the sequence of actions or time, for example:

   "我们先去上海,再去广州。"

3. "上菜,上汤":

   "上"是动词,意思是:端来,送来,在饭店吃饭时常用。

   The word "上" is a verb which means "serve", often used while eating in a restaurant.

练习 Exercises

一、用正确的语调读下边的句子：Read the following sentences in correct intonation：

1. 这个周末你打算怎么过？
2. 你一个人去吗？
3. 走，咱们吃饭去吧。
4. 我想先洗个澡，再去吃晚饭。
5. 你也刚来吧？一块儿吃好了。
6. 你别笑。

二、替换练习：Substitution drills：

（一）

1. <u>我等你</u>，不过，<u>你得快一点儿</u>。
   我可以借给你钱　你得早点儿还我
   我能来　　　　　我要晚来一会儿
   你可以问他　　　他也许不想告诉你
   这次我听你的　　下次你得听我的

2. <u>食堂关门了</u>，只好<u>出来吃了</u>。
   没邮票了　　　去邮局买
   银行关门了　　向你借钱
   你不在　　　　回去了
   起晚了　　　　饿着肚子去上课

3. 你快给我们<u>介绍介绍</u>吧。
   　　说
   　　走
   　　去
   　　进来
   　　告诉他
   　　给我看看

4. 先<u>往前走</u>，再<u>往右拐</u>……
   去医院　去邮局

123

睡觉　　　学习
取学生证　去买书
上车　　　买票

（二）
替换划线部分的词语,并将句子补充完整:
Substitute the underlined parts and then complete the statements accordingly:

1. 快<u>到周末</u>了。→快到周末了,可以去爬山了。
   考试
   下课
   放假
   到我的生日

2. <u>边</u>喝酒　<u>边</u>　吃凉菜→热菜还没上,我们边喝酒边吃凉菜。
   说　　　笑
   唱　　　跳
   喝茶　　聊天儿
   听音乐　做练习

3. 过一会儿再<u>上热菜</u>。→先上饮料和凉菜,过一会儿再上热菜。
   回家
   上水果
   去吃饭
   喝汤

三、体会下边对话中加点儿短语的意思,并模仿对话:
Make sure of the meanings of the dotted phrases and produce dialogues following the two examples:

1. 甲:我能跟你们一起去吗?
   乙:当然!

2. 甲:你也刚来吧?
   乙:谁说我刚来? 我都来了半个小时了。

四、根据课文内容回答问题: Answer the questions according to the text:

1. 周末杰夫约王平去哪儿玩儿?

2．杰夫为什么开始没约安妮一起去旅行？
3．他们的旅行怎么样？
4．安妮为什么以为王平和她们一样也是刚去饭馆？
5．中餐上菜有什么习惯？

五、成段表达：Oral composition：

1．周末我想这么过。
2．我们国家上菜的习惯。
3．一个好玩儿的地方。

第二十课 今天比昨天冷一点儿

(在女生宿舍公共盥洗室)
女生甲:不知道今天外边冷不冷?穿什么衣服合适?
女生乙:天气预报说(今天)比昨天冷一点儿。
女生甲:是吗?
女生丙:(刚从外边回来)外边挺冷的。要是去上课的话,得穿上大衣。

(去上课的路上)
李文静:杰夫,穿这么少,不冷吗?
杰 夫:少吗?我觉得不少。这是我最暖和的衣服了。
李文静:冬天快到了,你得买件厚一点儿的大衣。
杰 夫:不用了吧?听说这儿的冬天没有我们那儿冷。
李文静:可是教室里有时不太暖和,你不怕感冒吗?
杰 夫:不怕,——嗯,怕。周末我就去买一件。要是你有时间(的话),帮我看看,好吗?

(在商场的冬装部)
李文静:这件(衣服)怎么样?
杰　夫:样子还可以,颜色不太好看。
李文静:那件呢?右边那件?
杰　夫:小姐,看一下儿右边那件。(售货员取下来给杰夫)可以试试吗?
售货员:可以,那边有镜子。
(杰夫试衣服)
杰　夫:哎呀,又瘦又短,太小了。
李文静:不是衣服小,是你的个子太高太大了。小姐,有没有特大号的?
售货员:(找了半天找出一件)这是最大的了。请再试一下儿。
李文静:这件比那件长一点儿,也比那件肥一点儿。
杰　夫:还是不合适。等我长小了再来买吧。

(杰夫对彼得说)
　　冬天快到了,一天比一天冷了。我没带过冬的大衣。昨天李文静陪我去商店买大衣,我试了半天,没有一件合适的。

Dì-èrshí kè　Jīntiān bǐ zuótiān lěng yìdiǎnr

(Zài nǚshēng sùshè gōnggòng guànxǐshì)
Nǚshēng jiǎ: Bù zhīdào jīntiān wàibian lěng bu lěng? Chuān shénme yīfu héshì?
Nǚshēng yǐ: Tiānqì yùbào shuō (jīntiān) bǐ zuótiān lěng yìdiǎnr.
Nǚshēng jiǎ: Shì ma?
Nǚshēng bǐng: (Gāng cóng wàibian huílai) Wàibian tǐng lěng de. Yàoshi qù shàng kè dehuà, děi
　　　　　　　chuānshang dàyī.

(Qù shàng kè de lùshang)
Lǐ Wénjìng: Jiéfū, chuān zhème shǎo, bù lěng ma?
Jiéfū: Shǎo ma? Wǒ juéde bù shǎo, zhè shì wǒ zuì nuǎnhuo de yīfu le.
Lǐ Wénjìng: Dōngtiān kuài dào le, nǐ děi mǎi jiàn hòu yìdiǎnr de dàyī.
Jiéfū: Bú yòng le ba? Tīngshuō zhèr de dōngtiān méiyǒu wǒmen nàr lěng.
Lǐ Wénjìng: Kěshì jiàoshì li yǒushí bú tài nuǎnhuo, nǐ bú pà gǎnmào ma?
Jiéfū: Bú pà,……ńg, pà. Zhōumò wǒ jiù qù mǎi yí jiàn. Yàoshi nǐ yǒu shíjiān (dehuà), bāng
　　　wǒ kànkan, hǎo ma?

(Zài shāngchǎng de dōngzhuāngbù)
Lǐ Wénjìng: Zhèi jiàn (yīfu) zěnmeyàng?

127

Jiéfū: Yàngzi hái kěyǐ, yánsè bú tài hǎokàn.

Lǐ Wénjìng: Nèi jiàn ne? Yòubian nèi jiàn?

Jiéfū: Xiǎojie, kàn yí xiàr yòubian nèi jiàn. (Shòuhuòyuán qǔ xiàlai gěi Jiéfū) Kěyǐ shìshi ma?

Shòuhuòyuán: Kěyǐ, nèi bian yǒu jìngzi.

(Jiéfū shì yīfu)

Jiéfū: Āiyā, Yòu shòu yòu duǎn, tài xiǎo le.

Lǐ Wénjìng: Bú shì yīfu xiǎo, shì nǐ de gèzi tài gāo tài da le. Xiǎojie, yǒu méiyǒu tè dàhào de?

Shòuhuòyuán: (Zhǎole bàntiān zhǎochū yí jiàn) Zhè shì zuì dà de le. Qǐng zài shì yí xiàr.

Lǐ Wénjìng: Zhèi jiàn bǐ nèi jiàn cháng yìdiǎnr, yě bǐ nèi jiàn féi yìdiǎnr.

Jiéfū: Háishì bù héshì. Děng wǒ zhǎng xiǎo le zài lái mǎi ba.

(Jiéfū duì Bǐdé shuō)

Dōngtiān kuài dào le, yì tiān bǐ yì tiān lěng le. Wǒ méi dài guò dōng de dàyī. Zuótiān Lǐ Wénjìng péi wǒ qù shāngdiàn mǎi dàyī, wǒ shìle bàntiān, méiyǒu yí jiàn héshì de.

注释 Notes

1. "挺……的"：

"挺"相当于"很"，口语中常用。"挺"和"的"中间是形容词，如："天气挺好的""他挺聪明的"，有时，"的"可以省略。

The expression "挺……的", with an adjective or a verb in between, is often used in spoken Chinese, same as "很", for example: "天气挺好的" "他挺聪明的", "的" can sometimes be omitted.

2. "要是……的话"：

表示假设，"要是"和"的话"可以一起使用，也可以省略其中的一个。如：

Indicating a supposition, "要是" and "的话" can be used together or separately. Compare the three examples all meaning "If it rains, I'm not going."

"要是下雨的话，我就不去了。""要是下雨，我就不去了。""下雨的话，我就不去了。"

3. "不是衣服小，(而)是你的个子太高太大了"：

句中"不是……，(而)是……"，前后两个部分，前一部分否定，后一部分肯定。如：

In "不是……，(而)是……", the first part is negative, the second part is affirmative, for example:

"不是我不想来,(而)是没时间。"

4."还是不合适":

"还是"表示情况没有变化,仍旧和先前一样。如:

"还是"indicates that the situation remains unchanged, or the same as before. For example:

"他又讲了一遍,我还是不明白。""这些橘子尝了一个是酸的,又尝了一个还是酸的。"

5."半天":

"半天"有两个意思:

"半天" has two meanings:

(1)指白天的一半,如:

"half of a day", for example:

"半天上课,半天参观。"

(2)是说话人感觉比较长的一段时间,如:

The speakers feel it took a long time to do sth.

"等了半天,他才来。""我看了半天也不明白。"

练习 Exercises

一、用正确的语调读下边的句子:Read the following sentences in correct intonation:

1. 今天比昨天冷一点儿。
2. 外边挺冷的。
3. 穿这么少,不冷吗?
4. 这是我最暖和的衣服了。
5. 听说这儿的冬天没有我们那儿冷。
6. 样子还可以,颜色不太好看。
7. 还是不合适。
8. 一天比一天冷了。
9. 我试了半天,没有一件合适的。

二、替换练习:Substitution drills:

(一)

1. 这儿的冬天没有我们那儿 冷。

他　　　　　我　　　　高
　　这件　　　　那件　　　合适
　　我的发音　　你　　　　好
　　逛街　　　　爬山　　　累

2. 不是<u>衣服小</u>，是 <u>你的个子太高太大了</u>。
　　不想去　　　没时间
　　你胖　　　　她太瘦了
　　不喜欢　　　没钱买
　　我不告诉你　我真的不知道

3. <u>这件</u>比<u>那件</u> <u>长</u>一点儿。
　　今天　昨天　冷
　　家里　学校　暖和
　　蓝的　黑的　肥
　　苹果　香蕉　便宜

4. 这是最<u>大</u>的了。
　　　　　厚
　　　　　瘦
　　　　　长
　　　　　便宜
　　　　　合适

5. <u>李文静</u>　陪　<u>我</u>　　<u>去商店买大衣</u>。
　　我　　　　妈妈　　去医院看病
　　他　　　　我们　　去上海旅行
　　我　　　　女朋友　逛街
　　王阿姨　　李文静　在宿舍聊天儿

6. 我<u>试</u>了半天,<u>没有一件合适的</u>。
　　找　　还是没找到
　　想　　也想不起来他叫什么
　　听　　也没听懂
　　看　　还是没看清楚

（二）
替换划线部分的词语，并将句子补充完整：
Substitute the underlined parts and then complete the statements accordingly：

1. 要是<u>去上课</u>的话,<u>得穿上大衣</u>。→外边挺冷的,要是去上课的话,得穿上大衣。
   有空儿　　来我家玩儿吧
   不能去　　早一点儿告诉我
   想去　　　就请和我们一起去吧
   不舒服　　就回去休息一下儿

2. 等<u>我长小了</u>　再　<u>来买</u>吧。→我太高太大了,等我长小了再来买吧。
   以后有时间　　聊
   我放了假　　　去旅行
   我有房子了　　结婚
   同学们都来了　开始

3. 一<u>天</u>比一<u>天</u>　<u>冷</u>→这儿的天气一天比一天冷。
   个　　个　　大
   年　　年　　多
   件　　件　　肥
   个　　个　　难
   辆　　辆　　快

三、根据课文内容判断对错：

Judge the right and wrong of the following statements according to the text：

1. 今天没有昨天冷。
2. 今天房间里很冷,得穿上大衣才暖和。
3. 杰夫不怕感冒。
4. 杰夫陪李文静买大衣。
5. 他们试了半天也没买到一件合适的大衣。

四、说一说：Talk about the following subjects：

1. 你们国家现在的天气怎么样？
2. 你在北京过冬习惯吗？
3. 你们教室暖和吗？
4. 你怕冷吗？

五、小对话：A short dialogue：

甲：你不爱看书吗？

乙：谁说我不爱看？

甲：你看，你书架上书那么少！

乙：你的意思是说，你的书比我的多？

甲：当然！我的书最多了！

乙：我买的书比你买的少，可我看的也许比你看的多多了！

甲：你说什么？不一定吧？

六、成段表达："这里和我想象的(不)一样"

　　Oral composition："It's not the same as I expected"

　　参考用语：words and expressions for reference

　　比　没有　一点儿　……多了　极了　……得多　不太　挺　最　天气
　　习惯

第二十一课　他们是做什么工作的？

（杰夫、王平在散步）

杰　夫：王平，听说你大学毕业后想去美国念研究生，到时候你可以去我家玩儿。
王　平：哦，那太好了！可是我又怕……
杰　夫：怕什么？我爸爸、妈妈都很好客。
王　平：他们是做什么工作的？
杰　夫：我爸爸是律师，妈妈是医生。
王　平：你家里还有什么人？
杰　夫：一个哥哥和一个妹妹。
王　平：他们都住在家里吗？
杰　夫：我哥哥在上大学，周末才回家；妹妹读中学，每天晚上回家。
王　平：他们也会欢迎我吗？
杰　夫：那还用说！

（杰夫对王平说）

　　要是你以后到美国上学，可以去我家玩儿。我家有五口人，我爸爸是律师，妈妈是医生，他们都很好客。我有一个哥哥和一个妹妹，哥哥是大学生，妹妹是中学生，他们也会欢迎你的。

（在安妮的宿舍）
彼　得：安妮，这是你的相册吗？
安　妮：嗯，是我的。里边都是去年的照片。
彼　得：我想看看，可以吗？
安　妮：你看吧。
彼　得：这张照片是你们全家的合影吗？
安　妮：对！
彼　得：哪个是你呀？
安　妮：连哪个是我都看不出来？你再找找。
彼　得：怎么有两个像你一样的女孩？……后边穿红衣服的是你，对不对？
安　妮：错了，那是我妹妹。
彼　得：原来前边的是你呀！你们俩长得太像了。

Dì-èrshíyī kè　Tāmen shì zuò shénme gōngzuò de？

(Jiéfū、Wáng Píng zài sàn bù)
Jiéfū：Wáng Píng, tīngshuō nǐ dàxué bìyè hòu xiǎng qù Měiguó niàn yánjiūshēng, dào shíhou nǐ kěyǐ qù wǒ jiā wánr.
Wáng Píng：Ò, nà tài hǎo le! Kěshì wǒ yòu pà……
Jiéfū：Pà shénme？Wǒ bàba、māma dōu hěn hàokè.
Wáng Píng：Tāmen shì zuò shénme gōngzuò de？
Jiéfū：Wǒ bàba shì lǜshī, māma shì yīshēng.
Wáng Píng：Nǐ jiāli hái yǒu shénme rén？
Jiéfū：Yí ge gēge hé yí ge mèimei.
Wáng Píng：Tāmen dōu zhù zài jiāli ma？
Jiéfū：Wǒ gēge zài shàng dàxué, zhōumò cái huí jiā；Mèimei dú zhōngxué, měi tiān wǎnshang huí jiā.
Wáng Píng：Tāmen yě huì huānyíng wǒ ma？
Jiéfū：Nà hái yòng shuō！

(Jiéfū duì Wáng Píng shuō)
　　Yàoshi nǐ yǐhòu dào Měiguó shàng xué, kěyǐ qù wǒ jiā wánr. Wǒ jiā yǒu wǔ kǒu rén, wǒ bàba shì lǜshī, māma shì yīshēng, tāmen dōu hěn hàokè. Wǒ yǒu yí ge gēge hé yí ge mèimei, gēge shì dàxuéshēng, mèimei shì zhōngxuéshēng, tāmen yě huì huānyíng nǐ de.

（Zài Ānní de sùshè）

Bǐdé：Ānní, zhè shì nǐ de xiàngcè ma?

Ānní：ng, shì wǒ de. Lǐbian dōu shì qùnián de zhàopiānr.

Bǐdé：Wǒ xiǎng kànkan, kěyǐ ma?

Ānní：Nǐ kàn ba.

Bǐdé：Zhèi zhāng zhàopiānr shì nǐmen quánjiā de héyǐng ma?

Ānní：Duì!

Bǐdé：Něi ge shì nǐ ya?

Ānní：Lián něi ge shì wǒ dōu kàn bu chūlái, nǐ zài zhǎozhao.

Bǐdé：Zěnme yǒu liǎng ge xiàng nǐ yíyàng de nǚhái? ……Hòubian chuān hóng yīfu de shì nǐ, duì bu duì?

Ānní：Cuò le, nà shì wǒ mèimei.

Bǐdé：Yuánlái qiánbian de shì nǐ ya! Nǐmen liǎ zhǎng de tài xiàng le.

注释 Notes

1．"念""读""上"：

这三个动词都可以指"上学"，如"他念(读、上)完中学就工作了。""明年他开始读(念、上)大学了。""她今年上(念、读)小学四年级。""念""上"口语中更常用。

"念"，"读" and "上" may all indicate "attending school", for example："他念(读、上)完中学就工作了。""明年他开始读(念、上)大学了。""她今年上(念、读)小学四年级。""念" and "上" are more commonly used in spoken Chinese.

2．"那还用说"：

表示不用多说，不需要怀疑，用反问的语气强调事实就是这样。如：

"Needless to say" "Without a doubt"：used as if asking a rhetorical question for emphasis. Another example：

甲："他在美国留学很多年，英语一定很好吧?"

乙："那还用说。"

3．"连……也/都……"：

"连"常与"也/都"相呼应，加强语气，有"甚至"的意思。可以强调主语，如"连老师也/都不知道""连爷爷都笑了"；也可以强调宾语，被强调的宾语要放在动词的前面或句首，如"连这么简单的问题也/都不明白。"(复杂的问题更不明白了)；还可以强调谓语动词，这时一般要重复动词，如"这本书他连看也/都没看就买了。"

The preposition "连" is used correlatively with "也" or "都" for emphasis, meaning "even". It can be used to emphasize the subject, for example: "连老师也/都不知道","连爷爷都笑了"; or to emphasize the object, in which case, the stressed object should precede the verb or begin the sentence, for example: "连这么简单的问题也/都不明白。"(let alone more complicated ones); "连" can also be used to emphasize the predicate verb, in which case, the verb is often repeated, for example: "这本书他连看也/都没看就买了。"

4. "(看)得出来""(看)不出来":

这是一组可能补语。"看得出来"是肯定式,意思是"能看出来"。否定式是把助词"得"改为"不"。后面可以带宾语,如:"看不出来她的年龄。"如果宾语较长,要把宾语提前,如:"她的年龄我看不出来"。把可能补语的肯定式和否定式并列起来,可以提问,如:"她今年多大了,你看得出来看不出来?"

注意:在"把"字句中和表示请求允许的句子中,谓语动词不带可能补语,可能性由能愿动词"能"表示。如:应该说"你能看出来她的年龄吗?"不能说"你把她的年龄看得出来吗?"

This is a pair of potential complements. "看得出来" is the positive form, meaning "I can tell". The negative is formed by changing "得" to"不". "看不出来" can take an object or an objective clause, for example: "看不出来她的年龄。" If the object is a long clause, it comes before the expression, for example: "她的年龄我看不出来。" The positive and negative forms of potential complements can be juxtaposed to form a question, for example: "她今年多大了,你看得出来看不出来?"

Notice that in questions using "把" or when asking for permission, the predicate verb can not take a potential complement, and the potentiality is expressed by using the optative verb "能" (can). For example: It's correct to say, "你能看出她的年龄吗?" But it's incorrect to say, "你把她的年龄看得出来吗?"

5. "像"和"(好)像……一样":

"像"做动词,表示在形象上相同或有共同点,如:"他的眼睛、鼻子都像爸爸。""(好)像……一样"常表示比喻,如:"他像猴子一样调皮。"

The verb "像" means "alike" or "resemble ", for example: "他的眼睛、鼻子都像爸爸。""(好)像……一样""like" or "as", often used in similar, does not necessarily mean "physical likeness", for example: "他像猴子一样调皮。"

练习 Exercises

一、读下边的句子，注意句中停顿：
Read the following sentences, paying attention to where to pause:

1. 听说你大学毕业后想去美国念研究生。
2. 他们是做什么工作的？
3. 我爸爸是律师，妈妈是医生。
4. 你家里还有什么人？
5. 后边穿红衣服的是你，对不对？
6. 原来前边的是你呀！
7. 你们俩长得太像了。

二、替换练习：Substitution drills：

（一）

1. <u>你们两个</u>长得像<u>你们的妈妈</u>。

妹妹	我母亲
哥哥	我父亲
我的眼睛	我爸爸
我朋友	他妈妈

2. <u>听说你大学毕业后想去美国念研究生</u>，到时候<u>你可以去我家玩儿</u>。

听说你快结婚了	别忘了告诉我
考完试我就放假了	我们可以好好儿玩玩儿
我打算买一辆自行车	咱们一块儿骑车去旅行
听说下个周末是你生日	我一定送你一件生日礼物

（二）

替换划线部分的词语，并将句子补充完整：
Substitute the underlined parts and complete the sentences：

1. 连<u>哪个是我</u>都<u>看不出来</u>。

孩子	听得懂
老师	不会写
晚饭	没吃
我妈妈	不知道

2. 原来右边的是你。
　　你还没走
　　是你找我
　　你就是王老师
　　您是我父亲的朋友

三、熟读课文叙述部分，并填出空格处的词语：
Read repeatedly the narrative part in the text and fill in the blanks：

（　　）你以后到美国上学，可以去我家玩儿。我家有五（　　）人，我爸爸是律师，妈妈是医生，他们都很（　　）。我有一个哥哥和一个妹妹，哥哥是大学生，妹妹是中学生，他们也（　　）欢迎你的。

四、以彼得的口气复述第二段会话：
Reproduce Dialogue 2 in the first person from Peter's viewpoint：

"今天我在安妮的宿舍看见了一本相册，就……我看了半天也没看出来哪个是安妮……"

五、根据课文内容，判断下边的各句是否符合原意：
Decide if the following statements are faithful to the original text：

1. 王平在美国念研究生的时候，在杰夫家住过。
2. 王平怕杰夫的家里人不欢迎他。
3. 杰夫的哥哥和妹妹都在上学。
4. 安妮的相册是去年买的。
5. 安妮的妹妹长得很像她。

六、请说说：Talk about the following subjects：

1. 你们国家小学一般要上几年？中学呢？你在哪儿上的大学？
2. 你家里都有什么人？他们都是干什么的？
3. 你长得像谁？

七、自由问答：选用左边表示疑问的句式提问，选用右边的词语回答：
Free questions and answers: Ask a question in each of the interrogative sentence patterns on the left and answer the question with a word or expression chosen from the right：

　　……是………吗？　　　　对！
　　……，对不对？　　　　　原来……

…… 怎么 ……？	当然
…… 会 …… 吗？	没问题
听说 ………… ，是吗？	错了
	不
	那还用说！

八、 带一张全家人的合影或你和朋友们的合影给全班介绍，听众可以问很多问题，如：照片是什么时候照的，照片上都有什么人，他们都是干什么的，等等。

Bring a family photo or a photo of yourself and your friends and introduce it to the whole class. The listeners may ask all kinds of questions, like: When the photo was taken; Who they are in the photo; What kinds of work they do and so on.

九、趣味游戏： "找出不同" —— 在两幅几乎一样的画中找出若干处不同的地方，全班分成几个小组比赛，看哪组找得快，说得清楚。

An interesting game: "Looking for differences" —— Find out the differences between two almost identical pictures. Divide the class into several competitive groups and see which group can find all the differences first and describe them clearly.

***

你知道吗？(6)　　　　**家庭与称谓**

中国人的家庭现在和过去相比发生了较大的变化。

按照传统，中国人喜欢大家庭，祖孙三代、四代一起生活，家务事都由妇女承担。现在已很少有这种大家庭了。儿女一旦结婚，一个新家庭就诞生了。按照中国现行的人口政策："一对夫妇只能生一个孩子"，所以现代中国三口之家特别多。因为夫妻都工作，所以洗衣、买菜、做饭、教育子女等家务事自然就由夫妻共同承担，并且还要利用节假日或者定期去看望和照顾双方的老人。

中国人的亲属称谓比较复杂，我们把家庭中亲属之间的关系与称谓用以下的简表来表示，它可以帮助你了解一些最基本的称谓。

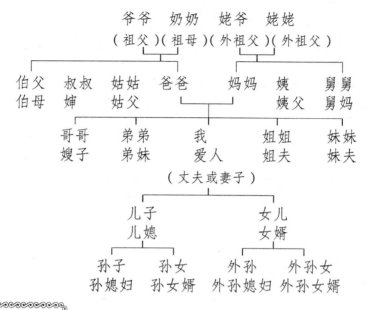

Do You Know? (6)   Family and Terms of Address

There have been considerable changes in the Chinese family as compared with the past.

The Chinese prefer extended families by tradition －－ three or four generations living under the same roof, with women undertaking most of the household duties. Nowadays, however, extended families are rare. As soon as a son or a daughter gets married, a new family is born. Under the current family-planning policies in China："Every couple (husband and wife) is allowed to give birth to one child only", so families of three abound in this country. Since husband and wife both have to work, they naturally have to share between them household duties such as washing, shopping, cooking and rearing children, and they also have to use their holidays and off days to visit and attend to their paternal and maternal parents. Chinese terms of address is quite complicated. The most basic family connections are shown in the following diagram to help you makes sense of the system：

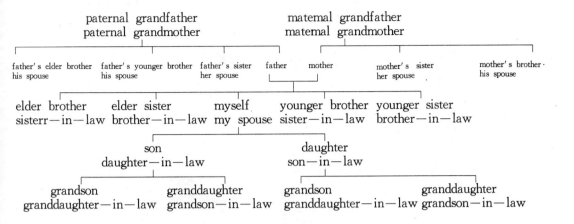

141

第二十二课　你今年多大了？

（下课以后）
杰　夫：彼得，一起去打球，好吗？
彼　得：真对不起，我得等我妈妈的电话，今天是我的生日。
杰　夫：是吗？祝你生日快乐！
彼　得：谢谢！
杰　夫：你今年多大了？
彼　得：都25岁啦，比你大多了！
杰　夫：你知道吗？下周安妮也过生日。
彼　得：真的？等安妮过生日的时候，咱们开个小小的生日晚会，怎么样？
杰　夫：好哇！要不要今天先为你开一个？
彼　得：不用了，下周跟安妮一起热闹吧！

（生日晚会就要开始了）
杰　夫：还差几分钟就到八点了。王平应该来了呀？
丽　莎：他是不是忘了？
安　妮：不会吧，他可能有事，要不他会准时来的。

彼　得：咱们再等他一会儿。
杰　夫：给他打个电话吧。
彼　得：我来打,他的电话号码儿是多少?
安　妮：他宿舍楼的电话是62754021。
彼　得：我忘了,他住几号房间来着?
杰　夫：301。
(彼得拨电话)
杰　夫：通了吗?
彼　得：没有,占线。
(有人敲门,安妮把门打开)
安　妮：王平,你可来了。(向彼得、杰夫)别打了,他来了!
王　平：真抱歉,我迟到了,让你们久等了。
　众　：没关系,我们怕你不来了呢。
王　平：这么热闹的事,哪能不来! 安妮,生日快乐! 这是给你的生日礼物。
安　妮：哎呀,太谢谢了!

(彼得对王平说)

　　下星期三安妮过生日,我们想为她开一个小小的生日晚会。要是那天晚上你有空儿,也来和我们一起玩儿玩儿吧!

Dì-èrshíèr kè　Nǐ jīnnián duō dà le?

(Xià kè yǐhòu)
Jiéfū: Bǐdé, yìqǐ qù dǎ qiú, hǎo ma?
Bǐdé: Zhēn duìbuqǐ, wǒ děi děng wǒ māma de diànhuà, jīntiān shì wǒ de shēngri.
Jiéfū: Shì ma? Zhù nǐ shēngri kuàilè!
Bǐdé: Xièxie!
Jiéfū: Nǐ jīnnián duō dà le?
Bǐdé: Dōu èrshíwǔ la, bǐ nǐ dà duō le.
Jiéfū: Nǐ zhīdao ma? Xià zhōu Ānní yě guò shēngri.
Bǐdé: Zhēnde? Děng Ānní guò shēngri de shíhou, zánmen kāi ge xiǎoxiǎo de shēngri wǎnhuì, zěnmeyàng?
Jiéfū: Hǎo wa! Yào bu yào jīntiān xiān wèi nǐ kāi yí ge?
Bǐdé: Búyòng le, xià zhōu gēn Ānní yìqǐ rènao ba!

(Zài shēngri wǎnhuì shang, wǎnhuì jiù yào kāishǐ le……)

Jiéfū: Hái chà jǐ fēnzhōng jiù dào bā diǎn le. Wáng Píng yīnggāi lái le ya!

Lìshā: Tā shì bu shì wàng le?

Ānní: Bú huì ba, tā kěnéng yǒu shì, yàobu tā huì zhǔnshí lái de.

Bǐdé: Zánmen zài děng tā yíhuìr ba.

Jiéfū: Gěi tā dǎ ge diànhuà ba.

Bǐdé: Wǒ lái dǎ, tā de diànhuà hàomǎr shì duōshao?

Ānní: Tā sùshèlóu de diànhuà shì liù èr qī wǔ sì líng èr yāo.

Bǐdé: Wǒ wàng le, tā zhù jǐ hào fángjiān láizhe?

Jiéfū: sān líng yāo.

(Bǐdé bō diànhuà)

Jiéfū: Tōng le ma?

Bǐdé: Méiyou, zhàn xiàn.

(Yǒu rén qiāo mén, Ānní bǎ mén dǎkāi)

Ānní: Wáng Píng, nǐ kě lái le. (Xiàng Bǐdé、Jiéfū) Bié dǎ le, tā lái le!

Wáng Píng: Zhēn bàoqiàn, wǒ chídào le, ràng nǐmen jiǔděng le.

Zhòng: Méi guānxi, wǒmen pà nǐ bù lái le ne.

Wáng Píng: Zhème rènao de shì, nǎ néng bù lái! Ānní, shēngri kuàilè! Zhè shì gěi nǐ de shēngri lǐwù.

Ānní: Āi yā, tài xièxie le!

(Bǐdé duì Wáng Píng shuō)

Xià xīngqīsān Ānní guò shēngri, wǒmen xiǎng wèi tā kāi yí ge xiǎoxiǎo de shēngri wǎnhuì. Yàoshi nèi tiān wǎnshang nǐ yǒu kòngr, yě lái hé wǒmen yìqǐ wánrwanr ba!

注释 Notes

1. "没(有)"和"不"：

　　这两个副词都用在动词或形容词前面，表示否定。"没(有)"否定的是过去已经发生的动作或状态，如："我昨天没去上课。""不"否定的是现在或将来发生的动作或状态，如："明天我不去上课了。""不"也可以对一般通常的情况进行否定，如：

　　Both adverbials come before a verb or an adjective, forming the negative. "没(有)"(have not or did not) indicates a past action or state, for example: "我昨天没去上课." "不"(not, won't, not want to) indicates an action or state in the present or yet to come, for example: "明天我不去上课." "不" may also indicate a general situation, for example:

　　"他不抽烟""我不会英语""那里冬天不下雪"。

　　注意：单独回答问题时，对过去的否定不能只用"没"字，如：

Notice: When used by itself in reply of a question, "没有" or "没呢" is used instead of "没":

"你吃饭了吗——没有(或"没呢")。"

2. "要不":

①"要不"是"或者"的意思,表示对两种情况的选择,如:

"要不" means "otherwise", indicating a choice between two situations, such as:

"咱们去看电影怎么样,要不去听音乐会?"

②"要不"在本课中可以说成"要不然",意思是"要是不这样(的话)",表示如果同上文提到的情况相反,就会产生下面的结果或疑问。如:

In the text "要不", also "要不然", means "if it is not so". If the situation mentioned earlier is not the case, the following result or problem would ensue. For instance:

"快走吧,要不来不及了!""你多穿点衣服,要不会感冒的。"

3. "……来着":

助词,常用在句末,表示事情曾经发生过,或者回忆、追问过去曾知晓的情况。如:

Particle, used at the end of a sentence or question, indicating a past action or state or the recalling or questioning of some past situation. For instance:

"我昨天还看见来着。""你刚才说什么来着?""老师怎么教我们来着?"

4. "你可来了":

"可……了"表示强调,如:

"可……了" is used for emphasis, for instance:

"他可好了""风可大了""你可来了""你可别忘了"。

练习 Exercise

一、读下边的句子,找出重音部分:

Read the following sentences, make sure which parts to stress:

1. 你今年多大了?
2. 都二十五岁啦,比你大多了!
3. 还差几分钟就到八点了。
4. 他的电话号码儿是多少?

145

5. 他住几号房间来着？

6. 他是不是忘了？

7. 真抱歉，我迟到了，让你们久等了。

二、替换练习：Substitution drills：

（一）

1. 还差<u>几分钟</u>就<u>到八点</u>了。

  两分 及格

  几天 该放假

  一门 考完

  十分钟 上课

2. 他住几号房间来着？

 你叫什么名字

 我刚才说什么

 你家在哪儿

 上次念到什么地方

3. 我们怕<u>你不来</u>了。

 我 孩子生病

 他 不能准时到教室

 小王 没人帮他请假

 她 考不上大学

（二）

  替换划线部分的词语，并将句子补充完整：

  Substitute the underlined parts and then complete the statements accordingly：

1. <u>王平</u>怎么还<u>没来</u>？→快八点了，王平怎么还不来？

 你 不睡

 他们班 没下课

 妹妹 不回来

 哥哥 没起床

2. 他可能<u>有事</u>。→他现在还没来，可能有事。

  已经出来了

  不在家

不知道这件事

不太舒服

3. 你　可　来了。→我们等了你半天,你可来了。
　　电话　　通
　　衣服　　买到
　　钥匙　　找到
　　作业　　做完

三、体会加点儿短语的用法,并模仿再做几组对话:
Make sure of the use of the dotted phrases, and produce a few more dialogues following the examples:

1. (1) 甲:要不要为你开一个生日晚会?
　　　乙:不用了,下次吧。
　　(2) 甲:我陪你去医院吧。
　　　乙:不用了,我自己能去。

2. (1) 甲:王平怎么还没来?
　　　乙:他是不是忘了今晚的事儿?
　　　丙:不会吧,他可能有事。
　　(2) 甲:杰夫一定回国了。
　　　乙:不会吧,昨天我还看见他来着。

3. (1) 甲:王平怎么还不来?
　　　乙:他可能有事,咱们再等他一会儿吧。
　　　甲:要不给他打个电话吧。
　　(2) 甲:都七点了,银行可能关门了。
　　　乙:要不明天再去?

4. (1) 甲:这件事告诉他好还是不告诉他好?
　　　乙:告诉他吧,要不他该不高兴了。
　　(2) 甲:今天的电视真好看,我想再看一会儿。
　　　乙:太晚了,别看了,要不明天起不来了。

四、下边各句中应该填"不"还是"没"? Fill in the blanks with "不" or "没":
1. 我怕你(　)来了呢。
2. 我还(　)吃饭呢。
3. 我(　)太想去逛街。

4. 这么热闹的事,哪能( )来!
5. 电话打( )通,占线呢。
6. 我( )记住他的电话号码儿。

五、记住下边的词语搭配,并扩展成完整的句子:
Learn by heart the following collocations and extend them into complete sentences:

1. 过生日
2. 开晚会
3. 打电话
4. 等电话

六、情景会话:假设第二段会话中彼得的电话打通了……
Situational dialogue: Supposing Peter has reached Wang Ping on the phone in Dialogue 2……

彼得:喂,3号楼吗?麻烦您转一下儿301房间。
王平:喂?
彼得:王平!王平,是你吗?你怎么还没出来?都8点啦!
王平:不对吧,我的表才七点半哪!
彼得:你的表该扔了,慢了那么多! 快来吧,就差你了!
王平:哎,我正给安妮包礼物呢!
彼得:快点儿包吧,我们都等着你呢!
王平:好的,我包完就去!

七、看答句想问话:Ask the corresponding questions:

1. 甲:_____?
   乙:我都22岁啦。
2. 甲:_____?
   乙:62754401。
3. 甲:_____?
   乙:301号。
4. 甲:_____?
   乙:五口人。

八、成段叙述:Oral composition:

　　(安妮给妈妈打电话)妈妈,您寄来的生日卡我已经收到了,它真漂亮,我非常喜欢。您知道吗,今晚我的同学和我的中国朋友一起给我开了个生日晚会,可热闹了。我们一起唱歌、跳舞,吃蛋糕,吃水果,我还收到了一件礼物,您猜是什么?

九、谈一谈： Talk about the following subjects：

1. 你习惯别人问你的年龄吗??
2. 你觉得生日晚会怎么开好?
3. 你在中国过过生日吗？怎么过的？

第二十三课　离这儿有多远？

（在校园里）
杰　夫：咱们学校西边有座山，风景不错，你爬过吗？
安　妮：没爬过，离这儿有多远？
杰　夫：不远，大概十多公里，骑自行车半个多小时就到了。
安　妮：这几天天气挺好的。
杰　夫：所以呀，我想周末咱们带点儿吃的、喝的，去山上野餐，怎么样？
安　妮：好主意，准会玩儿得开心！

（安妮告诉丽莎）
　　学校的西边有座山，风景不错，离这儿也不远，骑自行车半个多小时就到了。杰夫出了个好主意，说这个周末带上吃的、喝的，到山上去野餐，你去不去？

（安妮去商店买胶卷）
安　妮：请问，哪儿卖胶卷？
售货员：往里走，右边。
安　妮：谢谢。

（在卖胶卷的柜台前）
安　妮：小姐，买个胶卷。
售货员：这儿有好几种，你要什么的？
安　妮：柯达的。
售货员：(开了一张票)先去交一下儿钱。

（杰夫和安妮在骑车去野餐的路上）
安　妮：咱们现在是往哪个方向走？
杰　夫：往北。
安　妮：你不是说山在西边吗？
杰　夫：是在西北方向。
安　妮：还有多远？
杰　夫：不远了，到前边路口往左一拐，就能看见山了。
（到了山下）
安　妮：咱们把车放在这儿吧。
杰　夫：别动，先在这儿给你照张相。
安　妮：这儿有什么好照的？
杰　夫：嗯，背景好极了！一，二，三，糟糕，胶卷还没装上呢！
安　妮：你这个马大哈，到山上再照吧！
杰　夫：唉，还得听你的。来，东西都给我背着吧。
安　妮：哈哈，和男生一起出来玩儿就是好！

Dì-èrshísān kè　Lí zhèr yǒu duō yuǎn？

(zài xiàoyuán li)
Jiéfū：Zánmen xuéxiào xībian yǒu zuò shān, fēngjǐng búcuò, nǐ páguo ma？
Ānní：Méi páguo, lí zhèr yǒu duō yuǎn？
Jiéfū：Bù yuǎn, dàgài shí duō gōnglǐ, qí zìxíngchē bàn ge duō xiǎoshí jiù dào le.
Ānní：Zhèi jǐ tiān tiānqì tǐng hǎo de.
Jiéfū：Suǒyǐ ya, wǒ xiǎng zhōumò zánmen dài diǎnr chī de、hē de, qù shān shang yěcān, zěnmeyàng？
Ānní：Hǎo zhǔyi, zhǔn huì wánr de kāixīn！

(Ānní gàosu Lìshā)
　　Xuéxiào de xībian yǒu zuò shān, fēngjǐng búcuò, lí zhèr yě bù yuǎn, qí zìxíngchē bàn ge duō xiǎoshí jiù dào le. Jiéfū chūle ge hǎo zhǔyi, shuō zhèi ge zhōumò dàishang chī de、hē de,

dào shān shang qù yěcān, nǐ qù bu qù?

(Ānní qù shāngdiàn mǎi jiāojuǎnr)
Ānní: Qǐng wèn, nǎr mài jiāojuǎnr?
Shòuhuòyuán: Wǎng lǐ zǒu, yòubian.
Ānní: Xièxie.
(Zài mài jiāojuǎnr de guìtái qián)
Ānní: Xiǎojie, mǎi ge jiāojuǎnr.
Shòuhuòyuán: Zhèr yǒu hǎo jǐ zhǒng, nǐ yào shénme de?
Ānní: Kēdá de.
Shòuhuòyuán: (Kāile yì zhāng piào) Xiān qù jiāo yí xiàr qián.

(Jiéfū hé Ānní zài qí chē qù yěcān de lùshang)
Ānní: Zánmen xiànzài shì wǎng něi ge fāngxiàng zǒu?
Jiéfū: Wǎng Běi.
Ānní: Nǐ bú shì shuō shān zài xībian ma?
Jiéfū: Shì zài xīběi fāngxiàng.
Ānní: Hái yǒu duō yuǎn?
Jiéfū: Bù yuǎn le, dào qiánbian lùkǒu wǎng zuǒ yì guǎi, jiù néng kànjiàn shān le.
(Dào le shān xià)
Ānní: Zánmen bǎ chē fàng zài zhèr ba.
Jiéfū: Bié dòng, xiān zài zhèr gěi nǐ zhào zhāng xiàng.
Ānní: Zhèr yǒu shénme hǎo zhào de?
Jiéfū: ng, bèijǐng hǎo jíle! Yī, èr, sān, zāogāo, jiāojuǎnr hái méi zhuāngshang ne!
Ānní: Nǐ zhèi ge mǎdàhā, dào shān shang zài zhào ba!
Jiéfū: Ài, hái děi tīng nǐ de. Lái, dōngxi dōu gěi wǒ bēizhe ba.
Ānní: Hā ha, hé nánshēng yìqǐ chūlai wánr jiùshi hǎo!

注释 Notes

1. "这儿有好几种,你要什么的(胶卷)":

"你要什么的?"是"你要什么样的胶卷?"的省略形式,还可以说"你要哪种(胶卷)?"再如:"这里都有什么的?""你喝什么的?"等等。

"你要什么的?" is elliptical for "你要什么的胶卷?" or "你要哪种胶卷?" More examples: "这里都有什么的?" "你喝什么的?", etc.

2. "这儿有什么好照的":

这句话中的"好"的意思是"值得""使人满意"。这句话是反问句,意思是"这里没有什么值得照的(风景)"。类似的句子如:

The word "好" means "worth" or "satisfactory". It is a rhetorical question, meaning "There isn't any scenery worth taking a picture in." Similar sentences:

"这有什么好看的,别看了。""这有什么好笑的。"

3."马大哈":

指粗心大意的人。如:

"Scatterbrain":a careless and forgetful person. For instance:

"他是个马大哈,常常忘了自己的东西在哪儿。"

4."听你的":

表示按你的意见做。"听……的"中间还可以加入别的代词或名词,如:

Meaning "to do as you say". Other pronouns or nouns can come in between "听……的", for instance:

"听我的""听大家的""听大夫的""听爸爸的""听老师的""听学校的"。

练习 Exercises:

一、读下边的句子,注意句中停顿和语调:

Read the following sentences, taking care of the pauses and the intonation:

1. 那座山离这儿有多远?
2. 大概十多公里。
3. 骑车半个多小时就到了。
4. 咱们现在是往哪个方向走?
5. 山在西北方向。
6. 到前边路口往左一拐,就能看见山了。

二、根据课文内容判断下边的说法是否正确:

Decide whether the following statements are true to the text:

1. 周末他们打算去爬山。
2. 那座山在学校西边。
3. 杰夫在山下给安妮照了一张相。
4. 上山时杰夫帮安妮背东西。

三、替换练习：Substitution drills：

1. <u>这儿有好几种(胶卷)</u>， <u>你要什么的？</u>
   这些饮料都不错　　　　你喝
   矿泉水有大瓶的有小瓶的　你买
   杂志有中文的有英文的　　你看
   这几种菜都挺好吃的　　　你吃

2. <u>到前边路口往左</u>一拐，就能<u>看见山</u>了。
   你　　　　　　尝　知道好吃不好吃
   你往窗外　　　看　看见那座山
   你到学校　　　问　找到他
   你走过去　　　听　听到

3. 别动，<u>先在这儿给你照张相</u>。
   　　　你头发上是什么
   　　　举起手来
   　　　汽车
   　　　等人都坐好了再吃
   　　　这些东西可不是咱们的

4. 这有什么好<u>照</u>的？
   　　　　　看
   　　　　　笑
   　　　　　买
   　　　　　玩
   　　　　　介绍

5. 糟糕，<u>胶卷还没装上呢</u>。
   　　　钥匙不见了
   　　　钱包放哪儿了
   　　　电池没电了
   　　　我忘了告诉小王了
   　　　又迟到了

四、体会加点的短语的意思，并模仿对话：
Make sure of the meanings of the dotted phrases and produce similar dialogues：

1. 甲：咱们周末去爬山怎么样？
   乙：好主意！准会玩儿得开心！
2. 甲：咱们到山上再照相吧！
   乙：好，听你的。

五、尽可能想出可与下边的名词搭配的动词，并将它们扩展为完整的句子：
Think out，as many as possible，verbs which can be collocated with the following nouns and then extend each collocation into a complete sentence：

（　　）主意
（　　）吃的
（　　）胶卷
（　　）东西
（　　）钱

六、请你回答：Answer the questions：

1. 你经常照相吗？你知道哪些牌子的胶卷？你喜欢用什么胶卷照相？
2. 照相时，你喜欢什么背景？
3. 你喜欢骑自行车旅行吗？为什么？
4. 你爬过什么山？那儿风景怎么样？
5. 你喜欢野餐吗？为什么？

七、找一份当地地图，找出几个地方，并给大家介绍一下儿。
Find a local map，locate a few places and introduce them to your classmates.

提示词语：Words and expressions for use

山　江　河　湖　公园　南　北　东　西　西南　西北　东南　东北

八、成段表达：一次开心的旅行 Oral composition：A happy tour

参考词语：Words and expressions for reference

爬山　风景　离　野餐　玩儿　骑车　走路　往　照相

155

| 你知道吗？(7) | 方位与文化 |

汉语中常用的单纯方位词有东、西、南、北、上、下、左、右、前、后、里、外、中。下面的方位图中，

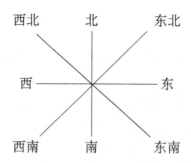

除东、西、南、北四个基本方位外，还有四个中间方位，四个中间方位的说法必须依次为"东南、东北、西南、西北"而不能说成"北东、南西"等。问路时，有的人习惯用"前、后、左、右"，如"往左拐""往右拐""往前走"等；有的人习惯用"东、西、南、北"，如"路南""路北""往西走再往南拐"等。北京地铁的出入口也用"东、南、西、北"表示，如"东南出口""西北口""西南口"等。

汉语的方位词在表示方位之外，有时还有一定的文化色彩，比如：中国人自古崇尚"坐北朝南"，人们以北为尊。一家一户院里的主要房屋都是门窗朝南的北房；请客时，让地位最高或年龄最大的人坐北面南，同是坐北面南，又要"东主西客"。

在你们国家，方位词有特别的意义吗？

| Do You Know? (7) | **Directions and Culture** |

Commonly used localizers in the Chinese language are: east, west, south, north, up, down, left, right, ahead, back, inside, outside, center. As shown in the following diagram, in addition to the four basic directions, east, west, south, north, there are four intermediate directions: "eastsouth, eastnorth, westsouth, westnorth" －－ their word order irreversible. In asking the way, some prefer to use "ahead, back, left, right", for example: "turn left" "turn right" "go ahead" and so on; others prefer to use "east, west, south, north", for example: "south side of the street" "north side of the street" "go west and turn south" and so on. At the entrances and exits of the Beijing Subway, "east, south, west, north" are also used to indicate directions, for example: "Northsouthern Exit" "Westnorthern Exit" "Westsouthern Exit" and so on.

In addition to indicating directions, Chinese localizers sometimes contain certain cultural implications, for instance: By tradition, the Chinese value the north. Therefore, the major rooms in the traditional Chinese quadrangle(四合院)are always on the north side of the courtyard with the doors and windows opening to the south; When giving a traditional banquet, the host together with the most senior or distinguished guests always sit at the north side of the table facing south -- with the host on the east side, the guest on the west side.

In your country, do localizers contain any special meanings?

第二十四课　她又聪明又用功

（上课前）

杰　夫：安妮，这是上次咱们去野餐时的照片，昨天刚洗出来。

安　妮：快给我看看！（看了一会儿）这张不错，这张也不错。……这张有点儿不清楚。

杰　夫：你挑几张吧，喜欢哪张挑哪张。

安　妮：都挺好的，这几张最好。我要给妈妈寄去。把底片给我吧，我再去洗几张。

杰　夫：好的。怎么样，满意吗？

安　妮：满意，谢谢你，杰夫。对了，我得给你多少钱？

杰　夫：算了，别客气，这是我送给你的，只要你满意就行了。

（安妮对丽莎说）

　　杰夫送给我的照片都是上次爬山时他给我照的，你看怎么样？我觉得这几张都不错，明天我要把这些寄给妈妈，另外再去洗几张放在自己的相册里。

（校园里）

丽　莎：王平，你好！好久不见了。

王　平：是啊，好久不见。最近忙吗？
丽　莎：还可以。你不是安妮的辅导吗？怎么样？她是个好学生吧？
王　平：安妮又聪明又用功，进步挺快的。
丽　莎：她说近来上课都能听懂了，可是，一到外边就听不懂了，越听不懂越着急。
王　平：着急可不行，慢慢来吧。
丽　莎：我也有同样的问题，不知道有什么好办法？
王　平：你还着什么急？说得不是挺好吗？
丽　莎：哪里，哪里，还差得远呢，我是认真地问你呢，有什么好办法？
王　平：办法很多，比如听录音啦、看电视啦，都是好办法，还可以经常找中国人聊聊天儿。
丽　莎：好哇，那我就经常来找你吧，你可不许烦哪！

Dì-èrshísì kè　Tā yòu cōngming yòu yònggōng

(Shàng kè qián)
Jiéfū: Ānní, zhè shì shàng cì zánmen qù yěcān shí zhào de zhàopiānr, zuótiān gāng xǐ chūlai.
Ānní: Kuài gěi wǒ kànkan! (Kànle yíhuìr) Zhèi zhāng búcuò, zhèi zhāng yě búcuò. …… Zhèi zhāng yǒudiǎnr bù qīngchu.
Jiéfū: Nǐ tiāo jǐ zhāng ba, xǐhuan něi zhāng tiāo něi zhāng.
Ānní: Dōu tǐng hǎo de, zhèi jǐ zhāng zuì hǎo, wǒ yào gěi māma jìqù. Bǎ dǐpiàn gěi wǒ ba, wǒ zài qù xǐ jǐ zhāng.
Jiéfū: Hǎode. Zěnmeyàng, mǎnyì ma?
Ānní: Mǎnyì, xièxie nǐ, Jiéfū. Duìle, wǒ děi gěi nǐ duōshao qián?
Jiéfū: Suànle, bié kèqi, zhèi shi wǒ sònggěi nǐ de, zhǐyào nǐ mǎnyì jiù xíng le.

(Ānní duì Lìshā shuō)
　　Jiéfū sònggěi wǒ de zhàopiānr dōu shi shàng cì pá shān shí tā gěi wǒ zhào de, nǐ kàn zěnmeyàng? Wǒ juéde zhèi jǐ zhāng dōu búcuò, míngtiān wǒ yào bǎ zhèixiē jìgěi māma, lìngwài zài qù xǐ jǐ zhāng fàng zài zìjǐ de xiàngcè lǐ.

(Xiàoyuán li)
Lìshā: Wáng Píng, nǐ hǎo! Hǎojiǔ bú jiàn le.
Wáng Píng: Shì a, hǎojiǔ bú jiàn. Zuìjìn máng ma?
Lìshā: Hái kěyǐ. Nǐ bú shi Ānní de fǔdǎo ma? Zěnmeyàng? Tā shi ge hǎo xuésheng ba!
Wáng Píng: Ānní yòu cōngming yòu yòng gōng, jìnbù tǐng kuài de.
Lìshā: Tā shuō jìnlái shàng kè dōu néng tīngdǒng le, kěshì, yí dào wàibian jiù tīng bu dǒng le, yuè tīng bu dǒng yuè zháo jí.

Wáng Píng: Zháo jí kě bù xíng, mànmānr lái ba.

Lìshā: Wǒ yě yǒu tóngyàng de wèntí, bù zhīdao yǒu shénme hǎo bànfǎ?

Wáng Píng: Nǐ hái zháo shénme jí? Shuō de bú shì tǐng hǎo ma?

Lìshā: Nǎlǐ, nǎlǐ, hái chà de yuǎn ne, wǒ shì rènzhēn de wèn nǐ ne, yǒu shénme hǎo bànfǎ?

Wáng Píng: Bànfǎ hěn duō, tīng lù yīn la, kàn diànshì la, dōu shì hǎo bànfǎ, hái kěyǐ jīngcháng zhǎo Zhōngguórén liáoliao tiānr.

Lìshā: Hǎo wa, nà wǒ jiù jīngcháng lái zhǎo nǐ ba, nǐ kě bù xǔ fán na!

注释 Notes

1. "喜欢哪张挑哪张":

前一个"哪张"是泛指,不定的,后一个"哪张"指前面喜欢的那张,是有定的。在这个句式中,有两个动词:V1:喜欢,V2:挑;V1 是 V2 的条件,V1 决定 V2。如:

The first "哪张" is indefinite and in a general sense, the second "哪张" is definite, indicating the preceding one that Anne likes. There are two verbs in the sentence pattern: V1: 喜欢, V2: 挑 ; V1 is the condition of V2 and decides V2. For instance:

"喜欢哪件(衣服)(就)买哪件""要哪个给哪个"。

注意:"哪"(nǎ)在口语中,后面跟量词或数词加量词时,常读作 něi。另外,类似的句型还有:

Attention: When followed by a measure word or a numeral plus a measure word in spoken Chinese, "哪" is often pronounced as "něi". More examples in similar pattern:

"爱吃什么吃什么""看见谁问谁"。

2. "对了":

口语词,突然想起什么事时用。如:

"对了" informal, used when one suddenly remembers something. For example:

"对了,(差点儿忘了)小王让我告诉你,他明天不来了。"

3. "算了":

口语词,本课表示不再计较,作罢。如:

"算了", informal, "let it be", "stop fussing about", "leave it at that". For instance:

"算了,别说了。""要是你不愿意就算了。"

4."哪里,哪里,还差得远呢":

谦词,听到对方称赞时,表示委婉的推辞和谦虚;"还差得远呢"谦虚地表示自己的水平还很不够,没有对方说的那么高。

Humble words, used as a polite reply to a compliment, indicating declination and modesty;"还差得远呢"means "I'm not as good as the you think." "There's still a great deal to be expected."

5、"什么":

①"有什么好办法""没说什么"

这两句话中的"什么"都表示不肯定的事物。如:

The"什么" in the two sentences indicates something indefinite. For instance:

"他们好像在谈什么。""我饿了,想吃点儿什么。"

②"着什么急""你笑什么"

这里的"什么"表示责备、否定,"着什么急"的意思是"不要着急";"你笑什么"的意思是"没有值得你笑的""你别笑"。类似的句型如:

The"什么" here indicates reproach, disapproval. "着什么急"means "Not to worry." "你笑什么"means:"There's nothing to laugh at." "Stop laughing." A similar sentence pattern:

"这么好的天气睡什么觉,出去玩一会儿吧!""你哭什么!"

6. 表示列举或举例子的句式(二):

Sentence patterns for listing or giving examples(二):

(1)"比如":举例子时的发语词:

"比如": a starter preceding an example:

"我的房间里有很多电器,比如:电视、洗衣机(什么的)。"

(2)"……啦……啦":用在列举的成分后面,可以有多项,如:

The word"啦" follows each of the items listed, for example:

"苹果啦,橘子啦,葡萄啦,我都喜欢吃。"

练习 Exercises

一、用正确的语调读下边的句子,注意重音:

Read the following sentences in correct intonation, be careful as to where to stress:

1. 快给我看看!
2. 这张有点儿不清楚。

3．安妮又聪明又用功。

4．一到外边就听不懂了。

5．越听不懂越着急。

6．你说得不是挺好吗？

二、替换练习：Substitution drills：

（一）

1．我也有同样的<u>问题</u>。
　　　　　　　相册
　　　　　　　习惯
　　　　　　　办法
　　　　　　　打算

2．越<u>听不懂</u>越<u>着急</u>。
　　想　　　怕
　　想早起　起不来
　　吃　　　胖
　　着急　　骑不快

3．<u>办法很多</u>，　比如　<u>经常找中国人聊聊天儿</u>什么的。
　　他去过很多地方　　四川、云南、东北
　　他会做不少中国菜　鱼香肉丝、香菇菜心
　　我想去很多国家旅行　法国、日本、美国
　　这儿衣服颜色很多　　黑的、蓝的、红的、绿的、白的

（二）
　　替换划线部分的词语，并将句子补充完整：
　　Substitute the underlined parts and complete the sentences：

1．<u>喜欢哪张　挑哪张</u>。→这些相片你喜欢哪张挑哪张。
　　要　　个　给　个
　　想吃　种　买　种
　　爱看　本　借　本
　　爱穿　件　穿　件

2．只要<u>你满意</u>就行了。→不用给我钱，只要你满意就行了。
　　　　他喜欢

在门口等我
　　　提前几分钟
　　　好好儿准备

3. 另外再去洗几张放在自己的相册里。→这几张我要寄给我妈妈,另外再
　　　　　　　　　　　　　　　　　　去洗几张放在自己的相册里。
　　　买几个送给朋友
　　　准备点儿喝的
　　　叫上王平和杰夫

4. 一到外边就听不懂了。→上课时都能听懂,可是一到外边就听不懂了。
　　　说话　　笑
　　　高兴　　唱歌
　　　下雨　　想睡觉
　　　写　　　错

5. 又聪明又用功。→小王又聪明又用功,所以学习很好。
　　　大　　　甜
　　　便宜　　好
　　　高　　　大
　　　瘦　　　短
　　　着急　　生气

6. 着急可不行。→着急可不行,慢慢来吧。
　　迟到
　　早退
　　不请假
　　不吃饭
　　不睡觉
　　不洗手

7. 你还着什么急? →你的汉语说得那么好,你还着什么急?
　　　生　　气
　　　睡　　觉
　　　吃　　饭

洗　澡
照　相
写　信

三、体会加点儿的短语的意思，并模仿对话：
Make sure of the meanings of the dotted phrases and produce similar dialogues：
1. 甲：怎么样，满意吗？
　　乙：满意，谢谢你，杰夫。对了，我得给你多少钱？
2. 甲：我得给你多少钱？
　　乙：算了，别客气，这是我送给你的。
3. 甲：你说得不是挺好吗？
　　乙：哪里哪里，还差得远呢。
4. 甲：办法很多，比如找中国人聊聊天儿。
　　乙：那我就经常来找你吧，……。

四、得体应答： Make appropriate replies：
1. 好久不见！
2. 最近忙吗？
3. 让你久等了！
4. 你汉语说得不是挺好吗？

五、给下边空格处填上适当的词语，并熟读这段话：
Fill in the blanks with suitable words or expressions and learn the passage by heart：

　　安妮，照片（　　）出来了，有几张（　　）不错的，你看看，（　　）几张好的给你妈妈（　　）去。她（　　）喜欢。要是你还想洗几张，我这儿有底片。怎么样，我（　　）得还可以吧？

六、体会下边各句中"什么"的用法，并用正确的语调读下边各句：
Make sense of the word "什么" in each of the following sentences and read the sentence in correct intonation：
1. 中午想吃点儿什么？
2. 我饿了，有什么可吃的？
3. 他俩好像在笑什么。
4. 你笑什么？有什么好笑的？
5. 还早呢，你急什么呀！

6. 你叫什么名字?

七、读下边的三组对话,再谈一谈,在你们国家人们听到别人夸奖时一般怎么应答?
Read the three dialogues and talk about what people in your country would often say in reply to a compliment.

1. 甲:你的汉字写得真好!
   乙:哪里哪里。
2. 甲:你的衣服真漂亮!
   乙:谢谢!
3. 甲:你的发音真不错!
   乙:我的老师也说我的发音比以前好多了。
4. 甲:你的女儿真漂亮!
   乙:你的孩子也挺可爱。

八、实践:摄影展评
A practice: Give a comment on a photographic exhibition.
要求:将自己最满意的照片拿出来介绍,供大家评价。
Requirements: Show and comment on the most satisfactory pictures you have taken and ask for comments from others.
参考用语:words and expressions for reference
背景　清楚　洗　照　合影　风景　远　近　胶卷

九、讨论:学汉语的好办法
Discussion: A good way to learn the Chinese language
参考用语:words and expressions for reference
辅导　进步　比如　聊天儿　懂　慢慢儿　只要……就……

第二十五课 便宜点儿吧

(在商店里)

杰　夫:小姐,苹果多少钱一斤?
售货员:三块五。
丽　莎:(拽杰夫衣袖)我觉得有点儿贵。
杰　夫:便宜点儿吧。三块怎么样?
售货员:我们这儿不讲价,这苹果多好哇! 又大又甜,这个价儿可不贵。
杰　夫:好吧,我买一斤。
丽　莎:要买就多买点儿吧。
杰　夫:刚才还说贵呢,现在花我的钱你又不怕贵了。
丽　莎:那我付钱好了。
杰　夫:跟你开个玩笑,你就认真了。小姐,来二斤。
售货员:好。还要别的吗?
杰　夫:不要了。

(在路上)

杰　夫:安妮,看你急急忙忙的样子,这是去哪儿啊?

安　妮：我得去接一个朋友，火车六点就到。现在四点半都过了，可我还……
杰　夫：你打算怎么去呢？
安　妮：我正想问你呢。
杰　夫：公共汽车又慢又挤，你"打的"去吧。
安　妮：车站离这儿挺远的，"打的"恐怕太贵了，再说，现在是下班时间，肯定堵车！
杰　夫：那只好骑车去了。
安　妮：骑车？来得及吗？
杰　夫：放心吧，来得及，我知道一条近路，骑车最方便了。
安　妮：可我不认识那条路哇，你看……
杰　夫：你别着急了，快走吧，你还不知道吗？我这个人最喜欢帮漂亮小姐的忙了！

（安妮对她的朋友说）

　　这是我的同学杰夫。今天我的课很多，出来的时候，已经快五点了，正是下班的时间，到处都堵车。要不是杰夫陪我骑车走近路来，肯定会晚的。

Dì-èrshíwǔ kè　Piányi diǎnr ba

(Zài shāngdiàn li)
Jiéfū: Xiǎojie, píngguǒ duōshao qián yì jīn?
Shòuhuòyuán: Sān kuài wǔ.
Lìshā: (Zhuài Jiéfū yī xiù) Wǒ juéde yǒudiǎnr guì.
Jiéfū: Piányi diǎnr ba, sān kuài zěnmeyàng?
Shòuhuòyuán: Wǒmen zhèr bù jiǎng jià, zhè píngguǒ duō hǎo wa! Yòu dà yòu tián, zhèi ge jiàr kě bú guì.
Jiéfū: Hǎo ba, wǒ mǎi yì jīn.
Lìshā: Yào mǎi jiù duō mǎi diǎnr ba.
Jiéfū: Gāngcái hái shuō guì ne, xiànzài huā wǒ de qián nǐ yòu bú pà guì le.
Lìshā: Nà wǒ fù qián hǎo le.
Jiéfū: Gēn nǐ kāi ge wánxiào, nǐ jiù rènzhēn le. Xiǎojie, lái èr jīn.
Shòuhuòyuán: Hǎo. Hái yào biéde ma?
Jiéfū: Bú yào le.

(zài lù shang)
Jiéfū: Ānní, kàn nǐ jíjí-mángmáng de yàngzi, zhè shi qù nǎr a?
Ānní: Wǒ děi qù jiē yí ge péngyou, huǒchē liù diǎn jiù dào. xiànzài sì diǎn bàn dōu guò le, kě wǒ hái……
Jiéfū: Nǐ dǎsuan zěnme qù ne?

Ānní: Wǒ zhèng xiǎng wèn nǐ ne.

Jiéfū: Gōnggòng qìchē yòu màn yòu jǐ, nǐ "dǎdī" qù ba.

Ānní: Chēzhàn lí zhèr tǐng yuǎn de, "dǎdī" kǒngpà tài guì le, zàishuō, xiànzài shì xià bān shíjiān, kěndìng dǔ chē!

Jiéfū: Nà zhǐhǎo qí chē qù le.

Ānní: Qí chē? Láidejí ma?

Jiéfū: Fàngxīn ba, láidejí, wǒ zhīdao yì tiáo jìn lù, qí chē zuì fāngbiàn le.

Ānní: Kě wǒ bú rènshi lù wa, nǐ kàn……

Jiéfū: Nǐ bié zháo jí le, kuài zǒu ba, nǐ hái bù zhīdao ma? Wǒ zhèi ge rén zuì xǐhuan bāng piàoliang xiǎojie de máng le!

(Ānní duì tā de péngyou shuō)

Zhè shì wǒ de tóngxué Jiéfū. Jīntiān wǒ de kè hěn duō, chūlai de shíhou, yǐjing kuài wǔ diǎn le, zhèng shi xià bān de shíjiān, dàochù dōu dǔ chē. Yàobúshi Jiéfū péi wǒ qí chē zǒu jìn lù lái, kěndìng huì wǎn de.

注释 Notes

1. "来得及":

表示还有时间,能赶上或能做某事。如:"飞机十点起飞,现在刚七点,来得及。"其否定式是"来不及",表示时间太少,不够、不能做某事或赶不上做某事。如:"明天就考试了,今天开始复习,来不及了。"

Indicating there's still time, being able to do something in time. For instance: "飞机十点起飞,现在刚七点来得及". The negative form is "来不及", indicating there's too little (or not enough) time to do something in time. For instance: "明天就考试了,今天开始复习,来不及了".

2. "帮忙":

离合词,常见的用法有:"请帮个忙""请帮帮忙""帮我个忙"。

注意:"帮忙"后不能加宾语,不能说"帮忙我",要说"帮我个忙"或"帮帮我的忙"。

"帮忙" is a verb phrase, the two words in it can be separated in use, common usage: "请帮个忙""请帮帮忙""帮我个忙".

Note that you can not say "帮忙我" because the phrasal verb never takes an object.

3. "再说":

①把某事放到以后再办或再考虑。如:

Means that put it off until some time later. For example:

"这件事先等一等,过几天再说。""这件事等小王来了再说。"

②表示进一步补充说明事情的原因。如:

Used to further explain the reason or cause of something. For example:

甲:"你为什么不去上海旅行了?"

乙:"我没有时间,再说我也没那么多钱。"

4. "你看":

征询对方的意见,如:"你看这件衣服怎么样?""你看他今天能来吗?"回答是:"我看……"。

Used to ask for the other party's opinion, for instance:"你看这件衣服怎么样?""你看他今天能来吗?" The reply is:"我看……".

5. "打的":

读"dǎdī"。"的"指出租汽车。也可以说"打(一)辆的"。"的"(dī)不单独用。

Pronounced as [dǎdī]. "的" means "a taxi", but the word cannot be used on its own. You can also say:"打(一)辆的".

练习 Exercises

一、用正确的语调读下边的句子:Read the following sentences in correct intonation:

1. 苹果多少钱一斤?
2. 我觉得有点儿贵。
3. 便宜点儿吧,三块怎么样?
4. 要买就多买点儿吧。
5. 还要别的吗?
6. "打的"恐怕太贵了。
7. 骑车? 来得及吗?
8. 放心吧,来得及。

二、下边各句中的"可"哪个重读,哪个不重读?

In which sentences, the word"可" should be stressed?

1. 我明天再去给你辅导,可以吗?

2．你可来了。

3．着急可不行。

4．风可大了。

5．这个价儿可不贵。

6．到时候我找你聊天儿，你可不许烦。

三、替换练习：Substitution drills：

（一）

1．苹果多少钱一斤？
　　啤酒　　　瓶
　　饺子　　　盘
　　那件蓝的　件
　　自行车　　辆

2．(现在)正是下班时间。
　　　　　　上班
　　　　　　吃午饭
　　　　　　休息
　　　　　　上课

3．车站离这儿　挺远的。
　　学校　机场　真远
　　宿舍　食堂　很近
　　我家　车站　不太远
　　医院　学校　挺近的

（二）

　　替换划线部分的词语，并将句子补充完整：
　　Substitute the underlined parts and complete the sentences：

1．我正想问你呢。→我也不知道他去哪儿了，我正想问你呢。
　　　　找你
　　　　买本汉英辞典
　　　　给他打电话
　　　　多洗几张

2. 打的 恐怕太贵了。→
   这个价儿　　太高了
   下午　　　　要下雨
   时间　　　　来不及了
   他说的　　　不是真的

3. 你看……？→
   　　我该怎么办
   　　咱们怎么走呢
   　　我买哪种好
   　　洗哪张好
   　　有什么好办法

4. (路上)肯定堵车。→
   打的去　　来得及
   你　　　　忘了我是谁了
   妈妈　　　给我寄生日卡了
   今晚　　　下雪
   现在家里　没有人

5. 到处都堵车。→
   　　是人
   　　是水
   　　这么挤
   　　有卖东西的
   　　没办法停车

四、先体会对话(1)中加点儿短语的意思，然后完成(2)：
First make sure of the meaning of the dotted words in Dialogue (1) and then complete Dialogue (2):

1. (1)甲：这个价儿太贵了吧？
   乙：放心吧，我这儿卖得最便宜!
   (2)甲：我怕找不到满意的工作。
   乙：放心吧，_____。
2. (1)甲：小王在吗？

171

乙:刚才还在这儿呢,现在不知去哪儿了。

(2)甲:不好了,我的钱包不见了。

乙:刚才还_____,_____。

3. (1)甲:明天的口语考试准备得怎么样了?

乙:明天考试?哎呀,要不是你问我,我还真忘了。

(2)甲:你怎么知道我病了?

乙:要不是_____,_____。

4. (1)甲:咱们坐公共汽车去吧。

乙:公共汽车太挤了,再说,现在公共汽车很少,恐怕来不及了,咱们还是"打的"吧。

(2)甲:周末咱们骑自行车逛街吧!

乙:_____,再说,_____。

5. (1)甲:这个菜太辣了吧?

乙:你还不知道吗,我最爱吃辣的啦!

(2)甲:这时候路上会堵车吗?

乙:你还不知道吗? _____。

五、以杰夫的口气叙述第一段会话:

Reproduce Dialogue 1 in the first person from Jeff's point of view:

"一天,我和丽莎去买水果……我和她开了个玩笑……"

六、模拟表演第二段会话。 Perform Dialogue 2.

七、请你说说: Talk about:

1. 你的学校离火车站远吗?
2. 你知道从学校到火车站怎么走吗?
3. 你在路上经常遇到堵车的情况吗?那时候你的心情怎么样?
4. 买东西时,你知道怎么讲价吗?在哪儿买东西可以讲价?你讲过价吗?

八、选择适当的词语进行情景会话:

Produce situational dialogues using the words and expressions properly:

觉得　　再说　　恐怕　　肯定

1. 请朋友和你一起骑车旅行。
2. 劝一个抽烟的人别再抽烟了。
3. 劝朋友别买那件衣服。

第二十六课　怎么了？

(在宿舍)

王　平：杰夫，这个周末咱们俩骑车进城转转好吧？
杰　夫：好是好，可是我去不了了。
王　平：怎么了？你有事吗？
杰　夫：唉，别提了，倒霉的事，我的自行车丢了。
王　平：什么？丢了？你是不是忘了锁车了？
杰　夫：没有哇。我锁得好好儿的，这不，钥匙还在我手里呢。
王　平：别着急，咱们下楼再好好儿找找。
杰　夫：不用了，我都找过几遍了，连个影子也没有，看来肯定是丢了。
王　平：算了，别想它了。"旧的不去，新的不来"，再买一辆吧。
杰　夫：这……下个月再说吧。

(两天以后在路上，王平看见杰夫骑着自行车)

王　平：杰夫，你的车不是丢了吗？
杰　夫：没丢。那天我去商店，把车停在外边，出来的时候，光顾和一个朋友聊天儿，忘了把车骑回去了。

王　平：你这个马大哈！

（课间休息，大家聊天儿）
丽　莎：快到圣诞节了，不知道咱们放不放假。
杰　夫：可能不放，因为中国没有过圣诞节的习惯。
彼　得：那是以前，现在不一定了吧。
丽　莎：要是不放假，就回不了家了。
杰　夫：那有什么关系，咱们大家在一起开个晚会什么的，不是也挺热闹吗？
安　妮：彼得，你的女朋友不是也想来中国看看吗？让她来中国过圣诞节，不就更热闹了吗？
彼　得：唉，别提她了，我们俩已经"吹"了。
安　妮：啊？抱歉，抱歉，我不知道……
彼　得：没什么，没什么。

（王平给安妮打电话）
　　安妮，真对不起，明天我有点儿事，所以下午不能给你辅导了。你看改在后天下午，怎么样？……对，后天下午，行吗？你方便吗？……方便？好，那就后天下午见？不好意思，给你添麻烦了。再见！

Dì-èrshíliù kè　Zěnme le？

（Zài sùshè）
Wáng Píng：Jiéfū, zhèi ge zhōumò zánmen liǎ qí chē jìn chéng zhuànzhuan hǎo ba？
Jiéfū：Hǎo shi hǎo, kěshì wǒ qù bu liǎo le.
Wáng Píng：Zěnme le？Nǐ yǒu shì ma？
Jiéfū：Ài, bié tí le, dǎoméi de shì, wǒ de zìxíngchē diū le.
Wáng Píng：Shénme？Diū le？Nǐ shì bu shì wàngle suǒ chē le？
Jiefu：Méiyǒu wa. Wǒ suǒ de hǎohāor de, zhè bú, yàoshi hái zài wǒ shǒu li ne.
Wáng Píng：Bié zháo jí, zánmen xià lóu zài hǎohāor zhǎozhao.
Jiéfū：Búyòng le, wǒ dōu zhǎoguo jǐ biàn le, lián ge yǐngzi yě méiyǒu, kànlái kěndìng shì diū le.
Wáng Píng：Suànle, bié xiǎng tā le. "Jiù de bú qù, xīn de bù lái", zài mǎi yí liàng ba.
Jiéfū：Zhè……Xià ge yuè zài shuō ba.

（Liǎng tiān yǐhòu zài lùshang, Wáng Píng kànjiàn Jiéfū qízhe zìxíngchē）
Wáng Píng：Jiéfū, nǐ de chē bú shi diūle ma?
Jiéfū：Méi diū. Nèi tiān wǒ qù shāngdiàn, bǎ chē tíng zài wàibian, chūlai de shíhou guāng gù hé

yí ge péngyou liáo tiānr, wàngle bǎ chē qí huíqu le.
Wáng Píng: Nǐ zhèi ge mǎdàhā!

(Kè jiān xiūxi, dàjiā liáo tiānr)
Lìshā: Kuài dào Shèngdànjié le, bù zhīdao zánmen fàng bu fàng jià.
Jiéfū: Kěnéng bú fàng, yīnwei Zhōngguó méiyǒu guò Shèngdànjié de xíguàn.
Bǐdé: Nà shì yǐqián, xiànzài bù yídìng le ba.
Lìshā: Yàoshi bú fàng jià, jiù huí bu liǎo jiā le.
Jiéfū: Nà yǒu shénme guānxi, zánmen dàjiā zài yìqǐ kāi ge wǎnhuì shénme de, bú shi yě tǐng rènao ma?
Wáng Píng: Bǐdé, nǐ de nǚ péngyou bú shi yě xiǎng lái Zhōngguó kànkan ma? Ràng tā lái Zhōngguó guò Shèngdànjié, bú jiù gèng rènao le ma?
Bǐdé: Ài, bié tí tā le, wǒmen liǎ yǐjing "chuī" le.
Wáng Píng: Á? Bàoqiàn, bàoqiàn, wǒ bù zhīdào……
Bǐdé: Méi shénme, méi shénme.

(Wáng Píng gěi Ānní dǎ diànhuà)
Ānní, zhēn duìbuqǐ, míngtiān wǒ yǒudiǎnr shì, suǒyǐ xiàwǔ bù néng gěi nǐ fǔdǎo le. Nǐ kàn gǎi zài hòutiān xiàwǔ zěnmeyàng?……Duì, hòutiān xiàwǔ, xíng ma? Nǐ fāngbiàn ma?……Fāngbiàn? Hǎo, nà jiù hòutiān xiàwǔ jiàn? Bù hǎoyìsi, gěi nǐ tiān máfan le. Zàijiàn!

注释 Notes

1. "好是好，可是我去不了了"：

意思是"虽然好，但是我去不了"。"A 是 A, 可是……"这个口语句式表示转折，好的情况中还有一点儿不如意的情况。如：

Means "It is a good idea, but I wouldn't be able to go". "A 是 A, 可是……" is an oral sentence pattern indicating a turn, indicating there is still something unsatisfactory in a satisfactory situation. For instance：

"那个菜好吃是好吃，可是有点儿辣。""衣服漂亮是漂亮，可是太贵了。"

2. "别提了"：

"提"的意思是"谈起，说起"。对某事表示不满意，不想谈到那件事时用。如：

"提" means "talk about, mention". Used to express the unhappy feelings about something and the reluctance to be reminded of it, for instance：

甲："昨天考试考得怎么样？"

乙："唉，别提了，考得不好。"

3."这不":

是反问句"这不是吗?"的省略形式,表示肯定,强调某物就在这儿。如果在远处,用"那不!"如:

"这不" is the elliptical form of a rhetorical sentence:"这不是吗?" It is used for emphasis. If the thing is away somewhere, say "那不!" For example:

甲:"我的笔呢?"

乙:"这不,就在桌子上呢。"

4."旧的不去,新的不来":

是一句俗语,意思是"旧的东西还存在的话,新的东西就不出现。"在旧的东西丢失了等情况之下,常用来表示安慰。如:

An old saying, it means "With the old things around, new things will not occur." It's often said as a consolation when something gets lost. For example:

甲:"我的手表又坏了。"

乙:"再买块新的吧,旧的不去新的不来嘛!"

5."吹":

动词,本义是"合拢嘴唇用力出气",如:"吹蜡烛""吹气球"。在口语中,可以引申表示事情不成功或关系结束。如:

"吹" is a verb, literally meaning "to send out a strong current of air through one's rounded lips", for instance:"吹蜡烛""吹气球". In spoken Chinese, it is extended to mean the failing of some attempt or the ending of a relationship. For example:

"别提了,那件事吹了!""他和女朋友吹了。"

6."不好意思":

①害羞,如:

To feel embarrassed:

"大家都看她,她觉得有点儿不好意思。"

"第一次在这么多人面前唱歌,真不好意思。"

②碍于情面而不便或不能做某事。如:

To find it difficult to do something for fear of hurting feelings:

"大家都请他去玩儿,他不好意思拒绝 ."

③客气话,表示抱歉。如:

To be sorry: a polite remark used as an apology:

"不好意思,给你添麻烦了。""这么晚来打扰你,真不好意思。"

7."添麻烦":

这里"添"是"加""增加"的意思。请别人帮忙以后,常用的表示感谢的话。如:
"添" here means "add" or "increase". Often used to express one's thanks for people's assistance. For instance:

甲:"太谢谢你了,给你添麻烦了!"　　甲:"真对不起,给你添了很多麻烦!"
乙:"哪里,不用客气。"　　　　　　　乙:"没什么,别客气。"

练习 Exercises

一、用正确的语调读下边的句子: Read the following sentences in correct intonation:

1. 怎么了? 你有事吗?
2. 唉,别提了。
3. 看来肯定是丢了。
4. 下个月再说吧。
5. 圣诞节可能不放假,因为中国没有过圣诞节的习惯。
6. 要是不放假,就回不了家了。
7. 抱歉,抱歉,我不知道……
8. 你看改在后天下午怎么样?
9. 你方便吗?
10. 不好意思,给你添麻烦了。

二、说出带点短语或句子的意思:

Explain the meanings of the dotted expressions or sentences:

1. "旧的不去,新的不来",再买一辆吧。
2. 我都找过好几遍了,连个影子也没有。
3. 要是不放假,就回不了家了。
4. 别提她了,我们俩已经"吹"了。

三、替换划线部分的词语,并将句子补充完整:

Substitute the underlined parts and complete the sentences:

1. 看来肯定是丢了。→自行车好几天都没找到,看来肯定是丢了。
　　来不及了
　　他真的不在家

你不喜欢他
我们给您添麻烦了
他有点儿不好意思

2. <u>下个月</u>再说→这个月太忙了,下个月再说。
以后
明天
下次
星期一上班的时候

3. 要是<u>不放假</u>,就<u>回不了家了</u>。→不知道圣诞节放不放假,要是不
　　　　　　　　　　　　　　　　　　放假,就回不了家了。

　　不舒服　　好好儿休息休息
　　不努力　　学不会
　　想家　　　睡不好觉
　　太麻烦　　不要做了

4. <u>好</u>　是　<u>好</u>,可是我去不了了。→你的主意好是好,可是我去不了了。
　漂亮　　漂亮　　太贵了
　喜欢　　喜欢　　不敢天天喝
　麻烦　　麻烦　　人人都爱吃
　挤　　　挤　　　有意思

四、注意加点短语的用法,并用它们完成后面的对话,然后再做几个小对话:
Note the use of the dotted phrases in the example dialogues, and complete the ensuing dialogues with them. Then produce a few more short dialogues:

1. (1)甲:今天天气不错,咱们去游泳好吗?
　　乙:好是好,可是我有辅导,去不了。
　(2)甲:这条裤子挺漂亮的。
　　乙:_____。
2. (1)甲:你好像有点儿不高兴?
　　乙:唉,别提了,我新买的自行车丢了,真倒霉!
　(2)甲:小王,考得怎么样?一定不错吧?
　　乙:_____。
3. (1)甲:圣诞节可能不放假,因为中国没有过圣诞节的习惯。

乙：那是以前,现在不一定了吧。
　(2)甲：听说这家饭馆很便宜,十块钱就能吃得很好。
　　　乙：_____。
4．(1)甲：你是不是忘了锁车了?
　　　乙：没有哇,这不,钥匙还在这儿呢!
　(2)甲：小王是不是已经回家了?
　　　乙：_____。

五、找出下边的句子中表示反问语气的短语,说说这些句子分别是什么意思?
Find the phrase, in each of the following, which forms the rhetorical question and explain what each sentence means：

1．那有什么关系,咱们大家在一起开个晚会什么的,不是也挺热闹吗?
2．你的女朋友不是也想来中国看看吗?
3．让她来中国过圣诞节,不就更热闹了吗?
4．你不是喜欢喝可乐吗?那我就来矿泉水好了。
5．你还着什么急?你汉语说得不是挺好的吗?
6．你还不知道吗,我这个人最喜欢帮漂亮小姐的忙了!

六、表演下边的对话：Perform the following dialogue：

甲：请问小王在家吗?
乙：不在,他刚出去。
甲：能不能麻烦您告诉他,一个叫刘方的来过了,请他给我回个电话。
乙：他知道你的电话号码吗?
甲：应该知道吧,不过我还是再留一下儿吧。哦,对不起,我没带笔。能用一下您的纸和笔吗?
乙：当然可以,请进来写吧。
甲：给您添麻烦了。
乙：别客气。

七、选用括号里的词或短语进行情景会话：
Make situational dialogues using the words or phrases in the brackets：

　　(怎么……?　别提了　因为　所以　可是　也许　抱歉　不好意思
　　　没什么　添麻烦)

1．寒假打算和朋友一块儿去南方旅行,可是去不了了,希望朋友原谅;
2．约好参加朋友的婚礼,可是有急事不能去了,打电话道歉;

3.下雪后,你骑自行车不小心滑倒了,有人把你和车扶起来,你向他表示感谢。

八、成段表达:Oral composition:

1.圣诞节我们这样过……

2.我们不过圣诞节,我们过……节……

你知道吗? (8)   "儿化"与语义

    在汉语普通话中有一种语音现象,就是在一些口语常用词后面加一个后缀[er],写成汉字是"儿"。这个"儿"不自成音节,而是和前面的音节合在一起,形成"卷舌韵母"。我们把这种现象叫"儿化"。儿化词大多数是名词,也有少数别的词类的词具有儿化形式。一个词是不是儿化,在语义上或语言表达色彩上会有所不同。

    (1)"儿化"可以改变词的含义,比如:

这——这儿　　　前门(北京地名)——前门儿(正门儿)

那——那儿　　　水——水儿(水果的汁等)

    (2)儿化词带有小、可爱、轻松、亲昵等语言表达色彩,比如:

冰棍儿　　小孩儿　　盘儿　　花儿

    (3)"儿化"可以改变词性,比如:

盖(动词)——盖儿(名词)　　　弯(形容词)——弯儿(名词)

画(动词)——画儿(名词)　　　干(形容词)——干儿(名词)

    (4)"儿化"可以使一些短语变成单词,在语义上也发生了变化,比如:

一块(数词+量词) —— 一块儿(副词,"一起"的意思)

一点 —— 一点儿

    在以北京话为代表的一些方言中,"儿化"现象比较多,除了以上列举的对语义有影响的儿化词以外,还有一部分可以儿化也可以不儿化的词,不必学习掌握,但对于有语义差别的儿化词,一定要注意学习掌握。

    你都学习了哪些儿化词了?你有信心说好儿化词吗?

Do You Know? (8)**The Retroflex Ending and It's Semantic Meaning**

    In the common speech of the Chinese language, there is a phenominon in pronunciation －－ adding a suffix [er] to some everyday expressions. Written in Chinese character, the suffix is "儿". "儿" is not a word by itself here. Preceding by a word, however, it forms "the retroflex final". We call this phenominon the "retroflex ending". Words with retroflex endings are often nouns. Some words in other parts of speech also have retroflex endings. A word with a retroflex ending often conveys a semantic meaning or implication somewhat different from the word without it.

(1) The retroflex ending may change the word's meaning, for instance: this -- here Qianmen (a place in Beijing) -- front door, main entrance that -- there water -- juice of fruit

(2) The retroflex ending implies the quality of smallness, loveliness, light-heartedness, intimacy, for example: popsicles, children, plates, flowers

(3) The retroflex ending may alter the word's part of speech, for instance: cover (verb) -- lid (noun) curved (adjective) -- curve (noun) draw (verb) -- drawing (noun) dry (adjective) -- raisins 葡萄干儿 (noun)

(4) The retroflex ending can turn some phrases into individual words, and change their semantic meanings, for example: a piece (numeral + measure word) -- together (adverbial) one o'clock -- a little

In some dialects represented by the Beijing dialect, there are more phenomina of retroflex endings. You don't have to pay too much attention to the words whose meanings do not change with or without a retroflex ending. But you must learn by heart the words that change their meanings with a retroflex ending.

Which words with retroflex endings have you already learnt? Are you confident of using them correctly?

第二十七课　要是下雨怎么办呢?

(中午,杰夫去王平的宿舍)

杰　夫:都一点了,你怎么还在睡觉?
王　平:我们中国人习惯午饭以后休息一会儿,这叫"午睡"。
杰　夫:是吗? 真对不起,打扰了。
王　平:没事儿,我已经睡够了,快请坐。
杰　夫:这个星期六要是你有空儿,到我那儿去坐坐好吗? 我有很多问题要请教你。
王　平:"请教"不敢当,随便聊聊吧。八点以后我都有空儿,那我八点去,行吗?
杰　夫:八点? 太早了,我还在睡觉呢。
王　平:八点还早? 我每天六点半就起床了。
杰　夫:起那么早干什么呢?
王　平:出去跑跑步,锻炼锻炼身体。
杰　夫:要是下雨怎么办呢?
王　平:下小雨没关系,要是下大雨,那就只好睡懒觉了。

（杰夫对彼得说）

　　我从王平那儿听说中国人有一个习惯，他们吃完午饭就睡午觉。我可不习惯午睡，中午我喜欢打球。王平说他每天早上六点半就起床，那么早我可起不来。我喜欢睡懒觉，睡懒觉多舒服哇！

（在一家饭馆里）

王　平：喜欢吃什么菜？你随便点，今天我请客。

安　妮：那我就不客气了。我爱吃辣的，来个辣子鸡丁吧。

王　平：这儿的麻婆豆腐最有名，要辣的，不如来个麻婆豆腐。

安　妮：好，听你的。我还没吃过……这个菜名字挺怪的，叫什么来着？

王　平：麻－婆－豆－腐。

（点菜后，小姐上菜）

王　平：请吧。

安　妮：（吃了一口）哎哟，怎么这么辣呀？

王　平：这是川菜，四川人就爱吃辣的。

安　妮：那别的地方的人呢？

王　平：一般来说，北方人爱吃咸的，南方人爱吃甜的，山东人爱吃辣的，山西人爱吃酸的。这就是：南甜北咸，东辣西酸。

安　妮：真有意思。每个地方有每个地方的习惯。哎，四川可不在东边。

王　平：你还挺认真！四川的辣是辣椒的辣，山东的辣是大葱的辣。

安　妮：原来是这么回事！

Dì－èrshíqī kè　Yàoshi xià yǔ zěnme bàn ne?

（Zhōngwǔ, Jiéfū qù Wáng Píng de sùshè）

Jiéfū: Dōu yì diǎn le, nǐ zěnme hái zài shuìjiào?

Wáng Píng: Wǒmen Zhōngguórén xíguàn wǔfàn yǐhòu xiūxi yíhuìr, zhè jiào "wǔshuì".

Jiéfū: Shì ma? Zhēn duìbuqǐ, dǎrǎo le.

Wáng Píng: Méi shìr, wǒ yǐjing shuì gòu le, kuài qǐng zuò.

Jiéfū: Zhèige xīngqīliù yàoshi nǐ yǒu kòngr, dào wǒ nàr qù zuòzuo hǎo ma? Wǒ yǒu hěn duō wèntí yào qǐngjiào nǐ.

Wáng Píng: "Qǐngjiào" bù gǎndāng, suíbiàn liáoliao ba. Bā diǎn yǐhòu wǒ dōu yǒu kòngr, nà wǒ bā diǎn qù, xíng ma?

Jiéfū: Bā diǎn? Tài zǎo le, wǒ hái zài shuìjiào ne.

Wáng Píng: Bā diǎn hái zǎo? wǒ měi tiān liù diǎn bàn jiù qǐchuáng le.

Jiéfū: Qǐ nàme zǎo gàn shénme ne?

Wáng Píng: Chūqu pǎopao bù, duànliàn duànliàn shēntǐ.
Jiéfū: Yàoshi xià yǔ zěnme bàn ne?
Wáng Píng: Xià xiǎo yǔ méi guānxi, yàoshi xià dà yǔ, nà jiù zhǐhǎo shuì lǎn jiào le.

(Jiéfū duì Bǐdé shuō)
　　Wǒ cóng Wáng Píng nàr tīngshuō Zhōngguórén yǒu yí ge xíguàn, tāmen chīwán wǔfàn jiù shuì wǔjiào. Wǒ kě bù xíguàn wǔshuì, zhōngwǔ wǒ xǐhuan dǎ qiú. Wáng Píng shuō tā měi tiān zǎoshang liù diǎn bàn jiù qǐchuáng, nàme zǎo wǒ kě qǐ bu lái. Wǒ xǐhuan shuì lǎn jiào, shuì lǎn jiào duō shūfu wa!

(Zài yì jiā fànguǎnr li)
Wáng Píng: Xǐhuan chī shénme cài? Nǐ suíbiàn diǎn, jīntiān wǒ qǐng kè.
Ānní: Nà wǒ jiù bú kèqi le. Wǒ ài chī là de, lái ge làzi jīdīng ba.
Wáng Píng: Zhèr de mápó-dòufu zuì yǒumíng, yào là de, bùrú lái ge mápó dòufu.
Ānní: Hǎo, tīng nǐ de. Wǒ hái méi chīguo……Zhèi ge cài míngzi tīng qíguài de, jiào shénme láizhe?
Wáng Píng: Má－pó－dòu－fu.
(Diǎn cài hòu, xiǎojie shàng cài)
Wáng Píng: Qǐng ba.
Ānní: (Chī le yìkǒu) Āiyō, zěnme zhème là ya?
Wáng Píng: Zhè shì chuāncài, Sìchuān rén jiù ài chī là de.
Ānní: Nà biéde dìfang de rén ne?
Wáng Píng: Yìbān lái shuō, běifāng rén ài chī xián de, nánfāng rén ài chī tián de, Shāndōng rén ài chī là de, Shǎnxī rén ài chī suān de. Zhè jiù shì: Nán tián běi xián, dōng là xī suān.
Ānní: Zhēn yǒu yìsi. Měi ge dìfang yǒu měi ge dìfang de xíguàn. Ái, Sìchuān kě bú zài dōngbian!
Wáng Píng: Nǐ hái tǐng rènzhēn! Sìchuān de là shì làjiāo de là, Shāndōng de là shì dàcōng de là.
Ānní: Yuánlái shì zhème huí shì!

注释 Notes

1. "没事儿":
　　意思是"不要紧, 没关系", 如:
　　Means never mind, It's nothing, for example:

甲:"用一下你的词典行吗?"
乙:"没事儿,用吧!"

对方表示感谢或道歉时,也可以用"没事儿"来回答。如:

It can also be used in reply to someone's thanks or an apology, for example:

甲:"耽误你半天时间,真过意不去。"
乙:"没事儿,有空儿欢迎你再来。"

2."睡够了":

"V+够了"表示某种行为动作已经得到满足,不想再继续进行下去了。如:

"verb+够了"means to have enough of something and to have no wish to have more. For instance:

"每天都吃大白菜,我都吃够了。""你玩儿够了没有? 该做作业了!"

3."不敢当":

谦辞,对方热情地招待或夸奖时,表示自己承当不起。

Humble words, used in reply to a warm reception or a compliment. For example:

"您这样热情地招待,真是不敢当。"
甲:"你的学习比我好,你就是我的老师。"
乙:"哪里,不敢当。"

4."随便":

①表示不加限制,选择什么、怎么决定都可以。当对方问到自己的意见,需要做出选择时,常用"随便"来回答。如点菜时,"甲:你吃点儿什么? 乙:随便。"在别人家里,"甲:您喝点儿什么? 乙:随便。""随便"之间可以加入指代决定、选择一方的词语"你、他"等,如:"甲:咱们什么时候去? 乙:随你的便。""随便"后也可加入动词,如:"你们随便吃,别客气。""这些杂志随便借。""你随便什么时候来都行。"

To make a choice or decision freely. "随便"is often used in response to a question asking for an opinion or a choice which has to be made. For instance:(in a restaurant)"A:你吃点儿什么? B:随便."(in someone's home)"A:您喝点儿什么? B:随便."Pronouns(such as"你"and"他"etc.)can come in between"随"and"便"."A:咱们什么时候去? B:随你的便."Verbs can also follow"随便",for example:"你们随便吃,别客气.""这些杂志随便借.""你随便什么时候来都行."

②用做形容词,表示怎么方便怎么做,想做什么就做什么,不加考虑,无所顾忌。如:

Used as an adjective, indicating the casualness in one's behaviour or one's doing things without thinking or scruples, for example:

"他说话很随便。"

5."睡懒觉":

早上起床很晚,或躺在床上不起来,是"睡懒觉"。如:

"睡懒觉"means to get up very late or to stay in bed awake. For example:

"早上应该早一点儿起床,别睡懒觉。"

"明天是星期天,没有课,可以睡(个)懒觉。"

6."起得来/起不来":

"起"指"起床",也说"起来"。"起"后加可能补语的标志"得/不"表示可能性。"起得来"是肯定式,意思是"能起来";"起不来"是否定式,意思是"不能起来"。如:

"起"or"起来"indicates get up or get out of bed. The word"起"is followed by the potential complement"得"or"不"。"起得来"is the affirmative, meaning be able to get up;"起不来"is the negative, meaning be unable to get up. For instance:

"早上五点出发,太早了,我起不来。"

甲:"六点半,你起得来起不来?"

乙:"起得来。"

7."不如":

表示比较,"不如"前面提到的人或事没有后面提到的好。如:

Used to form comparison, the person or thing preceding "不如"is not as good as the person or thing following "不如". For example:

"小张的学习不如小王。"(小王的学习比小张好)

"我一个人去有点儿害怕,不如你陪我一起去吧。"

8."一般来说":

意思是按照普通的通常的情况,对某事进行推测、判断。常用在句首。如:

Guessing or judging according to normal conditions, often used at the beginning of a sentence, for example:

"一般来说,感冒了吃这种药好得快。"

"一般来说,这儿的冬天不下雪。"

9."有意思":

就是"有趣""好玩儿""耐人寻味"。如:"昨天的晚会很有意思。""他说话非常有意思。"又如:"甲:昨天玩儿得怎么样?乙:可有意思了!"相反的词是"没(有)意思"。

Means amusing, fascinating, it affords food for thought, for instance:"昨天的晚会很有意思","他说话非常有意思". Another example:"A:昨天玩儿得怎么样?B:可有意思了!"The negative form:"没(有)意思".

练习 Exercises

一、用正确的语调读下边的句子:Read the following sentences in correct intonation:

1. 这个星期六要是你有空儿,到我那儿去坐坐好吗?
2. 我喜欢睡懒觉。睡懒觉多舒服哇!
3. 你随便点,今天我请客。
4. 那我就不客气了。
5. 真有意思!
6. 原来是这么回事!

二、读下边的句子,注意重音、停顿不同,含义不同:

Read the following sentences, note the different meanings resulting from different stresses and different pauses:

1. 我知道 他不知道。
   我知道他不知道。

2. 这儿的麻婆豆腐最有名。
   这儿的麻婆豆腐最有名。
   这儿的麻婆豆腐最有名。

3. 今天我请客。
   今天我请客。
   今天我请客。

三、替换练习:Substitution drills:

(一)

1. 那么早　我可　起不来。
   　　难　　　　　不会回答

晚　　　　不敢一个人出去
　　麻烦　　　不想学
　　有意思　　要去看看

2. 这儿的<u>麻婆豆腐</u>最有名。
　　　　饺子
　　　　水果
　　　　烤鸭
　　　　包子

3. 一般来说，<u>北方人爱吃咸的，南方人爱吃甜的</u>。
　　　　北方人高，南方人矮
　　　　瘦人怕冷
　　　　中国人有午睡的习惯
　　　　我一有问题就去请教他

(二)

替换划线部分的词语，并将句子补充完整：

Substitute the underlined parts and complete the sentences:

1. <u>要辣子鸡丁</u>不如<u>来个麻婆豆腐</u>。→这儿的麻婆豆腐最有名，
　　　　　　　　　　　　　　　　　　要辣子鸡丁不如来个麻婆豆腐。

　　买蓝的　　　买黑的
　　去你家　　　去我们家
　　挤公共汽车　骑自行车
　　住北方　　　住南方

2. 我已经<u>睡</u>够了。→ 我生病的时候，整天睡觉，我已经睡够了。
　　　　吃
　　　　看
　　　　听
　　　　玩儿

3. 随便<u>聊聊</u>吧。→我没什么事，随便聊聊吧。
　　　　看看
　　　　谈谈
　　　　逛逛

唱唱

四、掌握加点儿短语的用法,再模仿例句编几组对话:
Make sure of the use of the dotted phrases and produce a few more dialogues following the two examples：

1. 甲:真对不起,打扰你午休了。
   乙:没事儿,我已经睡够了。
2. 甲:我有很多问题要请教你。
   乙:不敢当,你可别这么客气。

五、下边的几种说法是否与课文原意相符: Are the following statements true to the text？
1. 一点了王平还在睡懒觉。
2. 杰夫一般早上六点起床去跑步。
3. 安妮没点菜。
4. 安妮没吃过麻婆豆腐。
5. 安妮觉得王平介绍的中国各地的饮食习惯很有意思。

六、请解释一下儿下边各项是什么意思: Explain the meaning of each of the following：
1. 午睡
2. 睡懒觉
3. 南甜北咸东辣西酸
4. 请客

七、得体应答: Provide an appropriate reply to each of the following remarks：
1. 甲:我有很多问题要请教你。
   乙:_____。
2. 甲:你随便点吧,今天我请客。
   乙:_____。
3. 甲:真对不起,打扰你午休了。
   乙:_____。

八、请你说一说: Talk about the following subjects：
1. 你一般怎么安排一天的时间?
2. 你有午睡的习惯吗?
3. 你喜欢什么户外活动？你喜欢跑步吗？为什么?

4．你知道哪些中国菜？什么味道？你最爱吃什么味道的菜？你知道怎么做吗？
5．你和朋友一起去饭馆吃饭习惯怎么付钱？

九、小讨论：Discussion：
中国有很多俗语，下边就有两条。你怎么理解？
There are a lot of Chinese old sayings , how do you understand the following two ?
1．一刻千金
2．病从口入

十、成段表达：介绍一个有关你们国家生活和饮食方面的习惯。
　　Make an oral composition : Introduce a habit in everyday life or the diet of your country .

第二十八课　天气越来越冷了

（在宿舍里）

安　妮：今天真冷啊！
丽　莎：是啊，天气越来越冷了。
安　妮：快考试了，真高兴。
丽　莎：考试还高兴？
安　妮：考完试就该放假了。我早就想家了。丽莎，放假你回家吗？
丽　莎：不回，我还要去旅行呢。
安　妮：你都想好了？打算去哪儿？
丽　莎：先去上海，然后去云南。
安　妮：什么时候出发？
丽　莎：那要看哪天考完了。一考完我就走。

（安妮对彼得说）

　　快考试了，考完试就该放寒假了。我想一放假就回国。丽莎打算去旅行，她先去上海，然后去云南。我也想去旅行，不过我更想回家，等放暑假的时候我再去旅行。

（在大街上，安妮从自行车上下来）

安　妮：(自语)奇怪，怎么骑不快了？杰夫！下来下来，帮帮我！
杰　夫：怎么回事？
安　妮：我的车有"病"了，快帮我看看！
杰　夫：可不是嘛，有"毛病"了——没气儿了！
安　妮：那怎么办呢？
杰　夫：打气呀！

（在彼得的房间里）

杰　夫：几点了？
彼　得：七点半了。
杰　夫：该播天气预报了，打开电视看看吧？
彼　得：你每天都听天气预报吗？听得懂听不懂？
杰　夫：听不懂。不过，老师常常说"听不懂也得听"。我差不多每天都听，现在能听懂一点儿了。比如："明天白天，晴"，还有"午后有小雨"，这就够了。

（彼得打开电视）

彼　得：还没到呢，现在是广告(节目)。
杰　夫：广告完了就是。
彼　得：我觉得天气预报一点儿都不准。昨天说今天有雪，可是到现在还没下呢。
杰　夫：那也可能是你听错了。
彼　得：我的听力这么好，还能听错？
杰　夫：你也学会"吹牛"了！

（安妮说）

　　天气越来越冷了。我又担心又高兴。担心的是冬天太冷，一不注意就很容易感冒；高兴的是我可以看到雪了。我特别喜欢看雪景。要是能滑冰，那就更好了。

Dì-èrshíbā kè　Tiānqì yuèláiyuè lěng le

(Zài sùshè li)

Ānní: Jīntiān zhēn lěng a!
Lìshā: Shì a, tiānqì yuèláiyuè lěng le.
Ānní: Kuài kǎoshì le, zhēn gāoxing.
Lìshā: Kǎoshì hái gāoxing?
Ānní: Kǎowán shì jiù gāi fàng jià le. Wǒ zǎo jiù xiǎng jiā le. Lìshā, fàng jià nǐ huí jiā ma?
Lìshā: Bù huí, wǒ hái yào qù lǚxíng ne.

Ānní: Nǐ dōu xiǎnghǎo le？Dǎsuan qù nǎr？
Lìshā: Xiān qù Shànghǎi, ránhòu qù Yúnnán.
Ānní: Shénme shíhou chūfā？
Lìshā: Nà yào kàn něi tiān kǎowán le. Yì kǎowán wǒ jiù zǒu.

(Ānní duì Bǐdé shuō)
　　Kuài kǎoshì le, kǎowán shì jiù gāi fàng hánjià le. Wǒ xiǎng yí fàng jià jiù huí guó. Lìshā dǎsuan qù lǚxíng, tā xiān qù Shànghǎi, ránhòu qù Yúnnán. Wǒ yě xiǎng qù lǚxíng, búguò wǒ gèng xiǎng huí jiā, děng fàng shǔjià de shíhou wǒ zài qù lǚxíng.

(Zài dàjiē shang, Ānní cóng zìxíngchē shang xiàlai)
Ānní: (Zì yǔ) Qíguài, zěnme qí bú kuài le？Jiéfū！Xiàlai xiàlai, bāngbang wǒ！
Jiéfū: Zěnme huí shì？
Ānní: Wǒ de chē yǒu "bìng" le, kuài bāng wǒ kànkan！
Jiéfū: Kě bú shì ma, yǒu "máobìng" le——Méi qìr le！
Ānní: Nà zěnme bàn ne？
Jiéfū: Dǎ qì ya！

(Zài Bǐdé de fángjiān li)
Jiéfū: Jǐ diǎn le？
Bǐdé: Qī diǎn bàn le.
Jiéfū: Gāi bō tiānqì yùbào le, dǎkāi diànshì kànkan ba？
Bǐdé: Nǐ měi tiān dōu tīng tiānqì yùbào ma？Tīng de dǒng tīng bu dǒng？
Jiéfū: Tīng bu dǒng. Búguò, lǎoshī chángcháng shuō "tīng bu dǒng yě děi tīng". Wǒ chàbuduō měi tiān dōu tīng, xiànzài néng tīng dǒng yìdiǎnr le. Bǐrú: "Míngtiān báitiān, qíng", hái yǒu "Wǔ hòu yǒu xiǎo yǔ", zhè jiù gòu le.
(Bǐdé dǎkāi diànshì)
Bǐdé: Hái méi dào ne, xiànzài shì guǎnggào (jiémù).
Jiéfū: Guǎnggào wánle jiùshì.
Bǐdé: Wǒ juéde tiānqì yùbào yìdiǎnr dōu bù zhǔn. Zuótiān shuō jīntiān yǒu xuě, kěshì dào xiànzài hái méi xià ne.
Jiéfū: Nà yě kěnéng shì nǐ tīngcuò le.
Bǐdé: Wǒ de tīnglì zhème hǎo, Hái néng tīngcuò？
Jiéfū: Nǐ yě xuéhuì "chuīniú" le！

(Ānní shuō)
　　Tiānqì yuèláiyuè lěng le. Wǒ yòu dānxīn yòu gāoxìng. Dānxīn de shì dōngtiān tài lěng, yí bu zhùyì jiù hěn róngyi gǎnmào; Gāoxìng de shì wǒ kěyǐ kàndào xuě le. Wǒ tèbié xǐhuan kàn

xuějīng. Yàoshi néng huábīng, nà jiù gèng hǎo le.

注释 Notes

1. "等放暑假的时候":

    "等……(的时候)"表示一个将来的时点,在那个时点将发生某事。"等"后面可以是时间词,如:"等下个月,我妈妈就来了"。更常用的是"等"后接词组或句子,表示时间,如:

    Indicating some event is going to happen at future point of time . "等" could be followed by a time word : "等下个月, 我就知道结果了". More common in use, "等" is followed by a word group or a clause indicating time:

    "等我大学毕业(的时候),我就去国外旅行。"

    "等他来了,咱们就走。"

2. "差不多":

    表示在时间、距离、程度等方面很相近,相差不多。如:

    Indicating almost the same in time , distance , or degree . For instance :

    "他和弟弟差不多高。""这两件衣服的颜色差不多。"

    "他们俩差不多同时走了进来。"

    甲:"买这件衣服得一个月的工资吧?"

    乙:"差不多。"

3. "一点儿都(也)不准":

    "一点儿都(也)不(没)……",表示完全否定,语气坚决,如:"那件事我一点儿也不知道。"除"一点儿"外,不同的情况还可以用不同的量词,如:"个、件、辆"等。如:

    "一点儿都(也)不(没)……" indicates a total and flat denial of something, for instance: "那件事我一点儿也不知道。" Under other conditions, different measure word could be used instead of "一点儿", such as "个、件、辆" and etc. For instance:

    "房间里一个人也没有。""我一件衣服也没买。"

4. "吹牛":

    夸口,说大话,有时也说"吹牛皮"。

    To boast, to talk big, sometimes also say "吹牛皮".

5. "担心的是……""高兴的是……"：

"……的是……"，"的是"的前面一般是表示思想情绪、心理状态的词语，如："痛苦、烦恼、怨恨、欢喜"等；"的是"的后面常是一个句子，表示前面的情绪、心理产生的原因。如：

In the usage, the words preceding "……的是……" indicate a certain sentiment or a psychological state of mind, such as "痛苦、烦恼、怨恨、欢喜" and so on; the words, usually a clause, following "的是" indicate the cause of the sentiment, for instance：

"我高兴的是明天可以回家了。"

练习 Exercises

一、读下边的句子，注意重音：

Read the following sentences, taking care of the stresses：

1. 天气越来越冷了。
2. 快考试了。
3. 考完试就该放假了。
4. 先去上海，然后去云南。
5. 我一放假就回国。
6. 等放暑假的时候我再去旅行。
7. 该播天气预报了。
8. 可能是你听错了。
9. 要是能滑冰，那就更好了。

二、根据课文回答问题： Answer the question according to the text：

1. 快考试了为什么安妮那么高兴？
2. 丽莎打算放假以后去哪儿？
3. 安妮骑车为什么越来越慢？
4. 为什么彼得说天气预报一点儿也不准？
5. 为什么杰夫说彼得吹牛？

三、替换划线部分的词语，并将句子补充完整：

Substitute the underlined parts and complete the sentences：

1. 先去上海，然后去云南。

    买菜　　　买肉

    去邮局　　去银行

去南方旅行　回国
念生词　　　念课文

2. 等放假的时候，我再去旅行。
　　你病好了　　　来辅导
　　天气好的时候　出去玩儿
　　下雪的时候　　去照雪景
　　这些钱花完了　去取

3. 听不懂也得听。
　　不想去　　去
　　不好喝　　喝
　　觉得难　　学
　　没时间做　找时间做

4. 差不多每天　都　听。
　　　天天　　　不吃早饭
　　　每年　　　去一次南方
　　　每次约会　迟到
　　　一个星期　没看见他

5. 天气预报一点儿也不准。
　　他　　　　不知道
　　我　　　　没听说
　　这儿冬天　不冷
　　你的话我　不觉得奇怪

6. 我特别喜欢看雪景。
　　　爱吃川菜
　　　怕辣
　　　喜欢滑冰
　　　爱听音乐

7. 要是能滑冰，那就更好了。
　　　你也能来

今天没有考试
我能多住几天
明天下雪

四、体会划线部分的意思,仿照例句完成对话:
Make sure of the meanings of the underlined parts and complete the dialogues following the example :

例:甲:你什么时候出发?
　　乙:那要看哪天考完了。一考完我就走。

1. 甲:你什么时候陪我去买衣服?
　　乙:_____。

2. 甲:妈妈,您说我能考好吗?
　　乙:_____。

3. 甲:这个照相机有毛病了,能修好吗?
　　乙:_____。

4. 甲:你打算和他结婚吗?
　　乙:_____。

五、模拟表演第二、第三段会话。 Perform Dialogue 2 & 3 .

六、填空并熟读这段话,注意加点儿的部分的用法,并模仿这种表达方式说一段话:
Fill in the blanks and learn the passage by heart , note the use of the dotted parts and produce a passage imitating the presentation .

天气越来(　　)冷了。我又担心(　　)高兴。担心的(　　)冬天太冷,一不注意(　　)很容易感冒;(　　)(　　)的是我可以看到雪了。我(　　)(　　)喜欢看雪景,(　　)(　　)能滑冰,那就更好了。

七、实践:了解当天的天气预报内容,第二天告诉同学们。
A practice : Learn the content of the weather forecast and brief your classmates about it the next day :

了解方式:
①打电话:天气预报台号码 121
②看电视:北京一台(6频道)18:55—19:00　　19:30—19:40

　　　　　中央一台（2频道）19:30—19:40

How to do it :

(1) Dial 121 ——the number of the Weather Forecast Telephone Service .
(2) Watch television : BTV Station 1 (Channel 6) 18:55-19:00 ;19:30-19:40
　　　　　　　　　　CCTV Station 1 (Channel 2) 19:30-19:40

第二十九课　我没买着火车票

（在宿舍里）

张　新：李文静，你去哪儿了？一整天都没看见你，看样子你挺累的。
李文静：我去买火车票了，累死我了。
张　新：是不是买票的人很多？
李文静：是啊，人太多了。我到车站一看，排了那么长的队，我都想回来了。
张　新：那你后来排队了吗？
李文静：没办法，我还是排了，一边排着队一边和旁边的人聊天儿。
张　新：到底买着了没有？
李文静：真倒霉！我排了两个多小时，可是快排到我的时候票卖完了。
张　新：你呀，走以前也不请教请教我。
李文静：买火车票有什么好请教的？
张　新：你不知道吧？可以预订啊！
李文静：哪儿可以预订？
张　新：咱们学校哇，提前三、四天去订就行。

(张新对李文静说)

春节快到了,买火车票的人很多,排几个小时的队也不一定买得着,所以最好预订。在学校预订的时候,要带上学生证,先填预订单,再交一些押金,就可以了。一般提前一天取票,不够的票钱取票的时候补交,另外还要交一些手续费。

(下课的时候)

杰　夫:听说你这个学期完了就回国,是吗?
安　妮:是啊,我太想家了。
杰　夫:还回来不回来?
安　妮:我想延长半年,不知道行不行。
杰　夫:我有个建议,考完试咱们聚一聚怎么样?
安　妮:我赞成!不过,这几天天气不太好,会不会下雪?
杰　夫:我看不会。就是下雪,也没关系,到外边去看看雪景,不是更有意思吗?
安　妮:那我给王平打个电话,叫他也来吧。
杰　夫:你现在就去打吧。

(王平告诉张伟)

昨天安妮打电话给我,说周末大家一起聚一聚。打算先出去玩玩儿,然后去我家。这几天我爸、我妈都不在家,我们可以一起去包饺子、聊天儿、看录相。你要是有空儿,也来吧。

Dì- èrshíjiǔ kè　Wǒ méi mǎi zháo huǒchē piào

(Zài sùshè li)

Zhāng Xīn: Lǐ Wénjìng, nǐ qù nǎr le? Yì zhěngtiān dōu méi kàn jian nǐ, kàn yàngzi nǐ tǐng lèi de.
Lǐ Wénjìng: Wǒ qù mǎi huǒchē piào le, lèisǐ wǒ le.
Zhāng Xīn: Shì bu shì mǎi piào de rén hěn duō?
Lǐ Wénjìng: Shì a, rén tài duō le. Wǒ dào chēzhàn yí kàn, páile nàme cháng de duì, wǒ dōu xiǎng huílai le.
Zhāng Xīn: Nà nǐ hòulái pái duì le ma?
Lǐ Wénjìng: Méi bànfǎ, wǒ háishi pái le, yìbiān páizhe duì yìbiān hé pángbiān de rén liáo tiānr.
Zhāng Xīn: Dàodǐ mǎizháo le méiyǒu?
Lǐ Wénjìng: Zhēn dǎoméi! Wǒ páile liǎng ge duō xiǎoshí, kěshi kuài pái dào wǒ de shíhou piào màiwán le.
Zhāng Xīn: Nǐ ya, zǒu yǐqián yě bù qǐngjiào qǐngjiào wǒ.
Lǐ Wénjìng: Mǎi huǒchē piào yǒu shénme hǎo qǐngjiào de?

Zhāng Xīn: Nǐ bù zhīdào ba? Kěyǐ yùdìng a!
Lǐ Wénjìng: Nǎr kěyǐ yùdìng?
Zhāng Xīn: Zánmen xuéxiào wa, tíqián sān-sì tiān qù dìng jiù xíng.

(Zhāng Xīn duì Lǐ Wénjìng shuō)

  Chūnjié kuài dào le, mǎi huǒchē piào de rén hěn duō, pái jǐ ge xiǎoshí de duì yě bù yídìng mǎi de zháo, suǒyǐ zuìhǎo yùdìng. Zài xuéxiào yùdìng de shíhou, yào dàishang xuéshēngzhèng, xiān tián yùdìngdān, zài jiāo yìxiē yājīn, jiù kěyǐ le. Yìbān tíqián yì tiān qǔ piào, bú gòu de piào qián qǔ piào de shíhou bǔ jiāo, lìngwài hái yào jiāo yìxiē shǒuxùfèi.

(Xià kè de shíhou)
Jiéfū: Tīngshuō nǐ zhèi ge xuéqī wánle jiù huí guó, shì ma?
Ānní: Shì a, wǒ tài xiǎng jiā le.
Jiéfū: Hái huílai bù huílai?
Ānní: Wǒ xiǎng shēnqǐng yáncháng bàn nián, bù zhīdào xíng bu xíng.
Jiéfū: Wǒ yǒu ge jiànyì, zánmen jù yi jù zěnmeyàng?
Ānní: Wǒ zànchéng! Búguò, zhè jǐ tiān tiānqì bú tài hǎo, huì bu huì xià xuě?
Jiéfū: Wǒ kàn bú huì. jiù shi xià xuě, yě méi guānxi, dào wàibian qù kànkan xuě jǐng, bú shi gèng yǒu yìsi ma?
Ānní: Nà wǒ gěi Wáng Píng dǎ ge diànhuà, jiào tā yě lái ba.
Jiéfū: Nǐ xiànzài jiù qù dǎ ba.

(Wáng Píng gàosu Zhāng Wěi)

  Zuótiān Ānní dǎ diànhuà gěi wǒ, shuō zhōumò dàjiā yìqǐ jù yi jù. Dǎsuan xiān chūqu wánr, ránhòu qù wǒ jiā. Zhè jǐ tiān wǒ bà、wǒ mā dōu bú zài jiā, Wǒmen kěyǐ yìqǐ bāo jiǎozi, liáo tiānr, kàn lù xiàng. Nǐ yàoshi yǒukòngr, yě lái ba.

注释 Notes

1. "看样子":

  表示根据某一情况进行某种推测。如:

  Used to make a deduction under circumstances. For instance:

  "天上有很多云,看样子要下雨。"

  "已经十点了,他还没来,看样子他不会来了。"

  "她的脸色不好,看样子她可能病了。"

2. "累死我了":

"形容词＋死"表示程度极深,如:"热死了""疼死了"等。当所要说明的主语是代词时,常把代词放在"……死"的后面,如:"热死我了""疼死我了"。

"形容词＋死"indicates the great extent of something, for instance:"热死了""疼死了"and so on. If the subject being modified is a pronoun, it comes after word"死":"热死我了""疼死我了".

3."没办法":

表示无可奈何,只能如此。如:"明天去上海的机票都卖完了,没办法,只能等后天的了。"为加深程度,也可以说"真没办法。"

To have no way out, to be utterly helpless; For example:"明天去上海的机票都卖完了,没办法,只能等后天的了．"To emphasize, can also say:"真没办法".

4."买着":

"着"读"zháo",用在动词后,表示已达到目的或有了结果,相当于"到"。如:"昨天丢的钥匙今天找着了""烟点着了""他睡着了",否定形式是"没找着""没点着""没睡着"等。表示可能与否,用"V得着""V不着"的形式来表示。如:"这本书现在还买得着吗？——买不着了,已经卖完了。"

"着", pronounced as [zhao], or "到" is used as a complement to the verb, meaning hitting the mark, succeeding in:"昨天丢的钥匙今天找着了""烟点着了""他睡着了", the negative is "没找着""没点着""没睡着"and so on."Verb＋得着"or"Verb＋不着"is used to indicate whether something is possible or not. for instance:"这本书现在还买得着吗？——买不着了,已经卖完了．"

5."会":

①表示有可能实现,如:

Indicating the likelihood of something:

"今天会不会下雪？——不会。""他会不会准时来？——会的。"

②表示具有某种能力,一般是指需要经过学习才能具备的能力。如:

Be able to, be good at, be skilled in, often indicating a skill or capability which could only be obtained after receiving certain training. For instance:

"这个孩子才一岁,还不会说话。""我不会游泳。""她会说五种外语。"

6."就是……也……":

表示假设的让步,意思和"即使……也……"相同,在口语中常用"就是……也……"。如:

To indicate the concession of supposition, the meaning is same as "即使……也……", often used in spoken chinese. For example:

"你就是送来，我也不要。""这么简单的问题，就是小孩子也能回答。"

练习 Exercises

一、读下边的句子，注意重音：Reading the following sentences and note the stresses：
1. 累死我了。
2. 我到车站一看，排了那么长的队，我都想回来了。
3. 没办法，我还是排了，一边排着队一边和旁边的人聊天儿。
4. 到底买着了没有？
5. 真倒霉！我排了两个多小时，可是快排到我的时候票卖完了。
6. 提前三、四天去订就行。
7. 我想延长半年，不知道行不行。
8. 我赞成！
9. 这几天天气不太好，会不会下雪？

二、替换练习：Substitution drills：

（一）

1. 看样子你挺累的。
　　　　你不太舒服
　　　　他知道这件事
　　　　今天不会下雨

2. 快排到我的时候票卖完了。
　　考试　　　我病了
　　放假　　　我妈妈来了
　　下车　　　我才发现她也在这辆车上
　　回到家　　我才想起来书包忘在学校了

3. 我有个建议，考完试咱们聚一聚怎么样？
　　　　　星期天全家一起去爬山
　　　　　今晚去听音乐会
　　　　　明天都到我家包饺子
　　　　　咱们班来个唱歌比赛

4. 就是<u>下雪</u>,　　　　也　　<u>没关系</u>
　　　不知道　　　　　　没什么
　　　钱不多　　　　　　能玩儿得好
　　　只有两三个人　　　可以在一起热闹热闹
　　　天天有考试　　　　不怕

(二)
替换划线部分的词语,并将句子补充完整:
Substitute the underlined parts and then complete the statements accordingly:

1. <u>累</u>死我了。→昨天爬了一天的山,累死我了。
　　气
　　急
　　热
　　冷
　　忙

2. 到底<u>买</u>着了没有?→你排了四个小时的队买票,到底买着了没有?
　　　知道不知道
　　　找着了没有
　　　有病还是没病
　　　想干什么

3. <u>提前三、四天去订就行</u>→订火车票提前三、四天去订就行。
　　　两天告诉我
　　　一个星期交给老师
　　　二十分钟起床
　　　五分钟出来

三、下边的句子中"着"应该怎么读?
How do you pronounce the word "着" in the following sentences?

1. 他说着说着,笑了。
2. 车票到底买着了没有?
3. 我的钥匙找着了,你看,这不!
4. 你好好儿听着,我有话要说!
5. 他俩一边说着一边走了进来。

205

四、选用"后来"、"以后"或"然后"填空:Fill in the blanks with "后来","以后",or"然后":

　　1．我很喜欢旅行,听说中国有很多美丽的地方,放假(　),我一定要去看看。

　　2．昨天我和小王进城去逛街,我们先买了几件衣服,(　)在一家小饭馆吃了午饭。午饭(　),小王说他想去书店看看,我觉得有点儿累,就先回学校了,不知道小王(　)买了什么书。

五、(一)根据张新的叙述说说订票有什么手续。
　　According to Zhang Xin's narrative, give a briefing on the procedures of ticket-booking.
　　(二)你能看懂下边的订票单吗?
　　Can you make sense of the following booking form?

预订人	时间	车次	终点站	预付款(押金)	经办人	取票时间
王海	1997.2.7	75次	兰州	400元	李湖	2月5日

六、将会话二和后边的叙述综合起来,编一段"安妮给王平打电话"的对话。
　　By summing up Dialogue 2 and the ensuing narration, produce a dialogue, with the following words and expressions, about "Anne phone call to Wang Ping"
　　　请用上以下词语:有空儿　建议　聚　打算　先……然后……　包饺子
　　　　　　　　　　聊天儿　看雪景　看录相　有意思

七、成段表达:Oral composition:
　　1．叙述一件事情(如生日晚会、圣诞晚会、一次考试、一场比赛、一个故事)的开始、进行和最后结果。
　　Describe the beginning, the process and the ending of some event (a birthday party, a Christmas party, an exam, a game, a story)
　　　参考句式:Sentence patterns for reference:
　　　　　……的时候　先……再……　然后　又　最后　快……的时候
　　　　　后来　……着　一边……一边……
　　2．介绍你的一个打算:
　　　Explain an idea of yours:
　　　参考句式:Sentence patterns for reference:
　　　　　我有个建议　打算　安排　有空儿　要是……就更好了

第三十课 杯子叫我打碎了

(在王平家门口儿)
彼　得：这雪下得真不小。
安　妮：你的衣服都湿了。
杰　夫：早上我告诉他有雪,可他不信。
王　平：好了,到家了,快进来吧。
(大家进了王平家)
王　平：随便坐吧,安妮,把雨伞给我,放在这儿了。先来点儿热茶,暖和暖和吧!
杰　夫：好极了!
安　妮：我来帮你,王平。
(安妮和王平端着茶进来,安妮不小心打碎了一个杯子。)
安　妮：哎呀,杯子叫我打碎了,真对不起。
王　平：没事儿,杯子我有的是。
(电话铃响了)
杰　夫：王平,电话!
王　平：你们先聊着,我去接电话。

（大家一边喝茶，一边聊天儿）

丽　　莎：杰夫，你会包饺子吗？

杰　　夫：我会吃饺子，味道好极了。

丽　　莎：你就会开玩笑，等会儿让王平好好儿教教你吧。

（王平打完电话）

王　　平：让我教什么？

丽　　莎：教杰夫包饺子。

王　　平：还是你来教他吧。你已经包得比我好了。

丽　　莎：哪里，哪里，怎么可能呢。

王　　平：饺子皮儿、饺子馅儿，我都准备好了，咱们说包就包吧。

杰　　夫：我建议咱们分成两个组，进行比赛，看哪组包得又快又好，我来做裁判。

众　　：你？！

王　　平：你真会想办法，让我们比赛，你等着吃呀！……这个裁判还是我来当吧！

（王平教杰夫包饺子）

　　先把饺子皮儿、饺子馅儿准备好。包的时候，把馅儿放在皮儿的中间，不要放得太多，然后把两边合上。先捏中间，再捏两边，就包好了。煮的时候，等水开了，再把饺子放进去，饺子都漂上来，就熟了。

Dì-sānshí kè　Bēizi jiào wǒ dǎsuì le

(Zài Wáng Píng jiā ménkǒur)

Bǐdé: Zhè xuě xià de zhēn bù xiǎo.

Ānní: Nǐ de yīfu dōu shī le.

Jiéfū: Zǎoshang wǒ gàosu tā yǒu xuě, kě tā bú xìn.

Wáng Píng: Hǎo le, dào jiā le, kuài jìnlai ba.

(Dàjiā jìnle Wáng Píng jiā)

Wáng Píng: Suíbiàn zuò ba, Ānní, bǎ yǔsǎn gěi wǒ, fàng zài zhèr le. Xiān lái diǎnr rè chá, nuǎnhuo nuǎnhuo ba!

Jiéfū: Hǎo jíle.

Ānní: Wǒ lái bāng nǐ, Wáng Píng.

(Ānní hé Wáng Píng duānzhe chá jìnlai, Ānní bù xiǎoxīn dǎsuì le yí ge bēizi.)

Ānní: Āiyā, bēizi jiào wǒ dǎsuì le, zhēn duìbuqǐ.

Wáng Píng: Méi shìr, bēizi wǒ yǒudeshì.

(Diànhuàlíng xiǎng le)

Jiéfū: Wáng Píng, Diànhuà!

Wáng Píng: Nǐmen xiān liáozhe, wǒ qù jiē diànhuà.
(Dàjiā yìbiān hē chá, yìbiān liáo tiānr)
Lìshā: Jiéfū, nǐ huì bāo jiǎozi ma?
Jiéfū: Wǒ huì chī jiǎozi, wèidào hǎo jíle.
Lìshā: Nǐ jiù huì kāi wánxiào, děng huǐr ràng Wáng Píng hǎohāor jiāojiao nǐ ba.
(Wáng Píng dǎwán diànhuà)
Wáng Píng: Ràng wǒ jiāo shénme?
Lìshā: Jiāo Jiéfū bāo jiǎozi.
Wáng Píng: Háishi nǐ lái jiāo tā ba. Nǐ yǐjing bāo de bǐ wǒ hǎo le.
Lìshā: Nǎli, nǎli, zěnme kěnéng ne.
Wáng Píng: Jiǎozi pír、jiǎozi xiànr, wǒ dōu zhǔnbèi hǎo le, zánmen shuō bāo jiù bāo ba.
Jiéfū: Wǒ jiànyì zánmen fēnchéng liǎng ge zǔ, jìnxíng bǐsài, kàn něi zǔ bāo de yòu kuài yòu
    hǎo, wǒ lái zuò cáipàn.
Zhòng: Nǐ?
Wáng Píng: Nǐ zhēn huì xiǎng bànfǎ, ràng wǒmen bǐsài, nǐ děngzhe chī ya! ……Zhèi ge
    cáipàn háishi wǒ lái dāng ba!

(Wáng Píng jiāo Jiéfū bāo jiǎozi)

　　Xiān bǎ jiǎozi pír、jiǎozi xiànr zhǔnbèi hǎo. Bāo de shíhou, bǎ xiànr fàng zài pír de zhōngjiān, bú yào fàng de tài duō, ránhòu bǎ liǎng biān héshang. Xiān niē zhōngjiān, zài niē liǎng biān, jiù bāo hǎo le. Zhǔ de shíhou, děng shuǐ kāi le, zài bǎ jiǎozi fàng jìnqu, jiǎozi dōu piāo shànglai, jiù shóu le.

注释 Notes

1."有的是":

　　强调数量多,相当于"很多""非常多"。如:

　　To emphasize the large quantity or number, same as "很多" "非常多", for instance:

　　"学习的机会有的是。""他有的是钱,去哪儿玩儿都行。"

2."你们先聊着……":

　　"先+动词+着"表示暂时先做某事,以便等待。如:

　　"先+verb+着" means to go on doing something until……. For example:

　　"你们先坐着,我去接个电话,一会儿就来。""各位先吃着,别的菜马上就来。"

3."怎么可能呢?":

反问句,意思是"不可能",对某事的可能性表示怀疑。如:

A rhetorical question, indicating something is impossible or some doubt about the possibility of something. For instance:

甲:"他没考上大学。"

乙:"怎么可能呢,他是我们班学习最好的学生。"

4."说包就包":

"说 V 就 V"这个句式,表示说起某事就马上做某事,或很快就发生了某种情况,不耽搁停留。如:

"说 verb 就 verb"is a sentence pattern meaning:to start doing something as soon as it is said:

"咱们说走就走。""孩子们说唱就唱,说跳就跳。""他每次都是说来就来,根本没有事先打个招呼的习惯。"

5."看哪组包得又快又好":

这句话中的"看"表示通过某种办法,进行观察比较之后,加以判断。如:

The word "看" in this sentence means to make a judgement after watching and making comparison. For instance:

"你们俩比一比,看谁跑得快?""听听天气预报,看什么时候下雪,咱们好去看雪景。"

练习 Exercises

一、用正确的语调读下边的句子,注意重音:

Read the following sentences in correct intonation, paying attention to the stresses:

1. 这雪下得真不小。
2. 你的衣服都湿了。
3. 把雨伞给我。
4. 味道好极了!
5. 杯子叫我打碎了。
6. 你就会开玩笑。
7. 怎么可能呢?
8. 饺子皮儿、饺子馅儿,我都准备好了。
9. 这个裁判还是我来当吧。

二、替换划线部分：Substitute the underlined parts：

1. 把<u>雨伞</u>　<u>给我</u>。
　　镜子　　给姐姐
　　书　　　放在这儿
　　作业　　交给老师
　　书　　　还给他
　　预定单　填好
　　杯子　　打碎了

2. <u>杯子</u>　叫　<u>我</u>　<u>打碎</u>了。
　　自行车　小王　借走
　　茶　　　他　　喝完
　　钥匙　　我　　丢
　　钱包　　小偷　偷走
　　衣服　　雨　　淋湿
　　饺子　　他　　煮破

3. <u>杯子</u>有的是。
　　茶叶
　　夏天的衣服
　　钱
　　学汉语的人
　　唱得好的人
　　爱吃饺子的人

4. 你们先<u>聊</u>着，我<u>去接电话</u>。
　　　　吃　　出去一下儿
　　　　忙　　以后再来
　　　　玩儿　去准备饭
　　　　等　　去找医生

5. 你就<u>会</u>开玩笑。
　　　知道睡觉
　　　想着玩儿

会让我生气
会出主意

6. 咱们说<u>包</u>就<u>包</u>吧。
　　去　去
　　走　走
　　干　干
　　写　写
　　唱　唱

7. 看<u>哪</u>组包得又快又好
　　谁跑得快
　　谁写得好
　　哪天有空儿
　　什么时候会下雪
　　哪位老师教得好

三、以安妮的口气叙述第二段会话。

Reproduce Dialogue 2 in the first person from Anne's point of view．

四、读下边的两段话，注意停顿、重音和语气：

Read the two passages, taking care of the pauses, the stresses and the intonation：

1.(王平说)杰夫说他爱吃饺子，我信，可是他说他会包饺子，我们都不信。他还说要当裁判呢，我们更不答应了。这个时候不学着包，以后哪儿有这么好的机会！最后还是我当了裁判，不过，我可没休息，我也参加了包饺子比赛。

2.(杰夫说)丽莎的饺子包得跟中国人一样，那不能让她跟王平分在一组。我和彼得差不多，可以分开。我要说的是，我们虽然不会包，可不一定学得慢，谁输谁赢还不一定呢。不信，咱们试试看！

五、填上合适的动词，并扩展成长句子：

Fill in the blanks with appropriate verbs and organize them into long sentences：

____菜　____饺子　____大学　____电话　____雨伞　____比赛　____办法

六、复述包饺子、煮饺子的过程(参考课文叙述)。

Repeat the process of making dumplings and boiling dumplings .

七、实践:"看谁包得又快又好"——包饺子比赛,老师当裁判。

A practise : See who can make dumplings faster and better －－ a race in dumpling－making , with the teacher as the judge .

八、成段表达:介绍你们国家的一种食品的做法。

Oral composition : Introduce a recipe for a kind of food in your country .

词语表　Cíyǔbiǎo

第一课

词语：

1. 你　　　（代）　　nǐ　　　　　you
2. 好　　　（形）　　hǎo　　　　good
3. 我　　　（代）　　wǒ　　　　 I
4. 叫　　　（动）　　jiào　　　 call；name
5. 什么　　（代）　　shénme　　 what
6. 名字　　（名）　　míngzi　　 name
7. 你们　　（代）　　nǐmen　　 you
8. 姓　　　　　　　 xìng　　　 surname；family name
9. 您　　　（代）　　nín　　　　you(respectful second person singular)
10. 老师　　（名）　　lǎoshī　　 teacher
11. 呢　　　（助）　　ne　　　　（modal particle）
12. 是　　　（动）　　shì　　　　to be
13. 他　　　（代）　　tā　　　　 he
14. 她　　　（代）　　tā　　　　 she
15. 我们　　（代）　　wǒmen　　 we
16. 都　　　（副）　　dōu　　　 all
17. 留学生　（名）　　liúxuéshēng　student studying abroad
18. 的　　　（助）　　de　　　　（structural particle）

专名：

1. 杰夫　　　　　　Jiéfū
2. 安妮　　　　　　Ānní
3. 田　　　　　　　Tián
4. 王平　　　　　　Wáng Píng

补充词语：

1. 汉语　　（名）　　Hànyǔ　　　chinese
2. 学生　　（名）　　xuésheng　 student
3. 张　　　（专名）　Zhāng
4. 李　　　（专名）　Lǐ

5. 刘　　　　（专名）　　　Liú
6. 陈　　　　（专名）　　　Chén

第二课

词语：

1. 现在　　　（名）　　　xiànzài　　　　　　now
2. 几　　　　（数）　　　jǐ　　　　　　　　how many
3. 点(钟)　　（量）　　　diǎn(zhōng)　　　（used to indicate time）o'clock
4. 早上　　　（名）　　　zǎoshang　　　　　morning
5. 哪国　　　　　　　　　nǎ guó(něi guó)　 which country
6. 人　　　　（名）　　　rén　　　　　　　 person
7. 吗　　　　（助）　　　ma　　　　　　　　（modal particle）
8. 不　　　　（副）　　　bù　　　　　　　　（an adverb expressing negation）
9. 谁　　　　（代）　　　shuí(shéi)　　　　who
10. 吧　　　（助）　　　ba　　　　　　　　（modal particle）
11. 对　　　（动）　　　duì　　　　　　　　yes
12. 在　　　（动）　　　zài　　　　　　　　in; at; on
13. 班　　　（名）　　　bān　　　　　　　　class
14. 一　　　（数）　　　yī　　　　　　　　 one
15. 二　　　（数）　　　èr　　　　　　　　 two
16. 也　　　（副）　　　yě　　　　　　　　 too
17. 了　　　（助）　　　le　　　　　　　　 （modal particle）
18. 两　　　（数）　　　liǎng　　　　　　　two
19. 该……了　　　　　　　gāi……le　　　　　 It's time for…
20. 上课　　　　　　　　 shàng kè　　　　　 attend class
21. 再见　　（动）　　　zàijiàn　　　　　　goodbye
22. 他们　　（代）　　　tāmen　　　　　　　they

专名：

1. 彼得　　　　　　　　 Bǐdé
2. 美国　　　　　　　　 Měiguó　　　　　　America
3. 法国　　　　　　　　 Fǎguó　　　　　　　France

补充词语：

1. 零　　　（数）　　　líng　　　　　　　　zero
2. 分　　　（量）　　　fēn　　　　　　　　 minute
3. 过　　　（动）　　　guò　　　　　　　　 past
4. 刻　　　（量）　　　kè　　　　　　　　 a quarter of an hour

215

5. 差	(动)	chà	short of
6. 早晨	(名)	zǎochen	morning
7. 晚上	(名)	wǎnshang	evening
8. 起床		qǐ chuáng	to get up
9. 吃饭		chī fàn	to have break-foot
10. 看电视		kàn diànshì	to wata TV
11. 洗澡		xǐ zǎo	to take a bath
12. 睡觉		shuì jiào	to go to bed
13. 中国	(专名)	Zhōngguó	China
14. 日本	(专名)	Rìběn	Japan
15. 德国	(专名)	Déguó	German
16. 韩国	(专名)	Hánguó	Korea
17. 田中	(专名)	Tiánzhōng	
18. 北京	(专名)	Běijīng	Peking, Beijing

第三课

词语：

1. 食堂	(名)	shítáng	dining room; mess hall
2. 哪儿	(代)	nǎr	where
3. 请问		qǐngwèn	May I ask…
4. 这	(代)	zhè	this
5. 教学楼	(名)	jiàoxuélóu	teaching building
6. 办公楼	(名)	bàngōnglóu	office building
7. 那	(代)	nà	that
8. 谢谢	(动)	xièxie	to thank
9. 教室	(名)	jiàoshì	classroom
10. 这儿	(代)	zhèr	here
11. 就	(副)	jiù	exactly; precisely
12. 不用		búyòng	needn't
13. 那边	(代)	nàbian(nèibian)	there
14. 哪边	(代)	nǎbiān(něibiān)	where
15. 宿舍	(名)	sùshè	dormitory
16. 旁边	(名)	pángbiān	side; nearby
17. 厕所	(名)	cèsuǒ	lavatory; toilet
18. 个	(量)	gè	(measure word)
19. 哦	(叹)	ò	oh
20. 不客气		bú kèqi	You are welcome; not at all.

21.	学校	（名）	xuéxiào	school
22.	很	（副）	hěn	very
23.	大	（形）	dà	big

专名：

山下		Shānxià	

补充词语：

1.	过路人		guò lù rén	passenger
2.	银行	（名）	yínháng	bank
3.	邮局	（名）	yóujú	post-office
4.	地铁站		dìtiě zhàn	subway station
5.	男孩	（名）	nánhái r	boy
6.	女孩	（名）	nǚhái r	girl
7.	狗	（名）	gǒu	dog
8.	猫	（名）	māo	cat

第四课

词语：

1.	一共	（副）	yígòng	altogether
2.	多少	（数）	duōshao	how many
3.	钱	（名）	qián	money
4.	要	（动）	yào	need; want
5.	哪	（代）	nǎ(něi)	which
6.	菜	（名）	cài	dish
7.	块	（量）	kuài	yuan (the basic unit of money in China)
8.	还	（副）	hái	too; also; as well
9.	买	（动）	mǎi	buy
10.	种	（量）	zhǒng	kind; type
11.	自行车	（名）	zìxíngchē	bike
12.	看	（动）	kàn	look
13.	颜色	（名）	yánsè	colour
14.	黑	（形）	hēi	black
15.	怎么样	（代）	zěnmeyàng	How about……
16.	喜欢	（动）	xǐhuan	like
17.	蓝	（形）	lán	blue
18.	想	（助动）	xiǎng	think
19.	劳驾		láo jià	Excuse me
20.	有	（动）	yǒu	have

21. 辆	（量）	liàng	measure word (for bicycle)
22. 百	（数）	bǎi	hundred
23. 了	（助）	le	(particle)
24. 花	（动）	huā	spend, cost

专名：

| 丽莎 | | Lìshā | |

补充词语：

1. 服务员	（名）	fúwùyuán	attendant
2. 商店	（名）	shāngdiàn	shop
3. 售货员	（名）	shòuhuòyuán	shop assistant; salesclerk
4. 元	（量）	yuán	yuan(a basic unit of money in China)
5. 角	（量）	jiǎo	jiao(a basic unit of money in China)
6. 毛	（量）	máo	(a basic unit of money in China)
7. 分	（量）	fēn	(a basic unit of money in China)
8. 卖	（动）	mài	to sell
9. 白	（形）	bái	white
10. 千	（数）	qiān	thousand
11. 字典	（名）	zìdiǎn	dictionary
12. 本	（量）	běn	meaure word (of book)
13. 支	（量）	zhī	meanre word (of pen, pencil, etc)
14. 笔	（名）	bǐ	pen
15. 红	（形）	hóng	red
16. 鞋	（名）	xié	shoe
17. 斤	（量）	jīn	a unit of weight (1 jin = 1/2 kilogram)
18. 苹果	（名）	píngguǒ	apple
19. 国旗	（名）	guóqí	national flag
20. 水果	（名）	shuǐguǒ	fruit
21. 双	（量）	shuāng	pair
22. 书	（名）	shū	book

第五课

词语：

1. 一起	（副）	yìqǐ	together
2. 去	（动）	qù	to go
3. 下午	（名）	xiàwǔ	afternoon
4. 课	（名）	kè	class
5. 下课		xià kè	after class

6. 以后	（名）	yǐhòu	after
7. 有空儿		yǒu kòngr	have spare time
8. 事	（名）	shì	thing; matter
9. 那儿	（代）	nàr	there
10. 晚上	（名）	wǎnshang	evening
11. 见	（动）	jiàn	to see
12. 对不起		duìbuqǐ	sorry
13. 没(有)	（副、动）	méi (yǒu)	have not
14. 几个		jǐge	several
15. 问题	（名）	wèntí	question; problem
16. 懂	（动）	dǒng	understand
17. 说	（动）	shuō	to speak
18. 明天	（名）	míngtiān	tomorrow
19. 给	（介、动）	gěi	for
20. 讲	（动）	jiǎng	to explain; to make clear
21. 太	（副）	tài	too
22. 今天	（名）	jīntiān	today
23. 和	（连）	hé	and

补充词语：

1. 兔子	（名）	tùzi	rabbit; hare
2. 跑	（动）	pǎo	to run
3. 肚子	（名）	dùzi	belly
4. 饱	（动）	bǎo	be full;
5. 上午	（名）	shàngwǔ	morning
6. 同学	（名）	tóngxué	classmate
7. 朋友	（名）	péngyou	friend
8. 玩儿	（动）	wánr	to play

第六课

词语：

1. 病	（名、动）	bìng	sick, to be sick
2. 能	（助动）	néng	can
3. 来	（动）	lái	to come
4. 怎么	（代）	zěnme	how
5. 感冒	（动、名）	gǎnmào	cold; flu
6. 知道	（动）	zhīdào	to know
7. 跟	（介）	gēn	to; towards

8. 请进		qǐng jìn	Come in, please.
9. 晚	(形、动)	wǎn	late, to be late
10. 才	(副)	cái	then and only then
11. 呀	(叹)	ya	used at the end of a sentence to convey query
12. 闹钟	(名)	nàozhōng	alarm clock
13. 睡觉		shuì jiào	to sleep
14. 所以	(连)	suǒyǐ	so
15. 停	(动)	tíng	to stop
16. 起床		qǐ chuáng	to get up
17. 大使馆	(名)	dàshǐguǎn	embassy
18. 请假		qǐng jià	to ask for leave

补充词语：

1. 坏	(形)	huài	to break; sth. wrong
2. 骑	(动)	qí	to ride
3. 咱们	(代)	zánmen	we (including both the speaker and the person or persons spoken to)
4. 见面		jiàn miàn	to meet
5. 表	(名)	biǎo	watch
6. 快	(形)	kuài	fast
7. 慢	(形)	màn	slow
8. 会	(动、助动)	huì	be likely to; be sure to
9. 从来	(副)	cónglái	always; all along
10. 机场	(名)	jīchǎng	airport
11. 接	(动)	jiē	to meet; to welcome

第七课

词语：

1. 喝	(动)	hē	to drink
2. 茶	(名)	chá	tea
3. 吃	(动)	chī	to eat
4. 豆	(名)	dòu	bean
5. 包子	(名)	bāozi	steamed stuffed bun
6. 听	(动)	tīng	to lesson
7. 就是		jiùshì	quite right; exactly
8. 哈哈	(象声)	hāha	Aha (indicating complacency or satisfaction)

9. 小姐	（名）	xiǎojie	Miss; young lady
10. 错	（动）	cuò	wrong
11. 豆包儿	（名）	dòubāor	steamed bean filling bun
12. 肉	（名）	ròu	meat
13. 哪	（助）	na	equivalent to "啊"
14. 欢迎	（动）	huānyíng	to welcome
15. 坐	（动）	zuò	to sit
16.（一)点儿	（名）	(yì) diǎnr	a bit; a little
17. 还是	（连）	háishi	or
18. 咖啡	（名）	kāfēi	coffee
19. 忘	（动）	wàng	to forget
20. 女士优先		nǚshì yōuxiān	Ladies first
21. 先生	（名）	xiānsheng	mister; gentleman
22. 又	（副）	yòu	again
23. 以前	（名）	yǐqián	before; in the past
24. 习惯	（名）	xíguàn	to be get used to
25. 非常	（副）	fēicháng	very

补充词语：

1. 啤酒	（名）	píjiǔ	beer
2. 饺子	（名）	jiǎozi	dumpling
3. 干	（动）	gàn	to do
4. 学	（动）	xué	to learn; to study
5. 抽烟		chōu yān	to smoke
6. 只	（副）	zhǐ	only
7. 家里人		jiā li rén	family members
8. 饮料	（名）	yǐnliào	drink

第八课

词语：

1. 干	（动）	gàn	to do
2. 好像	（动）	hǎoxiàng	seem; to be like
3. 高兴	（形）	gāoxìng	glad; pleased
4. 有点儿	（副）	yǒudiǎnr	somewhat
5. 想	（动）	xiǎng	miss
6. 家	（名）	jiā	home
7. 那(么)	（代）	nà(me)	then; in that case
8. 一会儿	（副）	yíhuìr(yìhuǐr)	a little while

9. 音乐	（名）	yīnyuè	music	
10. 咱们	（代）	zánmen	we (including both the speaker and the person or persons spoken to)	
11. 着	（助）	zhe	particle, indicating an action in progress	
12. 聊天儿		liáo tiānr	to chat	
13. 进来		jìnlái	to come in	
14. 做	（动）	zuò	to do	
15. 练习	（动、名）	liànxí	exercise	
16. 得	（助）	de	a structural particle	
17. 更	（副）	gèng	more; still more	
18. 真的		zhēnde	really	
19. 问	（动）	wèn	to ask	
20. 回答	（动）	huídá	to answer; to reply	
21. 昨天	（名）	zuótiān	yesterday	
22. 为什么		wèi shénme	why	
23. 就	（副、连）	jiù	at once; right away	

补充词语：

1. 饭	（名）	fàn	food
2. 电视	（名）	diànshì	TV
3. 累	（形）	lèi	tired
4. 贵	（形）	guì	expensive
5. 不舒服		bù shūfu	uncomfortable
6. 感冒	（名）	gǎnmào	to catch a cold
7. 作业	（名）	zuòyè	homework
8. 唱歌		chàng gē	to sing
9. 正在	（副）	zhèngzài	to indicate an action in progress
10. 时候	（名）	shíhou	time

第九课

词语：

1. 邮局	（名）	yóujú	post office
2. 寄	（动）	jì	to send
3. 信	（名）	xìn	letter
4. 封	（量）	fēng	measure word (for letter)
5. 一块儿	（副）	yíkuàir	together
6. 已经	（副）	yǐjing	already
7. 关门		guān mén	to close

8. 半	（形）	bàn		half
9. 张	（量）	zhāng		measure word (for paper, stamp and table, etc.)
10. 邮票	（名）	yóupiào		stamp
11. 到	（动）	dào		to
12. 本市		běn shì		this city
13. 取	（动）	qǔ		to fetch
14. 包裹	（名）	bāoguǒ		package; parcel
15. 啊	（叹）	a		used at the end of a sentence to convey confirmation
16. 得	（助动）	děi		have to
17. 外边	（名）	wàibian		outside
18. 真	（副）	zhēn		really
19. 没关系		méi guānxi		Not at all.
20. 自己	（代）	zìjǐ		oneself
21. 开门		kāi mén		to open the door
22. 先	（副）	xiān		first
23. 里边	（名）	lǐbian		inside
24. 国外		guówài		overseas; abroad
25. 告诉	（动）	gàosu		to tell

专名：

上海		Shànghǎi	name of a city

补充词语：

1. 时候	（名）	shíhou	time
2. 休息	（动）	xiūxi	to have a rest
3. 回	（动）	huí	to return
4. 因为	（连）	yīnwèi	because
5. 别人	（代）	biéren	other people
6. 哎	（叹）	āi	(showing surprise)
7. 贴	（动）	tiē	to stick; to paste

第十课

词语：

1. 天气	（名）	tiānqì	weather
2. 不错	（形）	búcuò	good
3. 热	（形）	rè	hot
4. 风	（名）	fēng	wind

5. 这里	（名）	zhèlǐ	here
6. 冬天	（名）	dōngtiān	winter
7. 冷	（形）	lěng	cold
8. 夏天	（名）	xiàtiān	summer
9. ……极了		……jíle	extremely
10. 春天	（名）	chūntiān	spring
11. 秋天	（名）	qiūtiān	autumn
12. 阿姨	（名）	āyí	a child's form of address for any woman of its mother's generation
13. 听说		tīng shuō	hear of
14. 身体	（名）	shēntǐ	body
15. 学习	（动）	xuéxí	to study
16. 忙	（形）	máng	busy
17. 生活	（名、动）	shēnghuó	life
18. 可是	（连）	kěshì	but
19. 饭	（名）	fàn	food
20. 好吃	（形）	hǎochī	dielicious
21. 还可以		háikěyǐ	not' bad
22. 爸爸	（名）	bàba	dad;father
23. 妈妈	（名）	māma	mum;mother

专名：

李文静　　　　　　　　　　Lǐ Wénjìng

补充词语：

觉得　　　　（动）　　　　juéde　　　　to feel

第十一课

词语：

1. 贵姓		guì xìng	What's your surname?
2. 办公室	（名）	bàngōngshì	office
3. 学生证	（名）	xuéshēngzhèng	student's identity card
4. 办	（动）	bàn	to do
5. 认识	（动）	rènshi	to know;to recognize
6. 一下儿		yí xiàr	(used after a verb to indicate a brief action)one time;once
7. 俩	**（数）**	liǎ	two
8. 新	（形）	xīn	new
9. 女	（形）	nǚ	female

10. 朋友	（名）	péngyou	friend
11. 哪里	（代）	nǎli	No.
12. 第		dì	prefix for ordinal numbers
13. 次	（量）	cì	time
14. 旅行	（动）	lǚxíng	travel
15. 学	（动）	xué	to study; to learn
16. 多	（副）	duō	indicating degree or extent
17. 长	（形）	cháng	long
18. 时间	（名）	shíjiān	time
19. 汉语	（名）	Hànyǔ	Chinese
20. 星期	（名）	xīngqī	week
21. 难	（形）	nán	difficult
22. 发音	（名）	fāyīn	pronunciation
23. 语法	（名）	yǔfǎ	grammar
24. 汉字	（名）	Hànzì	Chinese character
25. 介绍	（动）	jièshào	to introduce
26. 同学	（名）	tóngxué	classmate

专名：

刘		Liú	surname

第十二课

词语：

1. 刻	（量）	kè	quarter (measure word)
2. 节	（量）	jié	section (measure word)
3. 糟糕	（形）	zāogāo	too bad
4. 唉	（叹）	āi(ài)	a sigh of sadness or regret
5. 饿	（形）	è	hungry
6. 肚子	（名）	dùzi	belly
7. 嗯	（助）	ǹg	Uh-huh
8. 门	（量）	mén	measure word (for courses)
9. 口语	（名）	kǒuyǔ	spoken Chinese
10. 听力	（名）	tīnglì	listening
11. 每	（代）	měi	every
12. 上午	（名）	shàngwǔ	morning
13. 少	（形）	shǎo	few
14. 只有	（副）	zhǐyǒu	only
15. 学年	（名）	xuénián	school year

16. 学期	（名）	xuéqī	semester; term
17. 上(半年)		shàng (bànnián)	last (term)
18. 从……到……		cóng……dào……	from……to……
19. 月	（名）	yuè	month
20. 周	（名）	zhōu	week
21. 下(半年)		xià (bànnián)	next (term)
22. 放	（动）	fàng	have(a holiday or vacation)
23. 寒假	（名）	hánjià	winter vacation
24. 暑假	（名）	shǔjià	summer vacation

补充词语：

1. 课间	（名）	kèjiān	break
2. 饼干	（名）	bǐnggān	biscuit
3. 茶叶	（名）	cháyè	tea ; tea leaves
4. 换	（动）	huàn	to change
5. 分钟	（量）	fēnzhōng	minute
6. 走	（动）	zǒu	to go

第十三课

词语：

1. 动物园	（名）	dòngwùyuán	zoo
2. 走	（动）	zǒu	to go
3. 卖	（动）	mài	sell
4. 鞋	（名）	xié	shoes
5. 楼	（名）	lóu	building
6. 右边	（名）	yòubian	the right side
7. 大爷	（名）	dàye	address to an old man
8. 往	（介）	wǎng	towards
9. 前	（名）	qián	front
10. 马路	（名）	mǎlù	road, street
11. 左边	（名）	zuǒbian	the left side
12. 远	（形）	yuǎn	far
13. 分钟	（量）	fēnzhōng	minute
14. 牙科	（名）	yákē	department of dentistry
15. 清楚	（形）	qīngchu	clear
16. 再	（副）	zài	again
17. 别人	（代）	biéren	other people
18. 大夫	（名）	dàifu	doctor

19. 拐	（动）	guǎi	to turn	
20. 门	（名）	mén	door	
21. 写	（动）	xiě	to write	
22. 医院	（名）	yīyuàn	hospital	
23. 看	（动）	kàn	to cure	
24. 牙	（名）	yá	tooth	
25. 找	（动）	zhǎo	to find; to look for	
26. 上	（动）	shàng	to go (upstairs)	

补充词语：

1. 近	（形）	jìn	near
2. 住	（动）	zhù	to live
3. 路口	（名）	lùkǒu	crossing intersection
4. 前边	（名）	qiánbian	front
5. 层	（量）	céng	story; floor
6. 内科	（名）	nèikē	department of internal medicine
7. 外科	（名）	wàikē	surgical department
8. 花园	（名）	huāyuán	garden
9. 阳台	（名）	yángtái	balcony
10. 客厅	（名）	kètīng	drawing room
11. 熟悉	（形）	shúxi	to know sth. or sb. well; well acquainted with
12. 理想	（名）	lǐxiǎng	ideal; dream

第十四课

词语：

1. 位	（量）	wèi	polite form of address
2. 又……又……	（连）	yòu……yòu……	indicating the simultaneous existence of several conditions or characteristics
3. 酸	（形）	suān	sour
4. 甜	（形）	tián	sweet
5. 辣	（形）	là	hot
6. 来	（动）	lái	want to buy
7. 青菜	（名）	qīngcài	green vegetable
8. 爱	（动）	ài	like; be fond of
9. 等	（动）	děng	to wait
10. 饭馆	（名）	fànguǎn	restaurant
11. 味道	（名）	wèidao	taste

12. 便宜	（形）	piányi	cheap	
13. 早	（形）	zǎo	early	
14. 逛	（动）	guàng	to stroll	
15. 早市	（名）	zǎoshì	morning market	
16. 东西	（名）	dōngxi	thing	
17. 蔬菜	（名）	shūcài	vegetable	
18. 衣服	（名）	yīfu	cloth	
19. 比	（动）	bǐ	indicating difference in manner or degree by comparison	
21. 别的	（代）	biéde	other	
22. 地方	（名）	dìfang	place	
23. 香蕉	（名）	xiāngjiāo	banana	
24. 最	（副）	zuì	most	
25. 因为	（连）	yīnwèi	because	

专名：

1. 番茄肉片	Fānqié-ròupiàn	sliced meat with tomato ketchup
2. 糖醋鱼	Tángcùyú	fish in sweet and sour sauce
3. 古老肉	Gǔlǎoròu	Gu Lao pork
4. 鱼香肉丝	Yúxiāng-ròusī	fish-flavoured shredded pork
5. 香菇菜心	Xiānggū-càixīn	hearts of green vegetables with mushrooms

补充词语：

1. 米饭	（名）	mǐfàn	cooked rice
2. 碗	（量）	wǎn	bowl
3. 瓶	（量）	píng	bottle
4. 啤酒	（名）	píjiǔ	beer
5. 葡萄	（名）	pútao	grape
6. 海鲜	（名）	hǎixiān	seafood
7. 素菜	（名）	sùcài	vegetable dish
8. 主食	（名）	zhǔshí	staple food
9. 饮料	（名）	yǐnliào	drink

第十五课

词语：

1. 做	（动）	zuò	to be
2. 辅导	（名、动）	fǔdǎo	tutor
3. 行	（动）	xíng	OK

4. 最近	（名）	zuìjìn	recently
5. 小时	（量）	xiǎoshí	hour
6. 没问题		méi wèntí	no problem
7. 时候	（名）	shíhou	time
8. 希望	（动、名）	xīwàng	to hope, wish
9. 地	（助）	de	used after an adjective, a noun or a phrase to form an adverbial adjunct before the verb
10. 答应	（动）	dāying	to promise
11. 从……起……		cóng……qǐ……	starting from……
12. 房间	（名）	fángjiān	room
13. 葡萄	（名）	pútao	grape
14. 尝	（动）	cháng	to try; to taste
15. 斤	（量）	jīn	a unit of weight (1 jin = 1/2 kilogram)
16. 生日	（名）	shēngri	birthday
17. 玩儿	（动）	wánr	to play
18. 一定	（副）	yídìng	certainly
19. 祝	（动）	zhù	to wish
20. 快乐	（形）	kuàilè	happy; joy
22. 送	（动）	sòng	send; give
23. 件	（量）	jiàn	measure word (for things that can be counted)
24. 礼物	（名）	lǐwù	gift
25. 唱	（动）	chàng	to sing

补充词语：

1. 还	（动）	huán	to return
2. 岁	（量）	suì	year of (age)
3. 开始	（动）	kāishǐ	begin
4. 帮忙		bāng máng	to help

第十六课

词语：

1. 舒服	（形）	shūfu	comfortable
2. 回	（动）	huí	to go back
3. 休息	（动）	xiūxi	to have a rest
4. 头	（名）	tóu	head
5. 疼	（形）	téng	ache; pain

6. 回去		huíqù	to return ; to go back
7. 好好儿	(形)	hǎohāor	in a proper way
8. 也许	(副)	yěxǔ	maybe
9. 考试	(动)	kǎoshì	to test; to exam
10. 考	(动)	kǎo	to quiz
11. 准备	(动)	zhǔnbèi	to prepare
12. 努力	(形)	nǔlì	to try hard ; make great efforts
13. 多谢		duōxiè	Thank you very much.
14. 关心	(动)	guānxīn	concern
15. 出去		chūqù	to go out
16. 散步		sàn bù	to go out for a walk
17. 这么	(代)	zhème	so
18. 男	(形)	nán	male
19. 话	(名)	huà	word
20. 准	(形)	zhǔn	definitely
21. 快	(快)	kuài	quickly
22. 敢	(助动)	gǎn	dare
23. 慢	(形)	màn	slow
24. 哎	(叹)	āi	well
25. 别	(副)	bié	don't
26. 招待	(动)	zhāodài	to treat

专名：

张新　　　　　　　　　　Zhāng Xīn

补充词语：

1. 湖	(名)	hú	lake
2. 结婚		jié hūn	get married
3. 帮助	(动)	bāngzhù	to help
4. 父母	(名)	fùmǔ	parents
5. 出国		chū guó	go abroad
6. 练	(动)	liàn	to practise
7. 漂亮	(形)	piàoliang	beautiful

第十七课

词语：

1. 作业	(名)	zuòyè	homework
2. 复习	(动)	fùxí	to review
3. 旧	(形)	jiù	old

4. 预习	（动）	yùxí	to preview
5. 用功		yòng gōng	to study hard
6. 一般	（副）	yìbān	general; common
7. 电视	（名）	diànshì	TV
8. 周末	（名）	zhōumò	weekend
9. 爬	（动）	pá	to climb
10. 山	（名）	shān	hill; mountain
11. 累	（形）	lèi	tired
12. 街	（名）	jiē	street
13. 嗓子	（名）	sǎngzi	throat
14. 光	（副）	guāng	only
15. 顾	（动）	gù	to attend to
16. 让	（动）	ràng	to let
17. 拿	（动）	ná	to take; to carry
18. 饮料	（名）	yǐnliào	drink
19. 解渴		jiě kě	to quench ones thirst
20. 瓶	（量）	píng	bottle
21. 可乐	（名）	kělè	coca-cola
22. 矿泉水	（名）	kuàngquánshuǐ	mineral water
23. 好了		hǎole	indicate agreement, approval or conclusion
24. 觉得	（动）	juéde	to feel

补充词语：

1. 汽车	（名）	qìchē	car
2. 凉	（形）	liáng	cool
3. 小说	（名）	xiǎoshuō	novel
4. 明白	（形）	míngbai	to understand
5. 孩子	（名）	háizi	child
6. 交	（动）	jiāo	to hand in

第十八课

词语：

1. 书法	（名）	shūfǎ	calligraphy
2. 哇	（助）	wa	particle, a variation of "啊"
3. 过	（助）	guò	a particle, used as a grammatical suffix to indicate aspect
4. 正在	（副）	zhèngzài	to indicate an action in progress

5. 完	（动）	wán		over
6. 洗澡		xǐ zǎo		to take a bath
7. 洗	（动）	xǐ		to wash
8. 刚才	（名）	gāngcái		just now
9. 回来		huílái		come back
10. 打扰	（动）	dǎrǎo		to disturb
11. 嘛	（助）	ma		used at the end of a sentence to show what precedes it is obvious
12. 英语	（名）	Yīngyǔ		English
13. 胖	（形）	pàng		fat; plump
14. 喘	（动）	chuǎn		to pant
15. 可	（副）	kě		to worth
16. 笑	（动）	xiào		to laugh
17. 抱歉	（动）	bàoqiàn		to be sorry; to regret
18. 久	（形）	jiǔ		long time
19. 没什么		méi shenme		It doesn't matter.
20. 英文	（名）	Yīngwén		English
21. 报纸	（名）	bàozhǐ		newspaper
22. 边……边……		biān……biān……		(used before two verbs respectively to indicate simultaneous actions)
23. 念	（动）	niàn		to read
24. 以为	（动）	yǐwéi		think, believe
25. 句	（量）	jù		sentence
26. 意思	（名）	yìsi		meaning
27. 长	（动）	zhǎng		to grow

专名：

张伟　　　　　　　　　　Zhāng Wěi

补充词语：

跳　　　　　（动）　　　tiào　　　　　　to dance

第十九课

词语：

1. 打算	（动）	dǎsuàn	to plan; to intend
2. 快……了		kuài……le	will; will soon
3. 过（周末）	（动）	guò (zhōumò)	to spend (the weekend)
4. 小	（形）	xiǎo	small

5.	水	（名）	shuǐ	water	
6.	约	（动）	yuē	to invite; to make appointment with (sb.)	
7.	安排	（动）	ānpái	arrangement	
8.	当然	（副）	dāngrán	certainly	
9.	好玩儿	（形）	hǎowánr	have great fun; funny	
10.	晚饭	（名）	wǎnfàn	supper; dinner	
11.	不过	（连）	búguò	but	
12.	美丽	（形）	měilì	beautiful	
13.	只好	（副）	zhǐhǎo	have to	
14.	出来		chūlái	to come out	
15.	刚	（副）	gāng	just	
16.	顿	（量）	dùn	measure word (for meals)	
17.	汤	（名）	tāng	soup	
18.	碗	（名、量）	wǎn	bowl	
19.	饱	（动）	bǎo	to be full	
20.	中餐	（名）	zhōngcān	Chinese food	
21.	些	（量）	xiē	some	
22.	上	（动）	shàng	to serve	
23.	凉菜	（名）	liángcài	cold dishes	
24.	热菜	（名）	rècài	hot dishes	
25.	最后	（名）	zuìhòu	last	
26.	有时候(有时)		yǒushíhou (yǒu shí)	sometimes	

补充词语：

1.	房子	（名）	fángzi	house
2.	过冬		guò dōng	spend the winter
3.	想象	（动）	xiǎngxiàng	to imagine
4.	书架	（名）	shūjià	bookshelf

第二十课

词语：

1.	穿	（动）	chuān	to wear
2.	合适	（形）	héshì	suitable
3.	天气预报		tiānqì yùbào	weather forecast
4.	挺……的		tǐng……de	very; rather
5.	要是……的话		yào shi……dehuà	if

6. 大衣	(名)	dàyī	coat
7. 暖和	(形)	nuǎnhuo	warm
8. 厚	(形)	hòu	thick
9. 怕	(动)	pà	be afraid of
10. 帮	(动)	bāng	to help
11. 样子	(名)	yàngzi	style
12. 好看	(形)	hǎokàn	nice; beautiful
13. 试	(动)	shì	to try
14. 镜子	(名)	jìngzi	mirror
15. 瘦	(形)	shòu	tight
16. 短	(形)	duǎn	short
17. 个子	(名)	gèzi	height
18. 高	(形)	gāo	tall
19. 特大		tèdà	largest
20. 号	(名)	hào	size
21. 肥	(形)	féi	loose; wide
22. 带	(动)	dài	to bring
23. 陪	(动)	péi	accompany
24. 商店	(名)	shāngdiàn	shop
25. 半天	(名)	bàntiān	a long time

第二十一课

词语：

1. 工作	(名、动)	gōngzuò	job
2. 毕业		bìyè	graduate; finish school
3. 念	(动)	niàn	attend school
4. 研究生	(名)	yánjiūshēng	postgraduate
5. 好客	(形)	hàokè	hospitalble
6. 律师	(名)	lǜshī	lawyer
7. 医生	(名)	yīshēng	doctor
8. 哥哥	(名)	gēge	eld brother
9. 妹妹	(名)	mèimei	younger sister
10. 住	(动)	zhù	to live in
11. 上(大学)	(动)	shàng (dàxué)	to attend school
12. 大学	(名)	dàxué	university
13. 读	(动)	dú	to attend school
14. 中学	(名)	zhōngxué	high school

15. 会	（助动、动）	huì	can	
16. 用	（动）	yòng	to use	
17. 口	（量）	kǒu	measure word for the number of a family	
18. 相册	（名）	xiàngcè	album	
19. 去年	（名）	qùnián	last year	
20. 照片	（名）	zhàopiānr	photo	
21. 全	（形）	quán	all; whole	
22. 合影		héyǐng	group photo (or picture)	
23. 连……都/也		lián……dōu/yě	even	
24. 像……一样		xiàng……yíyàng	alike; resemble	
25. 女孩	（名）	nǚhái r	girl	
26. 红	（形）	hóng	red	
27. 原来	（形）	yuánlái	indicating discovery of the truth	

第二十二课

词语：

1. 多	（副）	duō	How (old)
2. 打(球)	（动）	dǎ (qiú)	to play
3. 球	（名）	qiú	ball
4. 电话	（名）	diànhuà	call; telephone
5. 岁	（量）	suì	year of age
6. 都	（副）	dōu	already
7. 开	（动）	kāi	to have (a meeting or party)
8. 晚会	（名）	wǎnhuì	party
9. 为	（介、动）	wèi	for
10. 热闹	（形）	rènao	lively; bustling with noise and excitement
11. 差	（动）	chà	to be short of
12. 可能	（助动）	kěnéng	probably
13. 要不	（连）	yàobù	otherwise
14. 打(电话)	（动）	dǎ(diànhuà)	give sb. a call
15. 号码	（名）	hàomǎ	number
16. ……来着		……láizhe	indicating a past action or state or the recalling or questioning of some past situation.
17. 通	（动）	tōng	through
18. 占线		zhàn xiàn	The line is busy
19. (恐)怕	（副）	(kǒng) pà	be afraid of

20. 哎呀	（叹）	āiyā	ah
21. 应该	（助动）	yīnggāi	should; ought to
22. 准时	（形）	zhǔnshí	on time
23. 迟到	（动）	chídào	be late

补充词语：

1. 转	（动）	zhuǎn	to connect
2. 规定	（动、名）	guīdìng	to get me through; to switch to
3. 要求	（动、名）	yāoqiú	request; to demand
4. 包	（动）	bāo	to wrap
5. 生日卡	（名）	shēngrìkǎ	birthday card
6. 它	（代）	tā	it
7. 猜	（动）	cāi	to guess
8. 及格	（动）	jígé	pass a test
9. 蛋糕	（名）	dàngāo	cake
10. 跳舞		tiào wǔ	dance
11. 扔	（动）	rēng	to throw away

第二十三课

词语：

1. 西	（名）	xī	west
2. 座	（量）	zuò	measure word (for mountain, building, etc.)
3. 风景	（名）	fēngjǐng	scenery
4. 离	（动）	lí	far from
5. 大概	（形、副）	dàgài	about
6. 公里	（量）	gōnglǐ	kilometer
7. 骑	（动）	qí	to ride
8. 野餐	（名）	yěcān	picnic
9. 主意	（名）	zhǔyi	idea
10. 开心	（形）	kāixīn	joy to; have a wonderful time
11. 出	（动）	chū	to go out
12. 胶卷	（名）	jiāojuǎnr	film
13. 方向	（名）	fāngxiàng	direction
14. 北	（名）	běi	north
15. 路口	（名）	lùkǒu	crossing
16. 看见		kàn jiàn	to see
17. 动	（动）	dòng	to move

18. 照相			zhào xiàng	to take a picture
19. 照	（动）		zhào	to take (a picture)
20. 背景	（名）		bèijǐng	background
21. 装	（动）		zhuāng	to load, to fill
22. 马大哈	（名）		mǎdàhā	scatterbrain; careless man
23. 背	（动）		bēi	to carry
24. 男生	（名）		nánshēng	boy student
25. 交(钱)	（动）		jiāo (qián)	to pay

专名：

柯达		Kēdá	Kodak

补充词语：

1. 牌子	（名）	páizi	brand
2. 中文	（名）	Zhōngwén	Chinese
3. 窗	（名）	chuāng	window
4. 钱包	（名）	qiánbāo	wallet
5. 电池	（名）	diànchí	battery
6. 电	（名）	diàn	electricity
7. 举手		jǔ shǒu	to raise (or put up) one's hand or hands
8. 头发	（名）	tóufa	hair
9. 彩色	（名）	cǎisè	colour
10. 黑白	（名）	hēibái	black and white
11. 江	（名）	jiāng	river
12. 公园	（名）	gōngyuán	garden
13. 南	（名）	nán	south
14. 东	（名）	dōng	east

第二十四课

词语：

1. 聪明	（形）	cōngming	clever
2. 洗(照片)	（动）	xǐ(zhàopiānr)	to develop (a negative)
3. 挑	（动）	tiāo	to choose
4. 把	（介）	bǎ	the usage of "把" often causes inversion with the object placed before the verb
5. 底片	（名）	dǐpiàn	negative
6. 满意	（形）	mǎnyì	satisfied
7. 对了		duìle	Oh, used when one suddenly remembers something.

8. 算了		suànle	Let it be.
9. 客气	(形)	kèqi	courteous
10. 只要……就		zhǐyào……jiù	so long as
11. 另外	(形)	lìngwài	other; in addition
12. 进步	(名)	jìnbù	progress
13. 近来	(名)	jìnlái	recently
14. 一……就……		yī……jiù……	once…; as soon as
15. 越……越……		yuè……yuè……	the more……the more……
16. 着急	(形)	zháo jí	worry
17. 同样	(形)	tóngyàng	same
18. 办法	(名)	bànfǎ	method
19. 录音		lù yīn	recording
20. 认真	(形)	rènzhēn	take seriously
21. 比如	(动)	bǐrú	for example; such as
22. 经常	(形)	jīngcháng	often
23. 不许		bùxǔ	don't allow
24. 烦	(形)	fán	annoyed

补充词语：

1. 门口	(名)	ménkǒu	entrance; doorway
2. 生气		shēng qì	be angry
3. 借	(动)	jiè	to borrow
4. 夸	(动)	kuā	to praise
5. 摄影		shèyǐng	to take a photograph or picture
6. 评价	(动、名)	píngjià	to appraise; evaluate
7. 展览	(动、名)	zhǎnlàn	exhibition
8. 绿	(形)	lǜ	green

第二十五课

词语：

1. 苹果	(名)	píngguǒ	apple
2. 贵	(形)	guì	expensive
3. 讲价		jiǎng jià	to bargain
4. 花(钱)	(动)	huā(qián)	to spend (money)
5. 付(钱)	(动)	fù(qián)	to pay
6. 开玩笑		kāi wánxiào	joke; make fun of
7. 急忙	(形)	jímáng	hurry
8. 接(朋友)	(动)	jiē(péngyou)	to meet; to welcome

9. 火车	（名）	huǒchē	train
10. 公共汽车		gōnggòng qìchē	bus
11. 挤	（形）	jǐ	crowded
12. 打的		dǎ dī	take a taxi
13. 车站	（名）	chēzhàn	station
14. 恐怕	（副）	kǒngpà	I'm afraid
15. 再说	（连）	zàishuō	besides；what's more
16. 下班		xià bān	come off work
17. 肯定	（副）	kěndìng	definitely
18. 堵车		dǔ chē	traffic jam
19. 来得及		láidejí	there's still time
20. 放心		fàng xīn	fell relieved；be at ease
21. 近	（形）	jìn	near
22. 方便	（形）	fāngbiàn	convenient
23. 条	（量）	tiáo	measure word (for road)
24. 帮忙		bāng máng	to help
25. 正	（副）	zhèng	just；right
26. 漂亮	（形）	piàoliang	pretty
27. 到处	（副）	dàochù	everywhere
28. 要不是	（连）	yàobushì	if……not……

补充词语：

1. 出租车		chūzūchē	taxi
2. 汉英辞典	（名）	Hàn-Yīng cídiǎn	Chinese–English dictionary
3. 遇到		yù dào	meet
4. 情况	（名）	qíngkuàng	situation；condition
5. 心情	（名）	xīnqíng	mood；state of mind
6. 劝	（动）	quàn	to advise

第二十六课

词语：

1. 进城		jìn chéng	go to down town
2. 转	（动）	zhuàn	to stroll
3. 倒霉		dǎo méi	bad luck
4. 丢	（动）	diū	to lose
5. 锁	（动）	suǒ	to lock
6. 钥匙	（名）	yàoshi	key
7. 手	（名）	shǒu	hand

8. 下(楼)	(动)	xià(lóu)		to go downstairs
9. 遍	(量)	biàn		indicating the process of an action from begining to end
10. 影子	(名)	yǐngzi		trace
11. 看来	(连)	kànlái		It seems
12. 它	(代)	tā		it
13. 旧	(形)	jiù		past;old
14. (回)不了		(huí) buliǎo		can't (go back)
15. 关系	(名)	guānxi		bearing
16. 大家	(代)	dàjiā		all;everybody
17. 提	(动)	tí		to talk about
18. 吹	(动)	chuī		to break up
19. 改	(动)	gǎi		to change
20. 后天	(名)	hòutiān		the day after tomorrow
21. 不好意思		bù hǎoyìsi		find it embarrassing (to do sth.)
22. 添	(动)	tiān		to add
23. 麻烦	(动、形)	máfan		trouble

专名:

圣诞节	(名)	Shèngdànjié	Christmas

补充词语:

1. 有意思		yǒu yìsi	interesting
2. 留	(动)	liú	to leave
3. 回(电话)	(动)	huí (diànhuà)	to call back
4. 纸	(名)	zhǐ	paper
5. 道歉		dàoqiàn	to apologize
6. 扶	(动)	fú	to support with the hand
7. 表示	(动)	biǎoshì	to show; to express; to indicate
8. 原谅	(动)	yuánliàng	to pardon
9. 婚礼	(名)	hūnlǐ	wedding ceremony
10. 滑倒		huádǎo	fall because the road is slippery

第二十七课

词语:

1. 下(雨)	(动)	xià(yǔ)	to fall
2. 雨	(名)	yǔ	rain
3. 午饭	(名)	wǔfàn	lunch
4. 午睡		wǔshuì	afternoon nap

5. 没事儿		méi shìr	It doesn't matter
6. 够	（动、形）	gòu	enough
7. 请教	（动）	qǐngjiào	consult
8. 不敢当		bù gǎndāng	I wish I could deserve your compliment; you flatter me
9. 随便	（形）	suíbiàn	do as one please
10. 那(么)	（副、连）	nà(me)	like that
11. 跑步		pǎo bù	run
12. 锻炼	（动）	duànliàn	take physical exercise
13. 懒	（形）	lǎn	lazy
14. 中午	（名）	zhōngwǔ	noon
15. 起来		qǐlái	to get up
16. 点	（动）	diǎn	to order
17. 请客		qǐng kè	to entertain guests
18. 有名	（形）	yǒumíng	famous
19. 不如	（动）	bùrú	not as
20. 怪	（形）	guài	strange
21. 哎哟		āiyō	expressing surprise
22. 北方	（名）	běifāng	north
23. 咸	（形）	xián	salty
24. 南方	（名）	nánfāng	south
25. 有意思		yǒu yìsi	interesting
26. 辣椒	（名）	làjiāo	hot pepper
27. 大葱	（名）	dàcōng	green onion
28. 回	（量）	huí	used to indicate frequency of action

专名：

1. 四川	Sìchuān	Si Chuan province
2. 山东	Shāndōng	province
3. 山西	Shānxī	province
4. 川菜	Chuāncài	Si Chuan dish
5. 麻婆豆腐	Mápó-dòufu	Pockmarked grandma's beancurd
6. 辣子鸡丁	Làzi-jīdīng	chicken cubes with hot pepper

补充词语：

1. 矮	（形）	ǎi	short
2. 户	（名）	hù	house; door
3. 外	（名）	wài	outside
4. 活动	（名、动）	huódòng	exercise
5. 金	（名）	jīn	gold

6. 口	（名）	kǒu		mouth
7. 入	（动）	rù		to enter

第二十八课

词语：

1. 然后	（副）	ránhòu		then; after that
2. 出发	（动）	chūfā		to start out
3. 天	（名）	tiān		sky
4. 奇怪	（形）	qíguài		strange
5. 下来		xiàlái		get off
6. 毛病	（名）	máobing		trouble; breakdown
7. 气	（名）	qì		air
8. 打(气)	（动）	dǎ (qì)		to pump up
9. 打开		dǎkāi		to turn on
10. 播	（动）	bō		to broadcast
11. 常常	（副）	chángcháng		often
12. 差不多	（副）	chàbuduō		almost
13. 白天	（名）	báitiān		daytime
14. 晴	（形）	qíng		fine; sunny
15. 午后	（名）	wǔhòu		in the afternoon
16. 广告	（名）	kuǎnggào		advertisement
17. 节目	（名）	jiémù		program
18. 雪	（名）	xuě		snow
19. 吹牛		chuī niú		boast
20. 担心		dān xīn		to worry
21. 注意	（动）	zhùyì		to pay attention to; to take notice of
22. 容易	（形）	róngyi		easy
23. 特别	（副）	tèbié		rather
24. 雪景	（名）	xuějǐng		snow scenery
25. 滑	（动）	huá		to skate
26. 冰	（名）	bīng		ice

专名：

云南		Yúnnán	province

补充词语：

1. 约会	（名）	yuēhuì		appointment
2. 照相机	（名）	zhàoxiàngjī		camera
3. 修	（动）	xiū		to repair

第二十九课

词语：

1. 着	（动）	zháo	used after a verb to indicate accomplishment or result
2. 票	（名）	piào	ticket
3. 整天	（名）	zhěngtiān	whole day
4. 看样子		kàn yàngzi	it looks as if
5.（累）死		(lèi) sǐ	extremely
6. 排	（动）	pái	line up
7. 队	（名）	duì	a row (of line) of people
8. 到底	（副）	dàodǐ	after all
9. 预订	（动）	yùdìng	to book in advance
10. 提前	（动）	tíqián	ahead
11. 订	（动）	dìng	to book; to order
12. 填	（动）	tián	to fill in
13. 预订单		yùdìngdān	booking form
14. 押金	（名）	yājīn	deposit
15. 补	（动）	bǔ	to make up for
16. 手续费		shǒuxùfèi	service charge
17. 申请	（动）	shēnqǐng	to apply
18. 延长	（动）	yáncháng	to extend
19. 建议	（名、动）	jiànyì	idea
20. 聚	（动）	jù	to get together
21. 赞成	（动）	zànchéng	to agree with
22. 包	（动）	bāo	to make (dumplings)
23. 饺子	（名）	jiǎozi	dumpling
24. 录相		lù xiàng	videotape

专名：

春节		Chūnjié	The Spring Festival

补充词语：

1. 比赛	（动）	bǐsài	match
2. 发现	（动）	fāxiàn	to discover
3. 音乐会		yīnyuèhuì	concert

第三十课

词语：

1.	杯子	（名）	bēizi	cup
2.	叫	（介）	jiào	used to introduce a passive construction
3.	打(碎)	（动）	dǎ (suì)	to break into pieces
4.	碎	（形）	suì	broken
5.	湿	（形）	shī	wet
6.	信(相信)	（动）	xìn (xiāngxìn)	to believe
7.	雨伞	（名）	yǔsǎn	umbrella
8.	有的是		yǒudeshì	have plenty of
9.	接(电话)	（动）	jiē(diànhuà)	to recieve (the phone)
10.	教	（动）	jiāo	to teach
11.	皮儿	（名）	pír	wrapper
12.	馅儿	（名）	xiànr	stuffing
13.	分	（动）	fēn	to divided
14.	组	（名）	zǔ	group
15.	进行	（动）	jìnxíng	to carry on
16.	比赛	（动）	bǐsài	race
17.	裁判	（名）	cáipàn	judge
18.	当	（动）	dāng	work as
19.	中间	（名）	zhōngjiān	middle
20.	合	（动）	hé	close
21.	捏	（动）	niē	mould
22.	煮	（动）	zhǔ	to boil
23.	(水)开(了)	（动）	(shuǐ)kāi (le)	boil
24.	漂	（动）	piāo	floating
25.	熟	（形）	shú(shóu)	cooked

补充词语：

1.	小偷	（名）	xiǎotōu	thief
2.	偷	（动）	tōu	to steal
3.	淋	（动）	lín	pour; drench
4.	机会	（名）	jīhuì	chance
5.	输	（动）	shū	lose
6.	赢	（动）	yíng	win
7.	不小心		bù xiǎoxīn	careless
8.	答应	（动）	dāying	to promise
9.	破	（动）	pò	broken

Translated text

Lesson One   How Do You Do

(First day of college, on the campus)
Jeff: How do you do!
Anne: How do you do!
Jeff: My name is Jeff. What is your name?
Anne: My name is Anne.

(In the classroom)
Teacher Tian: How do you do! My name is Tian.
Anne & Jeff: How do you do! Teacher Tian.
Teacher Tian: (to Jeff) What is your name?
Jeff: My name is Jeff.
Teacher Tian: (to Anne) And you?
Anne: My name is Anne.

(Outside the classroom)
Wang Ping: How do you do!
Jeff & Anne: How do you do!
Jeff: What is your name?
Wang Ping: My name is Wang Ping. You are ...?
Anne: I am Anne, He is Jeff.

(Jeff to Wang Ping) My name is Jeff, her name is Anne. We are both foreign students, Our teacher's name is Tian.

Lesson Two   What Time Is It

(On the street)
Peter: Good morning!

Anne: Good morning!
Peter: What's your name?
Anne: My name is Anne. And you?
Peter: My name is Peter. What is your nationality?
Anne: I'm British. Are you American?
Peter: No. I'm French.

(Peter and Anne are talking when Jeff approaches)
Anne: Jeff, how are you!
Jeff: Hello, Anne! Who's he?
Anne: This is Peter.
Jeff: How do you do, Peter! My name is Jeff!
Peter: How do you do! Are you American?
Jeff: Well, yes. Which class are you in?
Peter: Class 1. And you?
Anne: I'm in Class 2.
Jeff: So am I.
Peter: What time is it now?
Anne: It's two o'clock. It's time for class. Good-bye, Peter!

(Peter) I'm French, Anne is British, Jeff is American. I'm in Class 1, they are in Class 2. We have class at 2:00.

Lesson Three   Where Is The Dining Hall

(On the campus)
Anne: Excuse me, is this the classroom building?
Passerby: No. It's the office building. That one is the classroom building.
Anne: Thanks.
Passerby: Not at all.

(In the classroom building)
Anne: Excuse me, is the classroom for Class 2 here?
Student: Yes, it's right here.
Anne: Thank you.

Student: Don't mention it.

(On the campus)
Shan Xia: Could you tell me where the dining room for the foreign students is?
Passerby: Over there.
Shan Xia: Over where?
Passerby: Beside the dormitory building for the foreign students.
Shan Xia: Thanks.

(In the classroom building)
Jeff: Excuse me, where is the washroom, please?
Student: Next to the classroom. ... Oh, no. Next to that classroom.
Jeff: Thanks.
Student: You're welcome.

(Anne) This is our school. It's a very large school. This is the office building, that is the classroom building. The dining hall for the foreign students stands beside the dormitory building.

Lesson Four   How Much Is It Altogether

(In the foreign student's dining hall, Chinese food section)
Attendant: Which dish would you like?
Lisa: I'd like this one. How much is it?
Attendant: 6.50 yuan.
Shan Xia: I want this one, and that one, too.
Attendant: Which one?
Shan Xia: The one over there! How much is it altogether?
Attendant: 15.70 Yuan.

(Anne and Jeff are shopping together)
Jeff: I want this kind of bicycle, which color do you think is better?
Anne: How about the black one?
Jeff: Black ... ... but I like blue. I'd like to look at a blue one, too.
Anne: Excuse me, do you have a blue one like this?

Salesman: Which make?
Jeff: This one.
Salesman: Yes. We have both blue ones and black ones.
Jeff: I'll take a blue one. How much is it?
Salesman: 540 yuan.

(Jeff) I wanted to buy a bicycle. I looked at a black one and a blue one, too. I paid 540 yuan for a blue one.

Lesson Five Let's Go Together

(Before class)
Anne: Do you have class this afternoon?
Jeff: Yes, I do.
Anne: Will you be free after class?
Jeff: I'll finish class at six. Why?
Anne: Well, I want to go to Wang Ping's. Will you come along?
Jeff: I'd like to, I'll have time in the evening.
Anne: Let's go together in the evening then, shall we?
Jeff: Fine. See you in the evening!
Anne: See you in the evening!

(After the fourth period in the morning)
Anne: Teacher Tian, do you have time to spare now?
Teacher Tian: Sorry, I'm busy right now. Anything the matter?
Anne: (Opens a book) There are a few questions here I still don't understand.
Teacher Tian: Let me have a look. Oh, Shan Xia said he didn't understand these questions, either. I'll explain to you further in class tomorrow.
Anne: How wonderful! See you tomorrow!
Teacher Tian: See you tomorrow!

(Anne to Wang Ping) There are a few questions I still don't understand in today's lesson, Teacher Tian says she's going to further explain them to us tomorrow in class. Jeff and I will be free tomorrow evening, we'll go to your place together, OK?

Lesson Six   She Is Ill

(Before class)

Jeff: Teacher, Anne can't come to class.

Teacher Tian: What's the matter with her?

Jeff: She is ill. She has a cold.

Teacher Tian: Oh, I see. Thank you.

(Anne tells Jeff to ask leave for her)

　　Jeff, I have a cold and cannot go to class today. Please tell the teacher, all right?

(Half an hour into class, Lisa knocks at the door)

Teacher Tian: Please come in!

Lisa: Sorry I am late.

(Lisa sits down at her desk, the classmate sitting beside her whispers to her)

Classmate: Why are you late?

Lisa: Well, my alarm clock fell asleep, so ... ...

Classmate: What? Alarm clock asleep? Oh, I see, your alarm clock had stopped.

Lisa: Exactly, my alarm clock had stopped. I didn't get up until 8 and that's why I'm late.

Teacher Tian: Any problems?

Lisa: No, no. I'm sorry.

(After class, Peter asks the teacher for leave)

　　Teacher Tian, I must go to the embassy tomorrow and won't be able to come to class. I have to ask for leave.

Lesson Seven   I Like Tea

(At supper)

Jeff: What would you like?

Anne: Steamed buns with bean paste stuffing.

Jeff: What? I don't understand.

Anne: Steamed – buns – with – bean – paste – stuffing.

Jeff: Ha, ha! Miss, you're wrong!

Anne: How come?

Jeff: It's called steamed buns stuffed with bean paste, not steamed buns with bean paste stuffing.

Anne: Well, what is a bun with stuffing then?

Jeff: A bun with meat or vegetable stuffing is a bun with stuffing.

(Jeff and Anne entering Peter's room)

Jeff: Why, you're here, too, Wang Ping!

Wang Ping: Oh, it's you two!

Peter: Welcome! Welcome! Be seated, please.

Anne: OK, you sit over there, Jeff, and I'll sit here.

Peter: Jeff, what would you like, tea or coffee?

Jeff: Coffee. I like coffee.

Anne: Oh, you! How could you have forgotten "Ladies first"?

Peter: I'm sorry, lady. You like coffee, too, don't you?

Anne: Well, you're wrong there again, mister! I began to like tea after coming to China.

(Jeff to Anne) A bun with stuffing is a bun with stuffing, A bun stuffed with bean is a bun stuffed with bean. A bun stuffed with bean is not a bun with bean stuffing, Only a bun with meat or vegetable stuffing is a bun with stuffing.

(Anne) I used to like coffee when I was in Britain. But since I get to China, I get used to tea and I like tea very much now.

Lesson Eight   What Are You Doing

(Outside of Anne's dorm, Jeff knocks at Anne's door)

Jeff: Is Anne in?

Anne: (opens the door) Oh, it's you, come in, please! Do sit down!

Jeff: Thanks! What's the matter with you? You don't look very happy.

Anne: I am a little homesick.

Jeff: You're homesick? What about some music then?

Anne: OK, let's listen to music and chat.

(At Jeff's door)
Lisa: Jeff! Jeff … !
Jeff: Who is it? Come in!
Lisa: What are you doing?
Jeff: Doing exercise.
Lisa: Can you do them while listening to that music?
Jeff: I can do it even better with the music.
Lisa: Really? I have a question to ask, can you give me a correct answer?
Jeff: Go ahead!

(Jeff to Peter) Last night, I went to Anne's room. I noticed that she wasn't very happy. I asked her why and she said she was homesick. I said let's have some music. So we listened to some music and chatted happily for a while and she felt better.

Lesson Nine   I'm Going to The Post Office to Send a Letter

(Outside the dormitory)
Jeff: Anne, where are you going?
Anne: I'm going to the post office to send a letter.
Jeff: Well, I have a few letters to send, too.
Anne: Let's go together then!
Jeff: (looks at his watch) It's already 5:00, is the post office closed?
Anne: No, not until 5:30.

(In the school post office)
Anne: I want two 5.4yuan stamps.
Clerk: 10.8 yuan in all.
Jeff: Miss, this letter is for the U.S., this one's for Shanghai, and this is local.
Clerk: This one is 5.4 yuan. These two are 50 fen each.

(At the post office)
Anne: Why, Lisa, you're here to send letters, too?
Lisa: No. I came to pick up a parcel.

Anne: From your home?
Lisa: You're right!
Anne: In that case, you'll have to go to the larger post office outside the campus.
Lisa: Oh, Anne, can you come along with me?
Anne: I'm really sorry, I'm busy at the moment ...
Lisa: That's all right. I'll go on my own!

(Anne) Jeff and I both wanted to mail some letters. Jeff didn't know at what time the post office would close. I said it was only 5:00, the post office was still open and we could go together. In the post office, we got some stamps first. Jeff sent three letters, it was altogether 6.4 yuan. I mailed two letters, they cost me 10.8 yuan.

(Jeff) Lisa got a parcel from home, she didn't know that parcels from abroad do not come through the post office in our school, Anne told her she'd have to go to the larger post office outside for her parcel.

Lesson Ten What's the Weather Like Today

(Peter comes in from outside in the morning)
Jeff: What's the weather like today?
Peter: Oh, pretty good.
Jeff: Is it hot?
Peter: Not very.
Jeff: Is it windy?
Peter: Not at all.

(Anne and Wang Ping talk about the climate)
Anne: Is it cold in winter here?
Wang Ping: Well, quite cold.
Anne: Is it windy?
Wang Ping: Very windy.
Anne: What's the summer like?
Wang Ping: Extremely hot.
Anne: Well, the climate here is not good in winter, nor in summer.
Wang Ping: But there are spring and autumn.

(Aunt Wang, a friend of Li Wenjing's mother, comes from her southern hometown and visits Li Wen‑jing.)

Li Wenjing: Aunt Wang, how come you are here?
Aunt Wang: I heard that you were ill, so I wanted to see you. How did you get ill?
Li Wenjing: I'm not used to the climate here.
Aunt Wang: How are you feeling now?
Li Wenjing: Well, I'm all right now.
Aunt Wang: Have you been busy studying?
Li Wenjing: Not very much.
Aunt Wang: Have you gotten used to your life here?
Li Wenjing: Well, I haven't gotten perfectly used to it yet, but it doesn't matter.
Aunt Wang: Is the food good in the dining hall?
Li Wenjing: Passable.

(Li Wenjing) Aunt Wang, I'm so glad that you came to see me. Please tell my parents that It's very cold and windy here in winter, and extremely hot in summer. I am still not very used to the climate here. But it doesn't matter. I'm fine, and I haven't been very busy studying.

Lesson Eleven   May I Have Your Name

(At the office door)
Anne: Excuse me, is this the Foreign Students' Office?
Teacher Liu: Yes. Please come in! Anything the matter?
Anne: Teacher, I'd like to know if my student identity card is ready?
Teacher Liu: What is your name?
Anne: Anne.
Teacher Liu: So you are Anne? Your student identity card isn't ready yet, you can have it tomorrow.
Anne: Thanks. Teacher, may I know your name?
Teacher Liu: My name is Liu.
Anne: See you tomorrow then, Teacher Liu!

(On the campus, Jeff and Anne come across Wang Ping and Li Wenjing)

Wang Ping: Jeff, Anne, let me introduce you, this is Li Wenjing.
Jeff: Li Wenjing, how do you do! I'm Jeff.
Anne: My name is Anne. Glad to meet you.
Li Wenjing: How do you do! You've both students newly arrived?
Jeff & Anne: Yes.
Jeff: (whispering to Wang Ping) Your girlfriend?
Wang Ping: (whispering to Jeff) No. Just a female friend.
Li Wenjing: Well, what are you two talking about?
Wang Ping & Jeff: Nothing.

(On the way back to the dormitory)
Li Wenjing: Anne, is this the first time you are in China?
Anne: The second time. Last time I came traveling.
Li Wenjing: How long had you been learning Chinese before you came?
Anne: Two weeks.
Li Wenjing: Is it difficult to learn Chinese?
Anne: Well, the pronunciation is not difficult, the grammar is not very difficult, either. But Chinese characters are really difficult.

(Anne) Today we met a new friend introduced to us by Wang Ping. Her name is Li Wenjing, she's Wang Ping's classmate. I'm very glad to've met her.

Lesson Twelve   How Many Class Hours Are There in a Week

(In Anne's room)
Lisa: Anne, get up quickly!
Anne: What time is it?
Lisa: Quarter past 8!
Anne: Oh, no. I have class in the first period. Dear me, I'll have to attend class with an empty stomach again.

(On way to class)
Peter: Anne, going to class?
Anne: Uh-huh!
Peter: How many courses do you take in this term?

Anne: Three. Chinese Reader, Spoken Chinese and Listening. How many do you take?
Peter: Two. I didn't take the listening course.
Anne: How many periods do you have each week?
Peter: 20 periods.
Anne: 20 periods for two courses?
Peter: Yes, 10 periods each. How many periods do you have today?
Anne: Well, two in the morning and two in the afternoon, altogether four.

(Peter) I'm in Class 1, Anne's in Class 2. I take two courses, and she takes three. We both have 20 periods every week. There are too many students in our class -- 16, but fewer students in their class -- only 12.

(Teacher Tian briefing) There are two terms in a school year: The autumn term is in the second half of the year, from September to January the next year, lasting 20 weeks; The spring term is in the first half of the year, from February to July, lasting 18 weeks. There are a winter vacation and a summer vacation as well.

Lesson Thirteen   Could You Show Me the Way to the Zoo

(In a large bazaar)
Peter: Excuse me, miss, where can I get some shoes?
Clerk: The third floor, on the right side.
Peter: Thanks.
Clerk: Not at all.

(On the street)
Anne: Uncle, could you show me the way to the zoo, please?
Old man: Go straight ahead, it's on the left side of the street.
Anne: Is it far?
Old man: No. It's just a 5 - minute walk.
Anne: Thank you.
Old man: You're welcome.

(In the school hospital)

Jeff: Schoolmate, where is the Department of Dentistry, please?

A student: Well, I'm not sure, maybe it's on the second floor. You'd better ask someone else.

(on the second floor)

Jeff: Excuse me, doctor, is the Dentistry Department on this floor?

Doctor: Yes, walk ahead, turn right, the second door on the left. It's written on the door plate.

Jeff: Thank you very much.

(Jeff to Anne) I went to the hospital to see the dentist yesterday, but didn't know where the Dentistry Department was. I found it after asking two people for help. It was on the second floor. I went up the stairs, walked straight ahead and turned right, it was the second door on the left.

Lesson Fourteen   What Would You Like to Eat

(In a restaurant)

Jeff: Ladies, what would you like to eat?

Anne: I'd like something sweet and sour.

Jeff: What about you, Lisa?

Lisa: Well, I want something hot.

(Jeff summons a waitress)

Jeff : Miss, what dishes do you have both sweet and sour?

Waitress: Well, we have sliced meat with tomato ketchup, fish in sweet and sour sauce, and Gu Lao pork, too.

Lisa: A sliced meat with tomato then.

Jeff: For something hot, a fish − flavoured shredded pork.

Anne: How about a green vegetable, too?

Jeff: Let's have hearts of green vegetables with mushrooms.

Anne: Good, I love it.

Waitress: Three dishes in all. Anything to drink?

Jeff: Let's have tea.

Waitress: Please wait for a while.

(Jeff to Peter) Anne, Lisa and I went and dined in a restaurant yesterday. We ordered a sliced meat with tomato, which was sweet and sour, a fish-flavoured shredded pork which was hot, and a green vegetable which was good, too. That restaurant serves tasty and inexpensive food.

(At the dormitory)
Jeff: Early bird, Anne! Where are you going?
Anne: Well, I'm going to look around in the morning market.
Jeff: Morning market? What do they sell there?
Anne: Vegetables, fruits, clothes and the like, they sell everything.
Jeff: Fruits, too! Are they cheap?
Anne: Yes, cheaper than anywhere else!
Jeff: Really? I'm going with you! I want to get some bananas, I like bananas most.
Anne: Come along, then!
Jeff: OK, let's go.

(Anne) I enjoy looking around in the morning market, because lots of things are available there and they are cheap. Jeff liked bananas and wanted to get some, so he went with me. It was the first time he went shopping in a morning market.

Lesson Fifteen   Will You Be My Tutor

(In Wang Ping's room)
Anne: Have you been busy lately?
Wang Ping: Not very, why?
Anne: I'm asking you to be my tutor, is it OK?
Wang Ping: OK! What do you want to be tutored in?
Anne: Well, I want to practice spoken Chinese, two times a week, an hour each. Is there any problem?
Wang Ping: No problem! But when will it be more suitable?
Anne: How about every Monday and Thursday afternoon, 5:00 to 6:00?
Wang Ping: But I have class on Monday afternoon, is Tuesday all right?
Anne: OK. How much is it for an hour?

(Anne to Jeff) I want to practice spoken Chinese, so I ask Wang Ping to be my tutor. I wish to be tutored twice a week, each time for an hour. Wang Ping has gladly agreed. Starting from next week, Wang Ping will come to my room and tutor me every Tuesday and Thursday afternoon, from 5:00 to 6:00.

(In the morning market)
Anne: Are these grapes sour?
Pedlar: No. They're sweet.
Anne: Can I try one?
Pedlar: Well, go ahead. Don't pay me if they're not sweet.
(Anne tastes one)
Anne: It's really sweet! Give me two jin.

(On the street)
Jeff: Wang Ping, will you be free tomorrow evening?
Wang Ping: Anything the matter?
Jeff: Well, it's my birthday tomorrow, come and have fun.
Wang Ping: I certainly will.
Jeff: Thank you!

(Wang Ping) Jeff told me that tomorrow would be his birthday. He asked me to go to his room and have fun. I promised him readily. I want to give him a gift, and sing "Happy Birthday" to him.

Lesson Sixteen I Don't Feel Very Well

(In class)
Student: Excuse me, teacher, I don't feel very well. I want to go back to my room and take a rest, may I?
Teacher: What's the matter?
Student: Well, I have a slight headache.
Teacher: All right. Go and have a good sleep, perhaps you'll feel fine again.
Student: Thank you, teacher.

(After class)
Shan Xia: Anne, did you have your examination?
Anne: We did, last Friday.

Shan Xia: Well, how was it? Did you do well?
Anne: No. I didn't feel well last week and I wasn't well prepared for it.
Shan Xia: Never mind, isn't there a next time?

(In the room)
Zhang Xin: Li Wenjing, I hear you are not well. Are you feeling any better now?
Li Wenjing: Thanks a lot for your concern. I feel much better now.
Zhang Xin: Well, I'd like to go out for a walk, are you coming along?
Li Wenjing: I'm sorry I can't. A friend is coming to see me.
Zhang Xin: Who is it that's so concerned about you? Your boyfriend?
Li Wenjing: (silence) ...
Zhang Xin: Ha ha, I know from your silence I was right.
Li Wenjing: Oh, what do you know? Go away quickly!
Zhang Xin: How would I dare go slowly? Well, don't forget to give him a good treat.

(Anne to Shan Xia) We had the examination last Friday. But I hadn't been feeling very well before the exam, and wasn't well prepared for it. So I didn't do very well. I'll try harder next time.

Lesson Seventeen   It's Beyond My Comprehension

(Over supper)
Jeff: What do you do every evening?
Lisa: I write Chinese characters, do assignments, review the old lesson, preview the new lesson……
Jeff: You're really a good and conscientious student.
Lisa: Well, what do you usually do in the evening?
Jeff: Watch television, and chat.
Lisa: I enjoy chatting, too.
Jeff: Don't you like watching television?
Lisa: No, I don't.
Jeff: Why not?
Lisa: It's beyond my comprehension.

(Outside the dormitory building on Thursday afternoon)

Anne: What do you like to do this weekend?
Shan Xia: Mountain-climbing. How about coming with me?
Anne: You like mountain-climbing?
Shan Xia: Yes. Don't you like it?
Anne: Mountain-climbing is too tiring. I enjoy window-shopping.
Shan Xia: Well, I think window-shopping is even more tiring than mountain-climbing!

(Wang Ping tutoring Anne in her room)
Anne: You're really a good tutor! I understand everything you said.
Wang Ping: You did a good job yourself answering the questions. But my throat is on fire after all the talking. Let's have a break!
Anne: I'm so sorry. I just let you go on tutoring and forgot to offer you a drink. What would you like?
Wang Ping: Give me whatever you have, so long as it quenches my thirst.
Anne: I've got a bottle of Cocacola, and a bottle of mineral water.
Wang Ping: Don't you like Cocacola? I'll have the mineral water then.

(Lisa to Anne) Jeff likes watching television and chatting in the evening. I like chatting too, but I don't really like watching television because it's beyond my comprehension.

(Anne to Lisa) Shan Xia likes to spend his weekends climbing mountains. I think mountain-climbing is too tiring. I enjoy window-shopping. But Shan Xia says window-shopping is even more tiring.

Lesson Eighteen   I Was Taking a Lesson on Chinese Calligraphy

(At the classroom building)
Wang Ping: I went to your room last night, but you weren't in.
Zhang Wei: At what time?
Wang Ping: 8:00.
Zhang Wei: Oh, I was having class at 8:00.
Wang Ping: Having class in the evening?
Zhang Wei: Well, I was taking a lesson on Chinese calligraphy.

Wang Ping: But class finished at 9:30. Why weren't you in then?
Zhang Wei: 9:30? I was taking a bath. I didn't finish until 10:00 …… Anything the matter?
Wang Ping: Oh, nothing. I just wanted a chat with you.

(Zhang Wei) Last night at 8:00, I took a lesson on calligraphy. After class, I went and took a bath. It was already 10:00 when I finished. That was why Wang Ping looked for me twice but couldn't find me.

(Want Ping and Zhang Wei go to Anne's room to see her)
Wang Ping: Excuse me, is Anne in?
Lisa: She went out just now, but she'll be back soon. Please come in and wait for her.
Wang Ping: OK, sorry to disturb you.
Lisa: You're welcome. Please sit down! Do you want to read a paper? (handing him an English newspaper)
Wang Ping: Thank you. Um, I'll read a few sentences to you. …… What do you think of my pronunciation?
Lisa: It's not bad at all!
Wang Ping: The English teacher said so too in class.
Zhang Wei: Hey, you, told you're fat, you start panting.
Lisa: What did you say? He is not fat!
(Zhang Wei and Wang Ping shook with laughter, Anne comes in)
Anne: What's so funny? Sorry! Sorry to've kept you waiting for so long!
Wang Ping: It doesn't matter! It doesn't matter!

(Lisa to Anne) While waiting for you, Wang Ping picked up an English paper and began reading it aloud. I said his pronunciaton was pretty good. He told me that the teacher had said so, too. So Zhang Wei said, "Told you're fat, you start panting." I thought that sentence meant Wang Ping was fat. The three of us were laughing at it when you came in.

Lesson Nineteen   What are you going to do This Weekend

(Anne and Jeff talking over dinner in the dining hall)

Anne: Jeff, the weekend is coming soon, how are you going to spend it?
Jeff: I'm going on a short tour!
Anne: Where to?
Jeff: A nice place with hills and waters.
Anne: You're going alone?
Jeff: I've asked Wang Ping, the two of us will go together.
Anne: I don't have any arrangement yet for the weekend. Can I go with you?
Jeff: Certainly! I thought you'd go window-shopping again!

(In their room)
Lisa: Anne, back from the tour? Well, did you have fun?
Anne: We had great fun, It was a bit tiring, though.
Lisa: You haven't had supper yet. Let's go have supper together.
Anne: I want to take a bath first before supper.
Lisa: OK, I'll wait for you. But you have to hurry up, the dining hall will soon close.

(Anne to Lisa) Jeff, Wang Ping and I went on a tour today. We went to a beautiful place. There were hills and waters. We had great fun. It was a bit tiring though. I'm going to take a bath now, and then we'll go have supper together. Please wait for me.

(In a small restaurant off the campus)
Wang Ping: (having his soup, he sees Anne and Lisa come in) Ladies, how come you're here to dine, too?
Lisa: Well, I waited for her to finish her bath and the dining hall was closed. So we have to come out to dine.
Anne: You just came? Let's eat together.
Wang Ping: Who said I just came? Do you want me to have a second meal?
Lisa: Aren't you having your soup? A bowl of soup is enough for you?
Wang Ping: (laughs heartily) So you think soup is also served first in a Chinese restaurant!
Anne: Stop laughing. We don't really know all the rules in eating a Chinese meal. Tell us about them.
Wang Ping: Allow me then. In a Chinese meal, cold dishes are served first, people

eat over their drinks, hot dishes are served later, and the soup last, sometimes followed by some fruit.

Lesson Twenty It's Colder Today Than Yesterday

(In the public washroom of the girl students' dormitory)

Girl A: I wonder if it's cold outside today. What shall I wear?

Girl B: The weather forecast says it's a bit colder than yesterday.

Girl A: Is it?

Girl C: (coming in from outside) It's rather cold outside. Put on your overcoat if you're going to class.

(On way to class)

Li Wenjing: Jeff, aren't you cold wearing so little?

Jeff: So little? Well, I don't think I'm wearing too little. These are my warmest clothes.

Li Wenjing: Winter is getting near. You'll have to buy a heavier overcoat.

Jeff: It won't be necessary! I hear that winter here is not as cold as in my country.

Li Wenjing: But sometimes it's not very warm in the classroom. Aren't you afraid of catching a cold?

Jeff: No ... uh, yes. I'll go get one this weekend. Come along and help me with it if you have time, will you?

(In the winter clothing department of a store)

Li Wenjing: What about this one?

Jeff: The style is all right, but the colour is no good.

Li Wenjing: That one? The one on the right?

Jeff: Miss, I'd like to have a look at the one on the right. (the shop assistant takes it down and gives it to Jeff) Can I try it on?

Li Wenjing: This one is a bit longer than that one, and larger, too.
Jeff: But it still doesn't fit me. Well, I'll come and take it when I grow smaller.

(Jeff to Peter) Winter is coming. It's getting colder every day. I haven't brought a warm overcoat for winter. Yesterday, Li Wenjing accompanied me to a store to get one. I kept trying for a long time, but was unable to find even one that fits me.

Lesson Twenty One   What Do They Do

(Jeff and Wang Ping taking a walk)
Jeff: Wang Ping, I hear that you intend to go to the US for graduate work after you finish university here. When the time comes, you can stay with my family.
Wang Ping: Oh, how wonderful, but I'm afraid … …
Jeff: Of what? Both my father and my mother are hospitable people.
Wang Ping: What do they do?
Jeff: Well, my father is a lawyer and my mother is a medical doctor.
Wang Ping: Any other members in the family?
Jeff: An elder brother and a younger sister.
Wang Ping: Do they both live with the family?
Jeff: Well, my brother is in college. He goes home only on weekends; My sister is in high school and she goes home every evening.
Wang Ping: Would they welcome me, too?
Jeff: Needless to say!

(Jeff to Wang Ping) If you go to America to study, you can go visit my family. There are five people in my family. My father is a lawyer and my mother a medical doctor. They are both hospitable people. I have an elder brother and a younger sister. My brother is a college student and my sister a high school student. They'll both welcome you, too.

(In Anne's room)
Peter: Anne, is this your photo album?
Anne: Yeah, it's mine. The pictures inside were all taken last year.
Peter: I'd like to take a look at them, may I?
Anne: Go ahead.

Peter: Is this a group photo of your family?
Anne: Right!
Peter: Which one is you?
Anne: Well, you cannot even identify me? Try again.
Peter: Why, both girls look like you ... ... You are the one in red on the left, right?
Anne: Wrong, that is my sister.
Peter: So you are the one on the right! You two are so much alike.

Lesson Twenty Two   How Old Are You

(After class)
Jeff: Peter, let's go play tennis, OK?
Peter: Well, I'm very sorry. I have to wait for my mother's call, it's my birthday today.
Jeff: Really? Well, happy birthday!
Peter: Thank you!
Jeff: How old are you?
Peter: Already 25, much older than you!
Jeff: Well, you know, it'll be Anne's birthday next week.
Peter: Really? Let's hold a small evening party on Anne's birthday, what do you say?
Jeff: Fine! Shall we throw a party for you today?
Peter: There's no need. Let's have fun with Anne next week!

(Anne's birthday party is about to start)
Jeff: It's a few minutes to 8:00. Wang Ping should have arrived!
Lisa: Well, has he forgotten about it?
Anne: Not very likely. He's engaged probably. Or he would have come on time.
Peter: Well, let's wait for him a little longer.
Jeff: Let's give him a call. Peter: I'll do it. What's his telephone number?
Anne: The phone number of his dormitory building is 62754021.
Peter: I've forgotten his room number.
Jeff: 301.
(Peter dials)

Jeff: Getting through?

Bill: No, the line is busy.

(Someone knocking at the door, Anne opens it)

Anne: Wang Ping, here you are at last. (to Peter and Jeff) No need to call, here he is!

Wang Ping: Very sorry I'm late, I've kept you waiting.

All: It's all right. We were afraid that you weren't coming.

Wang Ping: How could I miss such fun! Anne, happy birthday! This is a birthday present for you.

Anne: Oh, thank you so much!

(Peter to Wang Ping) It'll be Anne's birthday next Wednesday. We're planning to hold a small birthday party for her that evening. If you'll be free, come and have fun with us.

Lesson Twenty Three   How Far Is It From Here

(On the campus)

Jeff: There is a mountain with beautiful scenery to the west of our school, have you ever climbed it?

Anne: No. How far is it from here?

Jeff: Well, not far, about a dozen km or so, you can get there half an hour or a little more on bike.

Anne: The weather's been pretty good these days.

Jeff: So I was thinking we could take some food and drinks and go have a picnic in the mountain, what do you say?

Anne: Good idea, I'm sure we'll have a wonderful time!

(Anne to Lisa) There is a mountain with beautiful scenery to the west of the school, it's not far from here, just a half hour bicycle ride. Jeff has come up with a good idea: We take some food and drinks and go picnicking in the mountain this weekend. Will you go?

(Anne buying a roll of film at a store)

Anne: Excuse me, where do I get a roll of film?

Salesman: Go inside, on the right.
Anne: Thanks.
(at the film counter)
Anne: Miss, I want a roll of film.
Salesman: There are several kinds, which do you want?
Anne: Well, a Koda.
Salesman: (makes out an invoice) Go and pay for it first.

(Jeff and Anne on way to the mountain for a pinic)
Anne: In what direction are we going now?
Jeff: North.
Anne: But didn't you say the mountain is to the west?
Jeff: Well, to the northwest.
Anne: How far away is it now?
Jeff: Not far, as soon as we turn left at the next crossing, we'll be able to see the mountain.
(at the foot of the mountain)
Anne: Well, let's leave the bikes here.
Jeff: Don't move, I'll take a picture of you here first.
Anne: Is there anything worth taking?
Jeff: The background is wonderful! One, two, three ... Oh, no, the camera isn't loaded yet.
Anne: You scatterbrain! Wait till we're up in the mountain.
Jeff: Oh, well, I ought to listen to you. Come on, I'll carry all the things.
Anne: Ha ... ha ... it's good to come out sight – seeing with a boy!

Lesson Twenty Four   She Is Bright and Conscientious

(Before class)
Jeff: Anne, here are the pictures taken last time we went picnicking. They were printed only yesterday.
Anne: Well, let me have a look, quick! (looks at the pictures for a while) This one is good, and that one too ... ... These few are not very clear.
Jeff: Well, choose a few. Take whichever you like.
Anne: They're all very nice, these are the best ones. I'll send them to my mother.

Oh, can you give me the negatives, I'd like to print a few more.

Jeff: OK. Now are you satisfied?

Anne: Sure, thank you, Jeff. Oh, I nearly forgot. How much shall I pay you?

Jeff: Forget it! They are free of charge. It's all right so long as you are happy.

(Anne to Lisa) Jeff gave me these pictures taken last time we went picnicking, what do you think of them? I think they are all very nice, I'm going to send them home to my mother tomorrow. I'll print a few more for my photo album.

(On the campus)

Lisa: Wang Ping, how are you! Well, we haven't seen each other for a long time.

Wang Ping: Yes, a long time. Are you very busy these days?

Lisa: So so. Aren't you Anne's tutor? How's she doing? She must be a good student.

Wang Ping: Well, Anne is bright and conscientious and making good progress.

Lisa: She says she can understand everything in class. But once she's outside, she cannot understand anything and the less she understands, the more worried she is.

Wang Ping: It's no good worrying, better do it slow and steady.

Lisa: I have the same problem, too. I wonder if there's an effective approach?

Wang Ping: Well, what are you worrying about? You speak quite well now, don't you?

Lisa: I'm flattered, but I still have a long way to go. I'm asking you in earnest, is there a better approach?

Wang Ping: There are many, such as listening to recordings, watching television ..., they're all good methods, you can often have a chat with a Chinese, too.

Lisa: Well, I'll often have a chat with you then. Don't you lose your patience!

Lesson Twenty Five Can You Make It Cheaper?

(In a shop)

Jeff: Miss, how much is a jin of apples?

Salesgirl: 3.5 yuan.

Lisa: (pulling Jeff's sleeve) I think it's a bit high.

Jeff: Can you make it cheaper. How about 3 yuan?
Salesgirl: No bargaining here, what good apples! They're big and sweet, the price isn't high at all.
Jeff: Well, then, I'll take one jin.
Lisa: Take some more.
Jeff: But you just said it was too high. Now at my expense, you don't mind the price any more.
Lisa: Let me pay then.
Jeff: It was only a joke and you took it to heart. Miss, give us two jin.
Salesgirl: OK. Anything else?
Jeff: Nothing else.

(On the street)
Jeff: Anne, what's the rush? Where are you going?
Anne: I have to meet a friend. The train is due at 6:00. Now it's already half past 4:00 and I ... ...
Jeff: How are you going to get there?
Anne: I was just about to ask you.
Jeff: Buses are slow and crowded, better take a taxi.
Anne: The station is pretty far from here, going there by taxi would be very expensive. Besides, It's rush hour now, the traffic will be jammed.
Jeff: Well, the only way is to go on a bike.
Anne: On a bike? Shall I be able to make it?
Jeff: I assure you'll make it. I know a short cut, very convenient for riding.
Anne: But I don't know the way, do you think ... ...
Jeff: Stop worrying and hurry up. Don't you know yet? What I enjoy most is helping pretty young ladies!

(Anne to her friend) This is my classmate Jeff. I took many lessons today. When I finished class, it was almost 5:00 - - rush hour. The traffic was jammed everywhere. Had it not been for Jeff's accompanying me through a short cut, I surely would have been late.

Lesson Twenty Six What's the Matter

(In their room)

Wang Ping: Jeff, let's go for a cycle ride to downtown this weekend, what do you say?

Jeff: It is a good idea, but I won't be able to go.

Wang Ping: What's the matter? Do you have an engagement?

Jeff: Oh, let's not talk about it. I had bad luck. I lost my bicycle.

WangPing: What? Lost? Did you forget to lock it up?

Jeff: No, I didn't. I locked it up all right. Look, isn't the key here?

WangPing: Don't worry, let's go down and look for it again.

Jeff: No need. I have looked for it several times but it's nowhere to be found. It's missing.

WangPing: Well, forget it. Don't think about it any more. "Old things not gone, new things won't come", just get a new one.

Jeff: Um ... ... I'll wait until next month.

(two days later, Wany Ping sees Jeff riding his bicycle)

WangPing: Jeff, didn't you lose your bicycle?

Jeff: No, I didn't. I went into a shop that day leaving my bike outside. I came out chatting with a friend and forgot to ride it back.

WangPing: Oh, you scatterbrain!

(The students chatting in a break)

Lisa: Well, Christmas is near, I wonder if we'd have holidays.

Jeff: Probably not, because they are not accustomed to having Christmas holidays here in China.

Peter: That was in the past, not necessarily so now.

Lisa: But we wouldn't be able to go home without holidays.

Jeff: What does it matter, we could have an evening party together, wouldn't that be exciting, too?

Anne: Peter, your girlfriend wants to come to China, too, doesn't she? Let her come to China for Christmas, wouldn't that be even more exciting?

Peter: Oh, let's not talk about her any more. We broke up.

Anne: Oh? I'm sorry, I'm sorry, I didn't know ... ...

Peter: That's all right. That's all right.

(Wang Ping to Anne on the phone) I'm sorry, Anne. I have an engagement tomorrow and won't be able to tutor you in the afternoon. Let's do it the next afternoon, what do you think? …… Yes, the afternoon after tomorrow, OK? Will it be convenient for you? …… Yes? All right, I'll see you the day after tomorrow. I'm sorry to've put you to trouble. Goodbye!

Lesson Twenty Seven   What If It Rains

(Noontime, Jeff in Wang Ping's room)
Jeff: It's already 1:00, you're still sleeping?
Wang Ping: We Chinese are used to taking a nap after lunch, it's called "noon nap".
Jeff: Really? Well, I'm very sorry to disturb you.
Wang Ping: It doesn't matter, I've had enough sleep. Please sit down.
Jeff: If you happen to be free this Saturday, come to my room, OK? I wish to consult you on a lot of questions.
Wang Ping: I'm flattered. We'll just have a casual chat. I'll be free after 8:00. So I'll be there at 8:00, OK?
Jeff: But 8 o'clock is too early, I'll be in bed sleeping.
Wang Ping: Too early? I get up at 6:30 every day.
Jeff: What do you do getting so early?
Wang Ping: Well, go out and run, build up physical strength.
Jeff: What if it rains?
Wang Ping: A drizzle won't stop me. But if it's rains hard, I just sleep late.

(Jeff to Peter) I learned from Wang Ping that the Chinese are used to taking a nap after lunch. I'm not in the habit of taking a nap. I like to play balls after lunch. Wang Ping says he gets up at 6:30, I'm unable to get up so early. I like to get up late. It' really a luxury!

(In a restaurant)
Wang Ping: What would you like? Just order anything you wish, It's on me today.
Anne: well, I will. I enjoy hot food, let's order chicken cubes with hot pepper.
Wang Ping: Pockmarked Grandma's Beancurd is famous dish here.

Anne : Ok, as you say. I've never tasted ……the dish has a strange name , what is it ?

Wang Ping: Pockmarked – – grandma's – – beancurd .

(they order , and the dishes are served)

Wang Ping : Well , help youself .

Anne : (tastes some beancurd) Dear me , it is hot .

Wang Ping : This is a Sichuan dish. Natives of Sichuan enjoy hot food .

Anne : What about people in other places ?

Wang Ping : Well , generally speaking , northerners like salty food , southerners like sweet food , natives of Shandong like hot food , and natives of Shanxi like sour food , that is to say : south sweet north salty east hot west sour .

Anne : How interesting ! Each place has its own cuisine . But Sichuan is not in the east .

Wang Ping : Well , you're really conscientious ! Natives of Sichuan like hot pepper , natives of Shandong like hot green onions .

Anne : well , I see .

Lesson Twenty Eight   It's Getting Colder Every Day

(In their room)

Anne : It's so cold today !

Lisa : Well , it's getting colder every day .

Anne : The examination is coming soon. I'm so glad .

Lisa : You're glad to take examinations ?

Anne : Well , we'll have a vacation after the exam . I've been feeling homesick for a long time . By the way , are you going home in the vacation , Lisa ?

Lisa : No , I'm not . I want to go touring .

Anne : You've made up your mind ? Where do you plan to go ?

Lisa : First Shanghai, then Yunnan.

Anne : When are you leaving ?

Lisa : That depends . As soon as the exam ends , I'm on my way .

(Anne to Peter) The exam is drawing near and we'll have a vacation afterwards . I want to go home as soon as the vacation begins . Lisa is planning to go touring . She' s going to Shang hai first and then Yunnan . I want to travel too , but I miss my family badly . I'll wait until summer vacation .

(In the street , Anne gets off her bike)
Anne : (talking to herself) That's strange , I can not ride fast . Jeff , get off your bike and help me !
Jeff : What's the matter ?
Anne : My bicycle is "sick" have a look at it .
Jeff : Well, you're right , it is "sick". The tire is flat .
Anne : What do we do then ?
Jeff : We pump it up .

(In Peter's room)
Jeff : What's the time ?
Peter : 7:30 .
Jeff : The weather forecast is coming up . Sha;; we turn on the television ?
Peter : Do you watch the weather forecast every day ? Do you understand it or not ?
Jeff : Well , no . But the teacher says , "You must listen to it even if you don't understand it ." So I listen to it almost every day and I can understand a little now , for example : "Tomorrow will be fine" and "there'll be light rain in the afternoon", and this is enough .
(Peter turns on the television)
Peter : It's not on yet . They are all commercials .
Jeff : Right after the commercials .
Peter : I don't think the forecast is accurate at all . Yesterday it said it's going to snow today , but so far it hasn't snowed yet .
Jeff : There's a possibility that you misunderstood it .
Peter : With my listening comprehension , how could I have misunderstood it ?
Jeff : Well , you've learn to boast now .

(Anne) The weather is getting colder every day . I am both worried and glad . What worries me is that winter is very cold here and I would catch a cold easily if I'm not careful ; What makes me glad is that it's going to snow soon . I enjoy watching a snow scene so much . It would be even more exciting if I can skate .

273

Lesson Twenty Nine I Didn't Get the Train Ticket

(In their room)

Zhang Xin : Where have you been, Li Wenjing ? I haven't seen you all day . You look very tired .

Li Wenjing : I went to get a train ticket and I am tired to death .

Zhang Xin : Was there a lot of people in line for tickets ?

Li Wenjing : Oh, there were a great deal of people . When I got there, I saw those long queues and wanted to come back at once .

Zhang Xin : Did you line up after all ?

Li Wenjing : Well, I did . I had no alternative . I just stood in the line while talking to a guy beside me .

Zhang Xin : Did you get it after all ?

Li Wenjing : I had bad luck ! I queued for more than two hours . But when I was almost there, the ticket were sold out .

Zhang Xin : Well, Why didn't you consult me before leaving ?

Li wenjing : Why should I consult you on buying a train ticket ?

Zhang Xin : You don't understand, do you ? You can book a train ticket !

Li Wenjing : Where can I book a ticket ?

Zhang Xin : Right here on the campus . You can book one 3 or 4 days ahead .

(Zhang Xin to Li Wenjing) The Spring Festival is drawing near . A great deal of people will need train tickets . You don't always get one even after queuing for hours. So the best way is to book a ticket in advance . You fill in a booking form, pay a deposit and that's it . Usually, you can get the ticket one day ahead, after making up the money to the right amount and paying a service charge .

(After class)

Jeff : I hear that you're going home when the term ends, is it true ?

Anne : Yes, I'm so homesick .

Jeff : But are you coming back ?

Anne : Well, I wish to extend my studies for a half year . I wonder if it could be arranged .

Jeff : I have an idea , let's have a get-together after the exam , what do you say ?

Anne : I'm for it ! But the weather is not very good lately , is it likely to snow ?
Jeff : Not very likely . Even if it snows , does it matter ? Wouldn't it be more exciting to enjoy a snow scene out in the open ?
Anne : Well , I'll call and tell Wang Ping to join us then .
Jeff : Call him now .

(Wng Ping to Zhang Wei) Anne called yesterday . she says that we are going to have a get - together at the weekend . We'll go out somewhere and then go to my place . My parents are not at home at present . We can make dumplings , chat , and watch videotapes together . If you happen to be free , come and join us .

Lesson Thirty I've Broken a Glass

(At the front door of Wang Ping's house)
Peter : It's really a heavy fall of snow .
Anne : Your clothes are all wet .
Jeff : I told him it was going to snow and he wouldn't believe me .
Wang Ping : well , here we are , come in quickly .
(all of them go in)
Wang Ping : Please sit down . Anne , give me the umbrella , just put it here . Well , what about some tea to warm up !
Jeff : Wonderful !
Anne : I'll help you with it , Wang Ping .
(Anne and Wang Ping come in with the tea - things , Anne breaks a cup)
Anne : Oh , no , I've broken a cup . I'm so sorry .
Wang Ping : Never mind , I have plenty of them .
(telephone ringing)
Jeff : Wang Ping , there's a phone call !
Wang Ping : You go on chatting , I'll answer it .
(Chatting over tea)
Lisa : Do you know how to make dumplings , Jeff ?
Jeff : Well , I know how to eat them , they're delicious .
Lisa : You're always joking . Wang Ping will teach you in a few minutes .
(Wang Ping hangs up)
Wang Ping : You want me to teach what ?

Lisa : Teach Jeff how to make dumplings .

Wang Ping : Well , you'd better teach him . You can do it better than I do now .

Lisa : I'm flattered . But how could it be possible ?

Wang Ping : Dumpling wrappers , dumpling stuffing , I have them all ready . Talking of making dumplings , let's begin doing it .

Jeff : I suggest that we divide into two groups for a race and see which group will do it faster and better . I'll be the judge .

All : You ?!

Wang Ping : What a bright idea ! You put us to a race while you sit back and wait for the feast ! I had better be the judge !

(Wang Ping teaching Jeff how to make dumplings)

First prepare some dumpling wrappers and stuffing . Put some stuffing , not too much , in the center of a wrapper , and fold the wrapper up . Then press the wrapper's edge from the middle to the two ends until it sticks and a dumpling is made . Put the dumplings into boiling water . When they come up floating , they're done .

北京大学出版社对外汉语书目

书名	编著者	定价
*汉语初级教程(1—4册)	邓懿等	120.00元
*汉语中级教程(1—2册)	杜荣等	48.00元
*汉语高级教程(1—2册)	姚殿芳等	50.00元
*汉语情景会话	陈如等	26.00元
趣味汉语	刘德联等	12.50元
*趣味汉语阅读	刘德联等	9.50元
*新汉语教程(1—3)	李晓琪等	85.00元
*新编汉语教程	李晓琪等	12.00元
*读报刊 看中国(初级本)	潘兆明等	20.00元
*读报刊 看中国(中级本)	潘兆明等	25.00元
*读报刊 看中国(高级本)	潘兆明等	25.00元
*汉语中级听力教程(上册)	潘兆明等	28.00元
*汉语中级听力教程(下册)	潘兆明等	32.00元
中高级对外汉语教学等级大纲(词汇·语法)	孙瑞珍等	29.00元
*对外汉语教学中高级课程习题集	李	
中国家常	杨	
中国风俗概观	杨	
外国留学生汉语写作指导	乔惠芳等	
*现代千字文	张朋朋	25.00元
*商用汉语会话	郭力	10.00元
*汉语交际手册	王晓澎等	15.00元
*中级汉语口语(上)	刘德联等	28.00元
*中级汉语口语(下)	刘德联等	28.00元
*高级汉语口语(上)	刘元满等	30.00元
*速成汉语	何慕	25.00元
汉语词汇与文化	常敬宇	8.80元
*标准汉语教程(上册1—4)	黄政澄等	100.00元
*标准汉语教程(下册1—2)	黄政澄等	50.00元
*英汉对照韵译毛泽东诗词	辜正坤译	18.00元
老子道德经(汉英对照)	辜正坤译	15.00元
*唐宋诗一百五十首(汉英对照)	许渊冲译	15.00元
唐宋词一百五十首(汉英对照)	许渊冲译	15.00元
汉魏六朝诗一百五十首(汉英对照)	许渊冲译	15.00元

元明清诗一百五十首(汉英对照)	许渊冲译	15.00元
*中国古代诗歌选读	钱华等	15.00元
汉语常用词用法词典	李晓琪等	58.00元
常用汉字图解	谢光辉等	85.00元
汉字书写入门	张朋朋	28.00元
实用汉语修辞	姚殿芳等	16.00元

标*号者均配有磁带,磁带每盘8.00元。

	李玉敬等	30.00元
	贺松	12.50元
	在田	16.80元
		26.00元